Highland Heritage

Highland Heritage

Scottish Americans in the American South

CELESTE RAY

The University of North Carolina Press

Chapel Hill and London

© 2001 The University of North Carolina Press

Designed by April Leidig-Higgins
Set in Monotype Bell by Keystone Typesetting, Inc.
Manufactured in the United States of America

The paper in this book meets the guidelines for permanence
and durability of the Committee on Production Guidelines
for Book Longevity of the Council on Library Resources.

Library of Congress Cataloging-in-Publication Data
Ray, Celeste.
Highland heritage: Scottish Americans in the American South
/ Celeste Ray.
p. cm. Includes bibliographical references (p.) and index.
ISBN 0-8078-2597-2 (alk. paper)
ISBN 0-8078-4913-8 (pbk.: alk. paper)
1. Scottish Americans—Southern States—Ethnic identity.
2. Scottish Americans—Southern States—Social life and
customs. 3. Scottish Americans—Southern States—Folklore.
4. Highland games—Social aspects—Southern States.
5. Southern States—Ethnic relations. 6. North Carolina—
Ethnic relations. I. Title.
F220.S3 R39 2001   305.891′63073—dc21   00-060722

05 04 03 02 01 5 4 3 2 1

Contents

CHAPTER SEVEN
Scottish Heritage, Southern Style
181

Illustrations

Maps and Figure

Preface

This book was supposed to be about the archaeology of Iron Age Europe. In 1990, I entered the University of Edinburgh to ponder the wonders of Celtic hill forts (one of those compelling fascinations that takes years of graduate school to shake). While in Scotland, I often heard mildly amused and occasionally indignant comments about America's "tartaneers"—dyed-in-the-wool fans of what Americans call plaid. I could not have been less interested in the loud, often downright tacky cloth that I have now come to appreciate. Nor was my imagination in the least seduced by the distribution of Highland clan names or by the Jacobite Period from 1689 to 1746. I did not venture beyond my favorite library shelves until, having been sufficiently exposed to pub tunes, museums, public monuments, and interpretative displays at battlefields, I noticed what can hardly go unnoticed in Scotland: how disproportionately the Highland image and the Jacobite period have shaped the Scottish national identity for both domestic and tourist consumption.

When I returned from Edinburgh to North Carolina, I began attending Scottish-related events. I went to the dances and the Highland Games simply because I was missing Scotland and the Scots, and I was surprised to meet people there who had never been to Scotland yet "missed" it too. They spoke often and with empathy of the nostalgia and homesickness felt by their Scottish immigrant ancestors. I was struck by their strong transnational identification and sense of place nine or more generations removed from the immigration experience. I began to wonder if my Scottish friends were perhaps too quick to assume insincerity in Americans' search for heritage (in whatever form the Scots might sell it to them). My research interests turned from Celtic hill forts to the North Carolinian settlement sites of Colonial Scottish immigrants—only to shift again when descendants of those immigrants introduced me to their genealogical and community lore and had little trouble convincing me that their persisting ethnic identity was, after all, far more intriguing than house foundations of any period.

After attending a handful of Scottish gatherings in North Carolina's

Cape Fear Valley, it was clear that these events were neither a fading practice of an older generation nor a completely new trend developing as Americans' interests in "roots" evolved into 1990s multiculturalism. Elsewhere across the nation, new Scottish Highland Games, Scottish country dance groups, and Scottish heritage societies were sprouting annually as Americans in general began to play with hyphenated identities and organize large public celebrations of ethnic origins. However, the church homecomings and family reunions I initially attended in the Cape Fear Valley drew on centuries-old links between people and places. As the Cape Fear was home to the largest settlement of Highland Scots in America, it remains a part of familial lore, a subject of genealogical research, and a point of pilgrimage for many Scottish Americans now dispersed across the nation. I began to explore North Carolina's unique perceptions of Scottish origins within the context of contemporary heritage celebrations and to consider how ethnicity and heritage survive through innovation and flexibility rather than any rigid continuity of tradition.

This book explores the nature of heritage and how people claim and reclaim it in mutable forms over the generations to identify with both forebears and with others in the present. Heritage always balances historical "truths" with idealized simulacra. Many cultural studies pass judgment on this creative side to culture—that which makes it interesting, adaptable, and eloquent. I prefer to examine the selection and variable expression of tradition as a cultural process, not only with reference to social and temporal frames, but as part of the pan-human experience. Because visions of heritage most commonly alter and even distort history in appealing ways, what we perceive as heritage replaces history and becomes our memory. When we choose to remember a selected past in a similar way, we celebrate our unity, but in doing so we also emphasize what divides us from all those with other memories or perhaps a different memory of the same selected past. For the individual and for collectives such as ethnic groups or nations, public memory charters action in the present. This alone should cause us to contemplate the ways in which history metamorphoses into heritage.

As a case study, this book examines Scottish heritage revival, celebration, and community at several levels. On the local level, certain places and people are constants in defining and celebrating a particular Scottish identity and heritage. Some of these constants also feature in the Scottish-American heritage movement at the state and regional scale, though specifics begin to blur with other defining aspects of state and regional identities. Scottish Americans from different states and regions may define both Scottish and American heritage in different ways, so that a Scottish-American identity and heritage conceived on a national level is conceived very broadly. At the international scale, on which many Scottish heritage organizations operate, defining a common heritage necessitates even further generalization of memory. How specifically we define a heritage depends upon the social context in which, and with whom, we are "remembering."

What all levels of the Scottish heritage movement have in common is a condensed, yet well-spiced conception of Scottishness. What is celebrated as a "Scottish" identity today is a blending of Scotland's regional cultures that were quite unassimilable into the eighteenth century. Highland themes and imagery strike the most pungent notes in the mix. The result is a bouquet unrecognizable as "Scottish" to Highlanders, Lowlanders, or Dorics of the early 1700s, yet it is the filter through which they are recalled by their descendants around the globe. While not static in interpretation, images of the Scot as Highlander have been long-lived and popular stereotypes since their fixation in the early nineteenth century. Their creation, and what one could call success, has always been inseparable from Scotland's inferior social, economic, and political situation within Great Britain. Yet the evolution—in fact sometimes convolutions—of culture allows stereotypes themselves to be eventually embraced as heritage.

Just as symbols often endure because their meanings transform, the shape of our memories also responds to the moment. The ethnographic and historical moment of this book is the last four decades. I am interested in how other moments in the Scottish past and an identity shaped in the late eighteenth and early nineteenth centuries have been selected and fashioned as heritage on a large scale in the last decades and how such visions of heritage blend with those on local scales.

This book itself is a product of a particular period. It draws upon nine years of ethnographic field work and ethnohistorical research. By ethnography, I mean describing the activities and beliefs I encountered through simultaneous participation and observation at community events, supplemented by interviews and the collection of oral histories. Events, such as Highland Games and heritage society dinners, constitute one of the few arenas where Scottish Americans interact face-to-face as a group, exchanging and debating community lore, rules, and traditions. In conjunction with informal and formal group and individual interviews between events, my fieldwork focused on the enacting of cultural beliefs about "the heritage" at events where community members with differing interests and differing perspectives of Scottish-American identity mingle. As Anthropologist Sally Falk Moore notes, "Events situate people in an unedited and 'preanalyzed' context, before

the cultural ideas they carry and the strategies they employ are ex-
tracted and subjected to the radical reorganization and hygienic order of
the anthropologists' analytic purpose" (1994:365).

I have been involved with members of the following groups that are
referenced throughout the text: the North Carolina Scottish Heritage
Society, founded in 1992; the Scottish Society of Wilmington, founded
in 1994; the Scottish Heritage Society of Eastern North Carolina,
founded in 1986; Scottish Heritage U.S.A., the American branch of the
National Trust for Scotland, founded in 1965; the Caledonian Foundation, relocated to North Carolina in 1991 and based at St. Andrew's
College in Laurinburg; the Burns Society of Charlotte, founded in 1955;
the Catawba Valley Scottish Society, founded in 1992; the Montreat
Scottish Society, founded in 1980; the Cape Fear Valley Clans, Inc.,
"revived" in 1993; and various reenactment and Scottish country dancing groups. I have also interviewed members of international, regional,
and state branches of over fifty clan societies in the United States and
Scotland. Additionally, and for comparative purposes, I have attended
heritage events and Highland Games in Scotland and throughout the
South in Georgia, South Carolina, Florida, Arkansas, Tennessee, Mississippi, Kentucky, and Virginia.

When I say this work has also involved ethnohistory, I mean attempts
at reconstructing ethnic and social histories through library and ar-
chival research about the Cape Fear settlement and eighteenth- and
nineteenth-century Scotland, combined with analysis of folk tradition
to trace the development of current conceptions of the past. I also
analyze and cite community literature throughout my writing. One of
the main vehicles for communication within a dispersed community, the
literature has enabled the phenomenal growth of the Scottish heritage
movement across the nation in the past decades. It is an essential part of
indoctrination into, and education within, the Scottish-American community at all levels. Literature originally replaced but now revives oral
tradition in supplying the knowledge of history, legends, genealogies,
and folklore that provide a sense of identity, heritage, and belonging.

Examining culture, the anthropological lens is trained on a moving
target. Heritage, like culture, is never firm. Both change as the times
require. Rarely would even those who claim a heritage or culture unanimously agree on its interpretation. Only when we stand back to celebrate or even analyze these ways of fashioning reality do we knit the
frays for smooth edges. I have attempted to reveal some of the tatters as
they tell us most about how and why humans construct their presents
from variously remembered pasts. Informants repeatedly told me, "Get
two Scots together in a room and you'll come out with three different

opinions." Some of my informants will no doubt take issue with various points, as many disagreed on the meanings of clan crest insignia or tartan origins within their own organizations. I have tried to present a broad picture of the basic themes, interests, and functions of the heritage movement. From community members' widely different interests, perspectives, and ranges of knowledge about Scotland and its history, I have discussed the opinions and beliefs I most frequently encountered.

Anthropologists Jean and John Comaroff caution that ethnography does not speak for others but about them, and "is an exercise in dialectics rather than dialogics, although the latter is always part of the former" (1992:8–11). My own experience of the community as insider/outsider cannot help but shape my writing, so I often resort to the first-person throughout the text to remind the reader that the black and white print represents the thoughts of the author. While separation of themes and their division into chapters is of course my own analytical construct, the emphases in this work are those of my informants.

Anthropologists no longer focus exclusively on aliterate natives in distant locales who will never see, much less read, what we write. We examine our own culture, being as "exotic" as any other, and most of us hope our informants will read what we write and perhaps continue the dialogue. The key here is to *continue* the dialogue, not begin it with a publication. More anthropologists now view their work as a collaboration. It is in this spirit that I circulated drafts of these chapters and repeated parts of interviews, lest my informants feel their words were taken out of context or that I had misinterpreted extemporaneous comments. The majority of my informants readily consented to being quoted by name. A few asked to be identified by surname (clan name) only and others preferred to be quoted without attribution. One informant, slightly unsure of her historical narrative, told me that if I found anything amiss to "say a Campbell said it"—the Campbells generally being one of the least-loved clans among the Highlanders, for reasons that will become clear in the course of the book.

While conducting many individual interviews, I relied most on group discussions: the actual debating over traditions and ideas. In the beginning, I tried not to ask specific questions at all, but to let my informants guide discussion around their own interests. When I began doing what anthropologists do, picking apart things to reassemble them in a (supposedly) "demystified" arrangement, I asked individuals and groups of informants for their opinions of my ideas. As I wrote, I asked community members for responses to my developing positions; I believe the result is something in which they will hear their own voices.

Acknowledgments

During the years of fieldwork toward this book, I have been gratified with my diversion from the Iron Age—not simply because transnational links between Scotland and America remain deeply interesting to me, but because of the truly delightful people I have met. I owe many thanks for the abiding welcome and patience of Scottish-American community members who included me in their activities and discussions, and in "the cousinhood." I especially wish to thank my own newfound fictive kin, Anna Ray, for her hospitality, friendship, and tours through Cape Fear Valley cemeteries and historic sites, despite the chiggers and the heat. Particular thanks also go to Charlie Rhodarmer for his enthusiastic explanations, for many informative debates, and for his thoughts as my work progressed.

Donald MacDonald and his nephew Jamie MacDonald were most helpful in acquainting me with the early history of the Cape Fear Valley and with present-day community events in addition to sites of community lore in Scotland. Their combined knowledge and devotion to all things Highland has inspired many. Ed Cameron and Bill Kern's tours of Ft. Bragg and areas of Highlander settlement in the area were much appreciated. Karen Becker and Sandy Gallamore cheerfully endured my many questions on Scottish country dancing and community organizations. Arnold Pope and Hugh Morton granted informative interviews on Scottish athletics and the Grandfather Mountain Highland Games. I must also thank Hugh Morton for his generous permission to use his photos of the games. Harvey Ritch shared his knowledge of the Grandfather Games and the bagpipe band scene. Dick and Keets Taylor supplied information on the founding and organization of Charlotte's Loch Norman Highland Games. Jacqueline Stewart of Scottish Heritage U.S.A. expertly fielded the most obscure questions and pointed the way to knowledgeable contacts. Peter MacDonald and Bob Martin tirelessly answered questions on tartan, weaving, and the wearing of the kilt. Hugh Cheape of the National Museum of Scotland has been a generous and inexhaustible source on tartan, Jacobites, and all things worth

knowing. Thanks also to Ken Bloom for explaining Scottish musical instruments, and to the 84th Highland Regiment, of which he is a member, for indulging my many queries and my presence at reenactments.

For sharing their knowledge of clan societies and for supplying that
marvelous orange shortbread, I thank Jim and Michaele Finegan of
Clan MacLachlan. I have appreciated the interest expressed in my studies by members of the North Carolina Scottish Heritage Society; especially Lieutenant Colonel Vic Clark, Glenn McGugan, Lieutenant Colonel David Cone, and George Roussos. Their stories about, and tours
throughout, the Cape Fear Valley exposed me to places of importance in
community lore. Muriel Piver and Danny MacDonald introduced me to
Scottish events in eastern North Carolina. Scott Buie's newsletters from
Texas were an invaluable source of information on community genealogical research. Penny Geffert and Elizabeth Holmes introduced me to
the resources at St. Andrew's University's DeTamble Library and Scottish Heritage Center in Laurinburg, North Carolina. At the Ellen Payne
Odom Library in Moultrie, Georgia, the national repository for Scottish clan and heritage society newsletters, I thank Beth Gay for her
assistance. Fred Hay and Dean Williams shared their time and knowledge at Appalachian State University's Appalachian Collection. Thanks
go also to the staff at the University of North Carolina's Carolina Collection and at the National Library of Scotland. Bob and Barbara Cain
kept me informed of many community events and familiarized me with
resources at the North Carolina State Archives for the study of the
eighteenth-century Highlander settlement. Far more people go un-
named than those named in these acknowledgments. To the many others who granted interviews in their homes, included me in family reunions, invited me to heritage society events, sent correspondence, and
gave freely of their time, beliefs, and family lore, I am indebted.

Many Scots and non-Scots have read drafts of this work and offered
invaluable comments and challenges. I have been thankful for the patience of my editor, David Perry; for the advice of Ian Ralston during
research in Scotland; for Glenn Hinson's editing and insight; and for
Norris Johnson's constructive reflections on my work. My gratitude
also goes to James Peacock for his support and interest in my ideas; for
generous gifts of his time and wisdom; and for engaging the McRowdies. He stimulated and refined my thoughts about the blending of
Scottish and southern heritage celebration. Carole Crumley's wide
range of interdisciplinary research and interests eased my transition
from the Ancient Celts to contemporary ethnicity. Her contagious joy in
the exploration of new ideas and linkages between disciplinary thought
has been an inspiration and example. I have been privileged to have her

encouragement. For friendship and support my deepest debt is, as always, to my mother Anna Jean Dickey Springer. Since the beginning of this research she has taken up genealogy to uncover our Scottish ancestry and found, ironically enough, surnames now associated with absolutely roaring tartans.

Highland Heritage

Introduction

What thou lovest well remains,
  the rest is dross
What thou lov'st well shall not be reft from thee
What thou lov'st well is thy true heritage . . .
—Ezra Pound, *Canto* LXXXI

Despite the diverse regional identities of their Scottish ancestors, to-day's Scottish Americans claim a Highland Scots identity constructed in the nineteenth century through romanticism, militarism, and tourism long after many of their forebears had immigrated from Scotland. Though not perhaps how the celebrated ancestors perceived themselves, their Highland representations have by now become traditional. This book considers the cultural processes that lead to a celebration of one form of identity over others, and the public rituals, symbolic costumes, social organizations, and beliefs that fortify ethnic identities and their revival. I examine an abiding awareness of Scottish heritage in North Carolina's Cape Fear Valley within the larger contexts of Scottish heritage revival at the state and southern regional levels. Through this case study, I wish to engage you in considering, more generally, the cultural construction of memory and the contemporary search for identity and community.

Individually and as groups, we imagine Technicolor pasts that may develop an authenticity of their own and fulfill various needs by doing so. Most of us value gaining or inheriting some conception of "the past," but rarely acknowledge the creative aspects of our recall, or openly consider how our ordering of the past orders our social relations in the present. Heritage and ethnic celebrations are exercises in remembering that remind people to consciously stand together as a group apart. The traditions and perspectives of the past that we select and celebrate as heritage are those that have a moral, instructive, emotional, or intellectual appeal and those we therefore find good to remember.

The Cyclic Popularity of a Scottish-American Identity

Visions of ethnicity and heritage are fluid, appearing more or less important in relation to their temporal and social frames. Contemporary celebrations of Scottish-American heritage have revitalized an ethnic identity that, seemingly forgotten by many contemporary Americans, has nonetheless been prominent in public consciousness for most of American history. A Scottish, especially Highland Scottish, identity carried many negative connotations in early Anglo-America. Political, cultural, linguistic, and social differences distinguished Highlanders from Lowlanders and from Ulster Scots well beyond the American Revolution. However, in the mid-nineteenth century, these discrete groups became more concerned with distancing themselves from Irish immigrants fleeing the famines than from each other. The popular romantic portrayals of Scotland and Scottish identity by Sir Walter Scott assisted a conceptual blending of these three groups in America, in contradistinction to the new immigrants who, for the first time in American history, came predominantly from Catholic and Jewish communities in southern and eastern Europe.

Across the nation in the period immediately preceding the Civil War, and in the North and West prior to World War I, the foundation of Scottish Highland Games and the introduction of new Scottish social fraternities experienced widespread popularity. However, the overwhelming and regionally unifying experience of the Civil War largely eclipsed such celebrations in the South, as the World Wars and Great Depression would generally do for the nation. Patriotism born of war and America's initial years as an emerging superpower temporarily obscured distinctively Scottish identities. The value placed on conformity in response to immigration, war, and economic despair created the absurd misconception of "white America." Regional and ethnic distinctions reemerged shortly after World War II as many Americans experienced renewed interest in "the old countries"; as second- and third-generation immigrants began reasserting identities that distinguished them from "the white norm"; and as the nation began to explore the extension of civil rights to all Americans.

The last decades of the twentieth century witnessed a dramatic surge of interest in Americans' cultural and ancestral ties to Scotland. Beginning with a handful of new heritage societies in the late 1950s and 1960s, the numbers of national Scottish-American clan and heritage societies had grown to the hundreds by the mid-1990s and accompanied an explosion of the Scottish Highland Games scene. Celebration of a Scottish-American identity is quite distinct from other post–World

War II, European ethnic revivals among, for example, Italian, Greek, Polish, or Scandinavian Americans. This is especially true in the South, where memory of Scottish ancestral tradition has merged with that of the southern experience, and particularly so in North Carolina, where the earliest and largest groups of Scots settled. Church and sporadic other commemorations in North Carolina nourished a lasting consciousness of Scottish roots. The celebration of Scottish heritage and identity in North Carolina is unique even among Scottish ethnic revivals. The Scottish heritage revival in North Carolina is not a second- or third-generation revival, but the revival of an identity and of a community from over two hundred years ago.

More Scots settled in North Carolina during the Colonial period than in any other state.[1] Many Lowland Scots and Scots-Irish traveled to North Carolina, as they did to other states, down the great wagon road from Pennsylvania. What makes Scottish immigration to North Carolina unique is the direct, large-scale immigration of Scottish Highlanders beginning in the 1730s; their localized settlement in the Cape Fear Valley; and the persistence of a Scottish identity in the area to the present. The memory of this Argyll Colony makes the state a symbolic homeland for many in today's Scottish-American community.

Historical Background

Based on a survey of land grants, historian Duane Meyer dates the first settlement of Highlanders on the Cape Fear to 1732 (1961:72).[2] The most celebrated group of emigrants are the 350 who traveled in 1739 aboard a ship called the *Thistle*, the *Mayflower* of the Cape Fear Scots. Most of the passengers aboard the *Thistle* came from Argyllshire in southwest Scotland. Other immigrants followed, from the northern areas of Ross, Sutherland, and the Isle of Skye (Graham 1956:50). North Carolina became such a desirable destination that historian James Hunter tells us of a Gaelic song that advocated seeking a fortune there: "dol a dh'iarraidh an fhortain an North Carolina" (1994:43). From his infamous tour of the Hebrides, James Boswell reported learning a dance on Skye called "America" in which "each of the couples . . . successively whirls round in a circle, till all are in motion; and the dance seems intended to show how emigration catches, till a whole neighbourhood is set afloat" (Rogers 1993:220).

Documentation is lacking to decisively assess the size of Highland immigration to the Upper Cape Fear from the 1730s to 1775. This was a period of social and economic change in the Scottish Highlands that accelerated the evolution and decline of the old clan system. The largest

Map 1. Scotland

numbers, an estimated 20,000, came in the eight years prior to the American Revolution (Meyer 1961:63–64). They came as families and as individuals, ranging in age from their teens to their eighties. They sometimes came in large groups organized by their tacksmen, retainers of the once powerful clan chiefs.[3]

   They also came because of the generous land grants and a ten-year tax exemption ensured by Governor Gabriel Johnston. Johnston, who governed North Carolina from 1734 until his death in 1752, was himself a native of Scotland and promoted the immigration of Highlanders. Similar offers from his successor, Governor Josiah Martin, and letters from settled immigrants further encouraged new arrivals. Martin issued Cape Fear land grants in return for an oath of loyalty to the

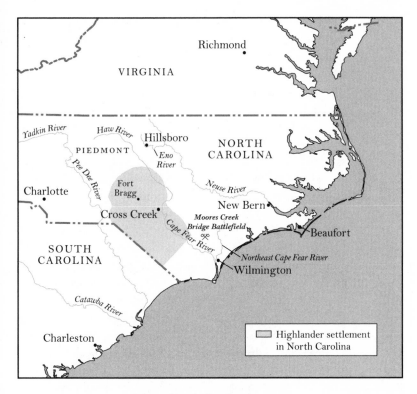

Map 2. North Carolina in 1770

Crown. By placing new Highland immigrants around the original settlement, he hoped that social pressure would encourage Highlanders to honor their oath in the trouble he knew was coming. Believing their loyalty unshakable, Martin actively sought Scots Highlander immigrants (as opposed to Lowland Scots and Scots-Irish settlers) right up to the beginning of the Revolutionary War. In the immediate period after the war, such inducements ceased. Though small numbers of Highlanders continued to come to the Cape Fear, their primary destination became Canada.

The pre-Revolution Highlanders originally settled in what was Bladen County. In 1754, much of their land became a part of the newly created Cumberland County—ironically named after the duke infamous for hounding and slaughtering Highlanders in Scotland during the lifetime of many Highland immigrants. Today the area of Highland settlement extends into Anson, Bladen, Moore, Cumberland, Richmond, Scotland, and Robeson Counties. Named for two creeks that reputedly intersected without mixing currents, Cross Creek formed the center of the Highland Settlement. The area became incorporated in 1762 with the Scottish name of Campbellton, but by 1783 the Highlanders had become uncomfortably synonymous with loyalism; hence Campbellton acquired its present name of Fayetteville, in honor of the patriots' hero, General Marquis de Lafayette.

Unlike the Scottish Highlanders who settled in Canada, Highlanders in North Carolina do not seem to have maintained strong distinctions between themselves; they shared, or at least had imposed on them at the time and by history, a unified identity in distinction from their Scots-Irish and German neighbors. On Prince Edward Island in Canada, groups that had moved from one area of the Isle of Skye remained distinct in settlement and in Gaelic dialect from communities of immigrants from other parts of Skye. While some groups from the same home areas clustered together in North Carolina, immigrants from across the Highlands mixed in one interdependent Highland settlement.

Despite the settlement's reputation as the Argyll Colony, it became home to settlers from many areas in the Highlands and also to many Scots-Irish and Germans. Meyer notes that Scots-Irish settlements were east and west of the Highlanders, "and in these settlements many names commonly considered as Highland names appeared. For example, the Campbells and McKays were leading families in both the Highlander settlement and the Scotch-Irish" (1961:90). Today's Scottish-American community also involves those of Scots-Irish and Highlander descent, but celebrates a "Scottish identity" through Highland symbols.

Heritage Celebration

In my initial forays to Scottish events, I was intrigued by the way in which Scottish Americans from across the country, of Highland, Lowland, and Scots-Irish ancestry alike, celebrate their ethnic identity with the imagery and material culture of Highland Scots. This gives the Highlanders of the Cape Fear a special preeminence nationally in community lore, yet current visions of Highland identity evolved long after the Cape Fear settlers had left Scotland. Though the form of heritage events and the traditions celebrated are largely creations of "Highlandism," a type of romanticism peculiar to nineteenth-century Scotland, their celebration nonetheless assumes continuity of practice and spirit between participants and their real or presumed Colonial Cape Fear ancestors. Assumed continuity of tradition from a period before Americans were Americans authenticates today's celebratory practices and makes Scottish-American heritage seem both unique and simultaneously more American (despite ancestral Loyalism).

Emotional investment in a heritage contributes to its celebration and therefore maintenance in public memory.[4] Especially when celebration involves solemn commemorations, we are less likely to question its inventiveness. Though a product of, and an impetus to, evolving versions of heritage, celebration often denies the historic dynamism of tradition to claim idealized, static, and ancient precedents that provide common ground in the interpretation of "the past" and a more secure sense of roots. The underlying assumption of celebration is that continuity, and therefore authenticity, of tradition was never completely lost, but, like ethnic identity, may be rekindled, restored, and reclaimed. In the Scottish-American ethnic revival, celebration focuses on the Cape Fear Valley as a hearth of "Scottish" (Highland) culture in America, and on today's descendants of the Highlander settlers as the preservers of a cultural inheritance.

What is the essence of heritage? Heritage is something of a rhapsody on history. The value of heritage lies in its perennial flexibility and the strength of emotions it evokes. Celebratory and commemorative reflections on ancestral experience merge historical incidents, folk memories, selected traditions, and often sheer fantasy to interpret a past in a form meaningful for a particular group or individual at a particular point in time. The bits of the past that seem most significant continuously change relative to the present.

Contemporary visions of Scottish heritage prioritize experiences of eighteenth-century Scots, both in Scotland and in America, as romanticized in the nineteenth and twentieth centuries. That memory of these experiences is often assumed to be continuous simply supports a heritage constructed around them. Claiming heritage may entail the selection, and often invention, of traditions, but what is most interesting about that process is how such cultural transformations of history become traditional and why. If temporal contexts elicit changing definitions of heritage, celebrations of heritage throughout history have always been, at some level, responses to contemporary social changes. Attempting to cope with transitions in behavioral or ideological standards, or in social status, groups and individuals rewrite their pasts for encouragement, security, glory, or as a critical commentary on their presents.

Contrasts between idealized pasts and the problems of the present are implicit, and often explicit, in Scottish-American heritage celebration. Specifically, celebration of a certain type of family, of patriarchal leadership within the family and Highland society, and of patriotism and the military emphasizes both resistance to current social changes in family structure and gender roles, and models of the past valuable to generations attuned to the Cold War. Generally, celebration focuses on what ancestral immigration and acculturation has culturally denied Americans of Scottish descent in terms of attachment to place, expressive tradition (music, dance, language), and a particular kinship system. Nonetheless, heritage lore also portrays the brief flourish of the Argyll Colony as a transplant of the kilt and bagpipe "lock, stock and barrel" to North Carolina. The objective of celebration is to bridge the gap between the Scottish identity and community in Colonial America with that claimed today. By restoring this link celebrants may somewhat replace both a continuing sense of lost connections with the Scottish homeland, and fresh grievances about social changes in their lifetimes, with celebration of an immutable past.

The presumed continuity of memory and celebration of tradition, rather than the unself-conscious practice of tradition, is what constitutes heritage. However, the point at which tradition ceased to be taken for granted and became celebrated, or entered into folk memory, must be accounted for in all heritage lore. At the core of most heritage revival is a sense of deprivation; a sense that particular historical moments and choices by groups and individuals have stripped a cultural inheritance from those who now highly regard it. North Carolinian Scottish Americans find the source of their loss in the motivations for ancestral emigration and favorably compare them with those of the Pilgrims.

The persecution of Highlanders for their values and way of life figures largely in celebratory addresses and conversation that ascribe Pilgrim-like qualities to early immigrants. Being exiled for political or religious beliefs and thereby deprived of one's native land and heritage seems more noble than to have voluntarily deserted the same for economic reasons (though these were undeniably compelling for many Highlanders). The reclaiming of a heritage denied is perhaps more impassioned than the reclaiming of one purposely shed or just forgotten. Historical perspective is then especially important in a study of ethnic identity formation, not to deconstruct that formation against a backdrop of "historical truths," but to study how perceptions of the past influence the selection of traditions and values in the construction, or synthesis, of identity.

Describing the early Cameron Hill Church of the Cape Fear settlement, local historian Ed Cameron writes (1992:ii):

> Cameron Hill stands tall, a place of interest to all who pause to contemplate the imprints of time that has passed. The essence of its history is not to be found in the rendering of facts. . . . In early days it was a wee bit of Scotland removed. A people, often honor-bound,

to favor a king that was hated. A people by nature clannish and nostalgic, thus bound to a homeland that had become too harsh to endure, when there was hope in America. Only the brave would come, seeking relief, land, and independence.

His words well summarize many Scottish Americans' view of the original Cape Fear settlers. He incorporates the essential imagery found in Scottish community literature and at heritage events: that of a homesick and exiled, yet honorable clanspeople, nostalgically retaining their treasured customs in a new land. He also praises their pioneer spirit and desire for independence; these traits transform them into "good Americans" and thereby provide a balance between pride in Scottish and American identities—a balance carefully maintained in today's heritage celebration.

While Scottish Americans compare the Highlanders with America's "ideal" immigrants, the *Mayflower* Pilgrims, they accentuate an all-important difference: that their immigrant ancestors were not Anglo-Saxon and neither, by extension, are they. This emphasis on a Highland/ Celtic Scots identity also distinguishes Scottish Americans as ethnic.

Heritage and Ethnic Revival

What we call heritage communicates our sense of self, as groups and as individuals, and often corresponds to what shapes ethnic identity. We mark ourselves off as ethnic through music, dress, foodways, linguistic styles, and particular expressions of religious faith—the same assemblages through which we celebrate heritage. In the United States, we take for granted that generation upon generation has merged intellectual, cultural, and historical legacies in the making of an American heritage, but Americans of the late twentieth century have attempted to sort out and reclaim particular cultural memories that they feel make them unique, and they hyphenate their identity to reflect this belief.

Distinguishing oneself in this fashion relates to, and seems to explain, social and economic realities of our historical moment. The claiming or reclaiming of identity also has the strong emotional appeal of distinctive roots among those with ancestors in the oldest immigrant groups, voluntary and involuntary. As a nation, we seem somewhat confused in that while demanding individualism, we face alienation; we challenge conformity, yet decry our lack of community. We want to embrace difference, but to do so in groups, so that communities based on difference, ease of transportation, the Internet, and so forth fill in for our lack of "good neighbors." Claiming particular dress or food customs as an inheritance provides the feeling of uniqueness, but not aloneness. Inheritors are linked in a group apart with a history and a sense of continuity through time.

The heritage and ethnic revivals of, for example, African, Irish, Hungarian and Portuguese Americans, in the last half-century reflect an awakening to our particular situation in history and the reprioritizing of cultural influences and historical events according to that awareness. Yet these revivals are not an entirely new phenomenon produced by postmodernism; they are the current expression of a continuing process that spans all of human history in oral and literate cultures. Tribal, chiefdom, and state-level societies around the globe have always turned to the ancestors and their presumed values for revitalization in times of rapid cultural change. The Pawnee Ghost Dance of the late nineteenth century was a doctrinal and ceremonial attempt to remember and again practice traditional ways and values that reasserted Pawnee ethnicity in the face of European cultural hegemony (Lesser 1978). In the Romanticism of the late eighteenth and early nineteenth centuries, northern Europeans embraced native folk cultures and the later arts and crafts movement in reaction to industrialism. Ethnic and cultural revivals of the last half-century reflect those of other centuries, borrow and merge their motifs, and revamp their public rituals. The Scottish-American community of the present further develops themes of cultural celebration that were employed among descendants of Cape Fear Scots in America intermittently since Colonial times and among those romanticizing Scots in late-eighteenth-century and nineteenth-century Scotland.

By stressing the impingement of our own time period on perceptions of the heritage, I do not mean to deconstruct the inventiveness of celebration, but rather to examine the current shaping of history and ethnicity as a fascinating process. I also mean to emphasize that Scottish-American ethnicity is not concocted, but that the surge of interest in this identity is a result of persistent folk memories, family and religious traditions, and continuing transnational links with Scotland being again recognized as such and recognized as important. Rather than a twentieth-century innovation, ethnic revivals seem to come in generational waves. With each revival, the heritage acquires new perspectives and emphases, some more enduring than others.

Scottish-American Ethnicity and the Fallacies of Multiculturalism

Is the Scottish-American community an ethnic group? When we speak of communities, we speak of groups that share conceptions of similarity and difference. Yet when we speak of ethnic groups as communities in this sense we must recall that these identities have evolved, not emerged, in America. Some of this community feeling results from the boundaries of hitherto distinct identities blurring in a new context. Though somewhat sharing linguistic or religious cultural attributes, people who thought of themselves as Umbrian, Tuscan, Piedmontese, or Sicilian become simply Italian in America. Not only are regional ethnicities sublimated to national identities, but racialist discussions of ethnicity in America further reduces the importance of such generalized identities to color.

Ethnicity is not race, yet persistent misassociation of these concepts in current academic exchange perpetuates such assumptions in popular culture. Multiculturalism calls for the decentering of European intellectual and cultural viewpoints to better reflect America's cultural diversity, but still frames diversity as "race *and* ethnicity." The symmetrical use of these terms nonetheless confirms rather than challenges notions of biological dimensions to culture in public consciousness. Recentering projects have reinforced rather than shaken off the deterministic marriage of race / color with culture, euphemized as ethnicity.

By equating race with ethnicity, multiculturalists critique Eurocentrism as a product of a monolithic European culture shared equally by all explicitly non-ethnic "whites." Scottish-American celebrations challenge the notion that so-called "white" ethnicity is race-related or merely a backlash to multiculturalism (as if multiculturalism meant nonracism) and demonstrate transnational links and the persistence of an ethnic identity over two centuries in American residence.

The reductionistic and ethnocentric feel of multiculturalism is both a product of, and an influence upon, social scientists' discussion of Americans as ethnic only because they are in America. Multiculturalism and much contemporary scholarship fails to consider the temporal and spatial dynamism of ethnicity: the fact that American ethnicities were in place in the homeland of origin only to be hyphenated and glossed fairly recently as Italian-American or Chinese-American, and now further reduced to continental descriptives of Euro-American, Afro-American, or Asian-American in a way that diminishes rather than enhances diversity. In current American discourse, ethnicity is reduced to "the big three," in less than coincidental reference to the hardly defunct notion of three races.

Much scholarly discourse ignores the voluntary aspects of ethnic identity and the important role that reclaiming / reasserting an identity plays in its meaning. Ethnic does not mean African-American and it does not mean "black." These terms have become interchangeable in

American discourse because both have been thought to describe an ascribed, minority identity within this country. Likewise, Americans of northern European descent are lumped together as "white"—seeming to lack any ethnicity—yet Scottish Americans and Irish Americans explicitly make clear that they are not Anglo-Saxons.

Anthropologist Roger Sanjek has written of his remarkable epiphany that "white ethnic persistence was a hoax," and that he "was delighted with the title of Richard Alba's revisionist paper 'The Twilight of Ethnicity among American Catholics of European Ancestry'" (1994:9). In his book *Racial and Ethnic Groups*, sociologist Richard Schaefer similarly claims, "The ethnicity of the 1990s embraced by English-speaking whites . . . does not include active involvement in ethnic activities or participation in ethnic-related organizations" (1996:127). The following account of Scottish Americans focuses on Americans of European descent who actively celebrate their ethnic awareness.

Composed of both those with a deep, transgenerational awareness of their heritage and those for whom a Scottish identity is a reclaimed ethnicity, these societies have ethnic events with particular dress, foods, religious services, and music throughout the year. These ethnic organizations maintain transnational links with the Scottish "homeland" by importing Scottish ministers, speakers, educators, and traditions, such as the Highland Games, invented or reinvented in Scotland after their ancestors left.

The ethnic revival of the 1960s and 1970s is not the "last gasp of white ethnicity," as many sociologists forecasted (Steinberg 1981). On nearly every weekend of the summer and early fall a Scottish Highland Games happens somewhere in America. These events may draw thousands of participants; one weekend games event at Grandfather Mountain in North Carolina sees over 30,000 participants annually. (Hardly a "gasp.")

North Carolinians, especially those from the Cape Fear Valley area, are unique in the country in that many trace their genealogies back to Colonial times with few exceptions to Scottish and Scots-Irish names in the family tree. In a 1997 proclamation of "Tartan Day," Governor James Hunt even made the grand claim that "North Carolina has the largest number of people of Scottish heritage of any other state or country in the world"—including Scotland!—a claim that many North Carolinians believe. Even elsewhere in the national Scottish-American community where the pattern of ethnic marriages were not so consistent or long-lived, community members stress a continuing sense of Scottish ethnicity by focusing on the Scottish branches of their genealogies. Whether the primacy granted to these ancestors and their customs has itself been a traditional family emphasis and awareness, or whether they have recently rediscovered roots and reclaimed ethnicity, Scottish Americans claim an identity that sets them apart from white Anglo-Saxon Protestant (WASP) America. Skeptical sociologists and anthropologists would argue that they do so simply *to* distinguish themselves from "the monolith of white America." However, is it not this monolith that is a hoax, rather than "white ethnic persistence"? The motivation for claiming and celebrating a heritage lies in a combination of our situation in time and the "swirling mists" and pan-pipe music of emotion where social scientists fear to tread.[5] Ethnic identities evoke emotions about the pasts and experiences that have led to one's present; though this of course has individualistic manifestations, group celebrations of identity operate on certain shared assumptions and feelings not often analyzed through the anthropological lens.

Beyond the emotional side of identity formation, social scientists have yet to comfortably address what genealogists describe as "voices in the blood" (Vandagriff 1993), or "psychic roots" (Jones 1994), though it is these notions, perhaps inelegant, of "genetic suction" to ancestral customs that shape the construction of heritage. *Communitas* is perhaps the best academic approximate, described by Victor Turner as a feeling of community spirit and an intense sense of togetherness (1974). Gwen Kennedy Neville extends this to "that feeling of well-being generated by participation in ritual" (1987:68). Expanded again, *communitas* might explain the feeling that my informants say brings them to celebrate their Scottish heritage: a sense of group cohesion through time and space within a community that members consider family. This feeling is strongest at gatherings and during commemorative rituals, but *communitas* may also be used to describe members' sense of connectedness with Scots of all varieties and time periods when community members are dispersed. *Communitas* perhaps best labels, in puffed and powdered academic terms, the feeling that has led to the tremendous growth of the Scottish heritage movement and the national appeal of the Scottish-American community.

Community and Clanship

The Scottish-American community at large consists of clan societies and their local branches, and non-clan-based Scottish interest groups (such as the St. Andrew's societies and state/local heritage societies), bagpiper bands, Highland and country dancers, Highland Games attendees, subscribers to Scottish newspapers, and so on—in short, anyone who holds an interest in things Scottish or who has a vague, passive awareness of having Scottish ancestry. The North Carolina Scottish community consists of many organizations and individuals with local, state, national, and international affiliations in addition to those who, more specifically, have attended Scottish-oriented religious gatherings or other events and are thereby actively aware of their Scottish heritage and genealogy. When speaking on the national scale, North Carolinians refer to the Scottish-American community, but may simply refer to those involved in state and local activities as the Scottish community. Unlike many other ethnic revivals, the Scottish-American movement assumes not just common cultural origins, but kinship ties among its members and with specific Scottish landscapes.

Over the last two centuries, "Scottish" heritage has been represented through essentialized Highland material culture, so that the Highland clan system has become the model for re-forming Scottish communities abroad. The clan system, on the way out by the time emigrants left the Highlands for North Carolina, has perhaps more relevance for Scottish Americans today than it did for the Cape Fear settlers of the Colonial period. Though one shares a special affinity with those in one's clan society, all the clans are thought to share more than a cultural kinship. For community members, what anthropologists call *communitas* arises from the most basic genetic level. The Scottish-American community is often described as a cousinhood. This is especially prominent in the southern states and particularly in North Carolina. North Carolinians emphasize not just Scottish ancestry, but Cape Fear ancestry; not just the cousinhood of the clans, but the genealogical proximity of "cousins."

This familial dimension distinguishes many groupings of Scottish Americans from what social scientists, after Benedict Anderson, have called imagined communities (1983). Ethnic groups, and even nations, are in a sense communities of the imagination in that most members will never meet each other or have, as sociologist Craig Calhoun notes, any "systematic web of interpersonal relationships" (1991:107). Descendants of Scots Highlanders, Scots-Irish, and Lowland Scots have entered into the creation of imagined communities (heritage organizations) on local, state, national, and international levels, although individually members may have little interaction with each other. Their interpersonal relationships may not be day to day, but they are based on more than what Calhoun calls "cultural or other external attributes" (108): they entail a presumption of kinship beyond shared group identity. The dual function of Scottish heritage societies as community and family asserts itself most strongly among those across the country with ancestral connections to the Cape Fear settlers, among whom actual family relationships are easiest to prove and who still gather at the annual homecomings of Presbyterian churches founded by Cape Fear Scots and their descendants.

Outline of the Book

I begin by considering the development of the identity embraced as Scottish by the Scottish-American community. Chapter 2 explores the origins of heritage revival and the unique history and personalities of Scottish heritage in North Carolina. The third chapter describes today's Scottish community and the perceptions of Highland social and kinship patterns upon which it is based. Heritage events are the focus of Chapter 4's discussion considering the process of selecting and innovating tradition. I examine Scottish Highland Games as both performance-based spectacles (standardized, yet responding to transnational developments) and as the physical expression of a dispersed community. Chapter 5 considers how themes in heritage lore direct the path of the heritage tourist in North Carolina and in the "auld sod" of the Scottish clanscapes. Travel and tourism have become pilgrimage in heritage revival as a physical actualization of transgenerational attachment to place. Chapter 6 explores military themes in the development and form of heritage events, and the overwhelming representation of career military people within the community. Drawing upon the themes of the previous chapters, Chapter 7 examines the southern style of Scottish celebrations in North Carolina.

Intentions

One of the chief ethics in anthropological study is cultural relativism. From the anthropological perspective, I have studied Scottish-American beliefs as valid and valuable parts of my informants' worldviews. I unravel many of these beliefs to examine the ways they developed and why they have become so meaningful to people, not to critique my informants' commitment to them.

Presentism, the intrusion of our present frame onto our interpretation and use of history, is of particular interest in both ethnographic and ethnohistorical analysis, not as something to be debunked, but as a particularly arresting aspect of the continuing renegotiation of history, culture, identity, and meaning. My inquiry is not directed at authenticating or disproving claims of continuity for traditions or identity, but examining the importance that continuity assumes for those who claim it. A diachronic perspective is then essential to my approach, not to explode myths or views of the past operative today, but to appreciate why and how today's understandings developed.

Short exegetical narratives of Scottish and American history appear throughout the text, especially in descriptions of activities at heritage events. There may be "no history" but what Lévi-Strauss calls "history for"; culture always references some past (1966:257). Recent or removed, imagined or written, however biased—the past supplies precedents and validation. The groups I have studied base their activities, their sense of identity, and their ideas of community on historical moments collectively celebrated as heritage. Heritage is a history told from a certain viewpoint, and told purposefully "for."

In discussing the construction of heritage, I discuss myth and mythologizing processes throughout my analysis. I do not use these terms in the derogative sense of common parlance, or to emphasize the inventiveness of the traditions discussed. I employ myth in the classical anthropological sense as a type of charter for a group or community, or even for individuals' sense of identity. In this study, myths are powerful accounts that effectively and meaningfully explain the customs and beliefs of the Scottish-American community and are set forth as facts—the various arrangements of which may be quite distinct from historical facts, but yield a malleable history for the extraction of heritage.

Later twentieth-century works on tradition have primarily, and somewhat gleefully, deconstructed its contrivance (Hobsbawm and Ranger 1983; Dorst 1989; Hewison 1983). This work instead focuses on the process and uses of fictionalizing history and on community formation through new rituals that are instilled with implied continuity from the past. Rather than invention, I trace the selection and reworking of tradition within the heritage movement—not to critique the validity or falsity of celebration and heritage lore, but to emphasize origins as a way of understanding to what the selection of tradition may be a response.

This work intends to show how the espousal and testimonial commemoration of certain histories fashions memories of far-removed and recent pasts that unite people in complex intellectual and emotional ways. The celebratory creation of such memories involves Americans with a transgenerational or a reclaimed Scottish ethnicity in heritage revival—a much criticized and deconstructed part of the postmodern condition that remains inadequately explored as a pre-postmodern and on-going process with historical precedents.

Highlandism and Scottish Identity

The Origins of Contemporary
Ethnic Expression

Plaintive strains of a lone bagpiper's lament fill the cool air of an early mountain evening. Conversations lull into enraptured reverence among the assembled Highland clans as dusk announces the beginning of an anticipated ritual. Burning pine torches replace the smell of Scottish meat pies and picnic dinners hurriedly packed away as the young are wrapped in warm tartan shawls and pushed to the front of the growing crowd to watch their fathers, uncles, brothers, and grandfathers enact an annual tradition with ancient origins.

Swathed in the tartans of their clans, a procession of men declare their clan's presence and hurl their torches on a central bonfire. Their brief and moving pronouncements of clan history and reputation, of battles fought and clansmen lost, elicit war cries and applause from the crowd. Well into the night, singing and storytelling relate the legendary demise of these same clans after the 1746 defeat of Charles Edward Stuart's Jacobite Rising. Men and women of all ages softly weep for the poignancy of the moment and for shared memories of that ancestral experience. As the described scene is the opening of a 1990s Highland Games in North Carolina, that experience is over 250 years and an ocean removed. How has this memory maintained such emotive power, and why has it become central to perceptions of Scottish heritage?

The identity embraced as "Scottish" by the Scottish-American community is a Highland identity that evolved into the Scottish national identity in the late eighteenth and early nineteenth centuries through romanticism, the re-creation of the kilt and the tartan, Highland soldiers' service in British empire-building, and the works of Sir Walter

Scott. The development of a Scottish national identity and the themes of Scottish-American heritage are both linked to Jacobitism and Highlandism. These cultural ideologies and the Scottish heritage movement, though ostensibly separated by space and time, are part of a continuous process of evolving tradition, meaning, and cultural memory.

How the Highlands came to represent the whole of Scotland is a tale similar to the way plantation owners came to represent white southerners generally. As southern identity references the Lost Cause of Jefferson Davis and Robert E. Lee, the Scottish identity of southern Scottish Americans centers on the lost cause of Bonnie Prince Charlie, whose bid to regain the British throne for the Stuart dynasty ended in 1746 on the Scottish Moor of Drummosie now called Culloden. Those who supported him against the Hanoverians were the Jacobites, and chief among them were the Highland Scots.[1] Though they suffered most for his defeat, their involvement resulted in a second-class status within Britain for all Scots; and a Scottish nation that was no longer trusted to control its regional groups became merely "North Britain" for over a century. Despite the fact that Lowland and other Highland Scots had been largely responsible for the defeat of the Jacobite Highlanders, Scotland as a whole became suspect, and Scotland as a whole shared in their defeat. Consequently, all Scots have acquired a Highland identity in the eyes of non-Scots.

Scotland's ethnic populations retained their distinct forms of cultural expression and political leanings well after the 1707 Act of Union with England. The Viking-influenced Gaelic Highlands and Islands singularly differed in terms of language (and dialects), subsistence, religious forms, ancestral origins, settlement pattern, and worldview from either the Eastern "Dorics" or the Anglo-Normanized Lowlands. However, with the passage of Jacobite passions into myth, a concomitant myth of a uniformly "Highland" Scottish population exemplified Scottish subservience to England. Once beyond all hope of resurrection in the political realm, Jacobitism became romantic; its former adherents became tragically charming subjects of the Crown instead of rebels. They also became the focus of a romanticism peculiar to Scotland, called Highlandism, or Balmoralism after Queen Victoria's Highland castle. Sir Walter Scott's writings ennobling the hitherto "savage" Highlander assisted this development of an internationally familiar, and militaristic, image of the Scot, not only as a Highlander, but as a bagpiping, kilted soldier. Through the romance of Highlandism, all Scots became defeated Highlanders and Jacobites.

As in the American South, cultural attributes of the vanquished became idealized once no longer a threat. Post-Culloden legal proscriptions against Highland cultural expression banned tartan as an emblem of Jacobitism and outlawed bagpipes as "instruments of war," with the intention of purposefully destroying Highland Gaelic culture.[2] Yet the fetishism of Highland culture ironically followed these prohibitions. Just decades later, Highlanders were fighting in the Hanoverian army, and the previously dangerous symbols of Highland independence and clan loyalty became symbols of "Scottish" valor. Kilts became the "national" Scottish attire. Lowlanders, for whom Gaelic and the clan system were foreign, forsook the ancient Highland/Lowland cultural divide to don tartans and an elaborated and accessorized version of the kilt. Scotland became a "Celtic" nation.

The late eighteenth and early nineteenth centuries cultivated a national identity that focused not on the unique systems of Scottish law, organized religion, or education, but on the material expressions of Highland culture—outlawed as "symbols of treachery" for forty years following the Battle of Culloden. It is this identity Americans of Lowland Scots, Scots-Irish, and Highland Scots ancestry alike have adopted as "Scottish."

As an identity inextricably linked to the Highlanders' defeat, it kept Scotland quiet under English rule, making it a playground for wealthy English and the testing grounds for new taxes and economic experiments; both circumstances brought mass eviction and emigration. Ascribing "quaint" Highlander stereotypes to the whole of Scotland continued to rationalize structures of inequality within Britain through the twentieth century. English incomers still own large percentages of the most scenic countryside in the Highlands and Islands; wide economic disparity continues between Scotland and the rest of Britain; and tourism thrives on kitsched-up images of identity that tether "Scottishness" to militarism and the Royal family. Edinburgh journalist George Rosie writes that "so far as the British establishment is concerned, Jacobite Scotland is a *safe* Scotland" (1991:7).

So how does such an identity appeal to Scottish Americans? This mythic sense of the Scottish identity takes on quite different meanings and significance in the American context. In the nineteenth century, continuing transnational links with Scotland, the popularity of Sir Walter Scott's novels, and the concurrent re-creation of Highland Games and establishment of clan "societies" brought Highlandism and its peculiar sense of the Scottish identity to America. In today's revival, this identity seems as much an inheritance as the games tradition and "clan membership." The difference in its operation here as opposed to in Scotland is that, in America, the sense of grievance that this identity communicates has a specific and terminal focus: ancestral emigration.

What developed in the nineteenth century, and has now become traditional, colors interpretations of ancestral motives for leaving a homeland so beloved. The negative impact of Highlandism on Scotland as a nation is little known or discussed in American heritage celebrations; most Scottish Americans view the identity that it spawned as an inheritance from the pre-Culloden land familiar to their ancestors. Those who do recognize nineteenth-century Highland Games and clan societies in the United States and Scotland as revivals are of course less concerned with the social context for these events in Scotland and more concerned with what they see as a break in their continuity from "clan times," in other words, why they had to be revived. The same explanation for this "break" in tradition also explains the reason why Scottish ancestors became Americans: the persecution of the Jacobites.

Heritage lore opens the tale of North Carolina's Cape Fear Highlanders with Culloden as the sole impetus for the demise of the Highland clan system and for the "exile" of Highlanders to Carolina. The distinction of exactly who fought whom 250 years ago in a short battle in the north of Scotland might not seem a pivotal point of an anthropological discussion of contemporary Scottish-American heritage and identity, but it is central to all subsequent argument. A brief synopsis and discussion of Jacobitism is necessary for understanding community lore and rituals discussed throughout the text.

Jacobitism

England and Scotland had been ruled by one monarch since 1603, when James VI of Scotland (a Stewart) inherited the throne of the childless Elizabeth I and became James I of England.[3] Though James I's successors had varying success retaining the throne—and their heads—it was with his grandson James VII & II that the Jacobite drama began. Suspected of Catholic sympathies, James II was forced to abdicate in 1688 by parliamentary leaders in favor of his daughter Mary and her very Protestant husband, William of Orange. James initially attempted to regain his throne in 1689–90. His son, James Francis Edward Stuart, known as "The Old Pretender," made subsequent attempts in 1708, 1715, and 1719. The failed efforts of James II's grandson Charles Edward Stuart, known as "Bonnie Prince Charlie" to his supporters and as "the Young Pretender" to his enemies, finished the cause in 1745–46. Supporters of all three men were known as Jacobites from the Latin for James, *Jacobus*. "Risings" in support of the "Pretenders" followed the 1707 union with England, which barred the succession of Catholic Stuarts to the throne and secured the Hanoverian claim.[4] Though individual monarchs had held the crowns of both England and Scotland for over a century, their formal union was contrived to reduce any chance of an exiled Stuart regaining the British throne by first taking the crown of Scotland. Union with England only exacerbated the divided loyalties of Scots (to the Protestant faith and to the Stuarts). From 1689, the Highland clans provided troops for the Jacobite cause. Their efforts were countered, mostly within the boundaries of Scotland, by their rival clans and by Lowlanders more interested in defending the powerbase that Hanoverian rule gave them than the Hanoverians themselves.

The last Jacobite Risings of the eighteenth century were largely a Scottish civil affair, with the main events playing out centuries-old clan rivalries and the Lowland/Highland divide. However, this is not what comes across in Scottish popular culture, nor is it the story told at North Carolina heritage events and Highland Games. The predominant vision of the Jacobite battles as an English defeat of the Scottish nation is slow to fade both in the Scottish-American community and among Scots in Scotland. Recognizing how Jacobitism dominates the portrayal of Scottish history and how that denies Scotland's long history apart from England can explain much of the success of English cultural hegemony in Britain and how the folklore and ethnic identity Scots brought to America has changed in response to changes "back home."

A "Scottish" identity developed through the articulation of historical events, historical responses to these events, and the myths that evolved about both. Scotland's recorded history details its struggle against a colonizing power. Including that history in museums and interpreting relevant historical sites is essential, as the very sense of struggle and of being allied against "The Auld Enemy" often becomes a part of what it means to be a member of a national society. However, this emphasis on the external "other" stems from our post-eighteenth-century thinking in terms of nation-states, rather than in terms of distinct regional or tribal units, and yields an undynamic image of the society in question. The focus on the Jacobite period in heritage events and in the Scottish tourism industry, and therefore the resulting "death" of Gaelic culture, is a focus on "what was lost." The impact of such a focus is more dramatic when one appreciates how the defeat of the Highlanders gradually became generalized to a defeat of Scotland in social memory and how regional cultural artifacts became symbolic of both Jacobitism and Scotland.

A Jacobite focus perpetuates the image of the bagpiping "Scot," perennially dressed in plaids of rainbow brilliance, and a defeatist view of

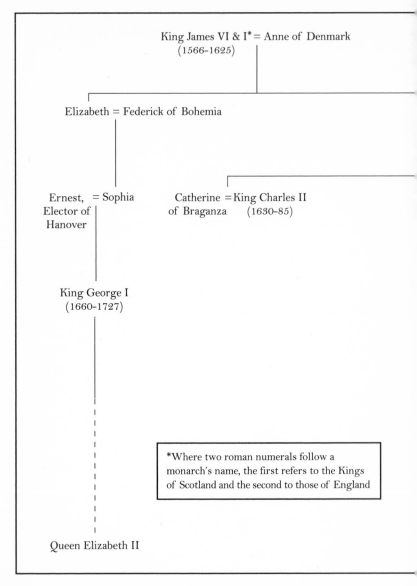

Figure 1. The Royal House of Stewart (Stuart) and the Hanoverian Branch

history that centers tragedy and grievance in the national consciousness. From the perspective of the French Annales School, we can see
the short-term sociopolitical "event" (Culloden in 1746) brought the
medium-term "conjuncture" (the Act of Proscription of 1747, to its
repeal in 1782), which has led to a new long-term "structure" (in which
Highlandism has provided new meanings for Highland material culture

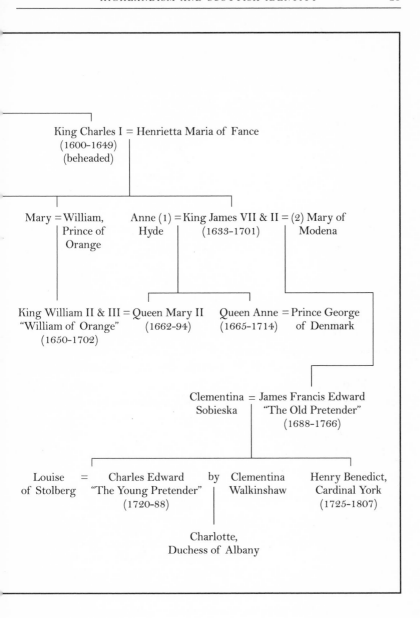

King Charles I = Henrietta Maria of Fance
(1600-1649)
(beheaded)

Mary = William,
Prince of
Orange

Anne (1) = King James VII & II = (2) Mary of
Hyde (1633-1701) Modena

King William II & III = Queen Mary II
"William of Orange" (1662-94)
(1650-1702)

Queen Anne = Prince George
(1665-1714) of Denmark

Clementina = James Francis Edward
Sobieska "The Old Pretender"
(1688-1766)

Louise = Charles Edward by Clementina
of Stolberg "The Young Pretender" Walkinshaw
(1720-88)

Henry Benedict,
Cardinal York
(1725-1807)

Charlotte,
Duchess of Albany

with the establishment of a Highlander identity for Scots in general)
(Braudel 1992). Repercussions from the passing event have produced
different and enduring perspectives on identity and history.[5]

My concern here is to understand how and why ethnic identities
change and the role of heritage revival / celebration in those changes. I
have so far laid out three important points: (1) after immigration to

Colonial America, Lowland, Highland, and Ulster Scots maintained the regional ethnic identities they had in their home areas; (2) after their immigration, one regional identity emerged as a national image in Scotland; and (3) that national identity is now traditionally considered a common heritage for the descendants of those who came to America before its evolution. Questions which then must be answered relate to how ethnic identities merge in America and how cultural changes in the old countries continue to be important for Americans' sense of identity and "roots." To answer these questions we must consider not only the important role of nostalgia in shaping cultural heritage, but the social, economic, political, and historical realities that give birth to nostalgia. We may begin by considering the origins of Highland romanticism in Scotland, the way it traveled to America, and how it shapes the meaning of Scottish-American heritage today.

The Beginnings of Highlandism

The tartanization of Scotland was perhaps accepted in the early nineteenth century not only because Highlanders developed a new folklore about the "Forty-Five" and Lowlanders had become genuinely nostalgic about Highland and Gaelic culture, but because it brought acceptance (even admiration) from the English ruling class.[6] The first reigning monarch to visit Scotland since 1641, and the first Hanoverian ever to do so, was George IV. In 1822, less than eighty years after the banning of Highland dress, he wore a kilt during his Edinburgh visit. Queen Victoria established the tradition of Royal summer holidays in the Highlands with her purchase of Balmoral Castle. She also joined the Church of Scotland (unusual for the Head of the Church of England!) and kept Highlanders in full regalia in her inner court circle (Brand 1978:127).[7] Many aristocrats and *nouveau riche* followed her example and bought country estates in the Highlands. Capitalizing on the new image of "Scottishness," the Highlands became the playground of the "sporting landlords."

Many Scots, Highland and Lowland, became dependent on lore of the defeated Jacobites to make a living, a dependency that continues through tourism today. Because the new "sporting" and absentee landlords preferred game deer, or more lucrative sheep, to human tenants, many Scots also faced eviction and immigration to Canada or New Zealand through the second half of the nineteenth century. Historian John Prebble notes that while "sporting landlords" Victoria and Albert enjoyed the Braemar Highland Games, they were also patrons of the

Society for Assisting Emigration from the Highlands and Islands of Scotland (1984:202).

Some authors (e.g., Jarvie 1989) have argued that the creation of the "Highlander" persona and the exaggerated displays of Celtic culture (of dress and accent by the Highland "ghillies" and at events such as "Highland gatherings")—while being just the stuff the sporting landlords expected to see—were actually a cultural form of resistance. If, indeed, these fantastic versions of Highland life were once resistance, they have become accepted as orthodox by many Scots and non-Scots alike. While the embellished style of Victorian entertainments ("traditional" dancing and singing, and sporting events) may have been acknowledged as contrived by the presenters, they have now been accepted, by outsiders and performers alike, as a legitimate and continuous tradition. Though not from the eighteenth century as often assumed, they have indeed become traditional traditions. The larger hotels in Edinburgh and Glasgow all have their "traditional Scottish evenings," being "traditional performances" of "traditional entertainments."

Social commentator Colin McArthur suggests that "Scotch Myths have had hegemony over Scots' perceptions of themselves to such an extent that they have a 'systemic' quality." Highlandism is now generally taken for granted by Scots. McArthur writes, "With two centuries to develop, it is now a durable and hegemonic system, the representation of one part of which can dredge up into consciousness the system as a whole, and the complex articulation of attitudes to history, to nationhood and to political decisions in the here and now" (McCrone 1989:167). Cultural performances of songs and dances with Jacobite themes and titles by performers costumed in tartan and kilt are a legacy of Highlandism and an expression of its "systemic" impact on national identity. That these nineteenth-century forms of expressive culture are embraced as heritage by Americans whose Scottish ancestors arrived on these shores in the century before their development is testimony to their enduring power and to the continuing transnational links between Scottish Americans and Scotland.

The Kilt: From Outlawed Seditious Symbol to National Badge of Valor

Highlandism produced what Jarvie calls "a symbolic tartan cultural identity" (1991:25). Certainly the tartan and the kilt, as re-created during the nineteenth century, today symbolize Scottish identity in Scotland and abroad. If people know one thing about Scotland, they know that it is the place "where men wear skirts" (though telling a man in a kilt that you like his skirt is highly unadvisable). In the Scottish-American community, one's choice of tartan and kilt style signals one's choice of a specific identity within the community—but how did this come to be?

The traditional kilt was a piece of cloth about four yards long called the plaid; the term most non–Scottish Americans now use for the tartan cloth of which it was made. The wearer wrapped and belted the plaid around his waist and used the remainder as a cape in cold weather or threw it over the shoulder as a sash. The type of kilt universally adopted across Scotland in the mid-nineteenth century, and that most commonly worn today, is the pleated feileadh-beag, anglicized as "philibeg" or small kilt, requiring between six and eight yards of cloth with no excess for a trunk wrap. As Jarvie notes, the kilt in its many splendid variations is not an "invented tradition" (1991:25).[8] Travelers' journals and government papers document the prominence of the kilt and the tartan for all ranks of Highland society hundreds of years before Culloden. What is interesting about the post-Culloden development of the kilt is the new national significance that the kilt acquired and the family associations assigned to the tartan.

Eighteenth-century Lowlanders had few interactions with and many negative stereotypes of Highlanders, associating tartan and the kilt with cattle thieves at the time of the Act of Proscription. To the rest of Britain, the kilt's strongest associations were with the "treason" of the Jacobite Risings. In the late 1740s, Highlanders appeared to the English, Welsh, and other Scots as traitorous barbarians, and yet, in fifty years time (much of it witnessing Highlanders fighting abroad in service of the Hanoverians), their image was that of loyal empire-builders. For nearly forty years, a Highlander wearing any form of tartan or kilt in Scotland could be jailed or transported for an act of defiance, yet wearing the same in the loyal military service of the Hanoverians (to whom it had previously been a symbolic threat) was never banned, and it is in this context that its form and meaning first changed. The revival, and in a sense the preservation, of the kilt began with the introduction of the philibeg in military service.

By its repeal in 1782, the Proscription Act had been fairly successful in ending the kilt's function as a daily garment in the Highlands. Though no longer utilitarian dress, the kilt and tartan certainly retained their appeal among Highlanders as a part of their identity and as something that had been denied them by law. Ironically, the British government used the very symbol of Highlanders' cultural autonomy to recruit Scots into the British army. The "garb of Old Gaul" was valo-

Reenactors and a volunteer demonstrate a theory about how Highlanders put on the early-eighteenth-century-style feileadh mor ("the big kilt"). This popular Highland Games demonstration requires that the wearer arrange his belt and a pleated cloth on the ground and then lay himself down to buckle it. The extra fabric above the belt would either be tucked in the belt or secured as a cape, depending on the weather.

rized as a symbol of Celtic bravery to which all Scots (Highland and Lowland) were expected to aspire.[9]

Highlanders joined the Hanoverians' military ranks because (with eighteenth-century changes in land tenure and the Highland economic and social situation) it was often the choice of "the King's shilling" or emigration. Scotland has always provided a disproportionate number of military personnel to the British forces. For success of its global agenda, the British government became dependent on soldiers drawn from the people whose local cultural and political autonomy it had most repressed. When it seemed that battles in the imperial quest might favor the natives, the officer in command would order the Highlanders to the frontlines with "Bring Forrit the Tartan." The same Crown that had tried to bury Highland culture in 1746 was waving its symbols to rally support by the turn of the nineteenth century. These tactics proved so successful that by 1881 the War Office required all the Lowland regiments as well as the Highland regiments to wear the kilt or tartan trousers and short Highland-style doublets. What was once dress associated with the most anti-Hanoverian element of the Empire became identified with Scottish regiments in loyal service of the same. Regional distinctions submerged in the conquest of "foreign" lands.

Downplaying Highland/Lowland distinctions, popular culture also incorrectly presented the Highland clans as a united front in "the matter of Prince Charlie." Four decades after Culloden, Jacobite nostalgia prompted a wave of poetry and "Jacobite" song-writing (the products of which still flavor today's heritage revival). In the romanticism of the times, many authors imputed older origins to their works and thereby further enhanced developing myths. In his book *The Jacobite Song*, William Donaldson prints the late-eighteenth-century "Gathering of the Clans":

> The King, he calls his men, his men;
> Rouse every clan, rise every man
> In tower, and town, and glen and glen
>   The French are coming, oho! oho!
>   Up wi' the Campbells—Hurra the MacDonalds,
>   Come out and beat the foe, the foe . . .
> The Gordons are forth afield, afield
> The Murrays and Grahames have quitted their hames,
> At the sound of the spear and shield, and shield. . . . (1988:91)

Donaldson notes that in the military songs of the Revolutionary and Napoleonic Wars, the "warlike traditions of the Gael [were] realigned to depict the French as the natural enemies." An additional point of interest is that in the same song, family names, which throughout Scottish history have been antagonistic, are linked as "natural" allies.

The unification of Campbells and MacDonalds, who fought on opposite sides in most every Scottish battle (especially the Jacobite ones), as the "King's men" demonstrates the late-eighteenth-century development of ideas about a historical Scottish unity and the sense that the whole of Scotland was "chastened" after Culloden. Donaldson writes that "as Highland soldiers gained acceptance as the guardians and restorers of national military glory, the image of Scotland itself began to change" (1988:70). It did not do so, however, as to benefit the Scottish. Ironically, Scots (all equally classed as reformed Jacobites) became known as the most pliant and loyal subjects through the manipulation of lore surrounding the rising and slaughter of a minority of Scots. The British military and the sporting landlords coopted and standardized Jacobite motifs and Highland dress for their own purposes.

Contemporary historical revisionists claim that the Jacobite defeats were actually triumphs since the true beginnings of a unified Scottish identity coincided with the Jacobites' demise. Donaldson believes the composers of Jacobite song and romantic writers of the eighteenth and early nineteenth centuries produced a new national consciousness and transformed "the Scottish identity" (1988)—which indeed they did, but writing in a defensive and tragic tone contra the English "other." Donaldson states that during the period in which Highlandism developed, "after centuries of conflict between the Highlands and the Lowlands a unified national image was achieved: Scots of every kind, regardless of ethnic, linguistic or regional background, began to consider themselves as part of an essentially Celtic nation" (1988:90). Scots were more unified after the Jacobite period, but they were unified under English hegemony and with symbols sanctioned by the English monarchs themselves. "Celtic" at the time meant "vanquished" and this association was instilled in the new unified national identity—an image of subjugation, not vibrant rebirth.[10] Current revisionism echoes Highlandism in posing Jacobitism as a matter between the Scots and the English and portraying the Jacobite period as the "climax of Scottish History."[11]

A new Scottish unity under England did develop in which the Jacobite story continues to feature. This story first became known to the world through the works of Sir Walter Scott. Scott had elaborately planned George IV's 1822 Edinburgh visit and had so revised the reputation of the Highlanders that George himself wore Royal Stewart Tartan. The head of the House of Hanover, wearing the tartan named for the family that sought his grandfather's overthrow, gave a toast proposing "health to the chieftains and clans" (Duff 1968:24).

The Scottification of Scottishness

If the Highlanders' international military service endeared them at home, Sir Walter's fantastic romanticizations of Highland life introduced them to an international readership. Inspiring many involved in the early-nineteenth-century European Romantic movement, Scott's writings were at the heart of Highlandism and the adoption of tartan as "the Scottish habit." Scott's "Waverley" novels were his most famous. The first bore the subtitle "60 Years Since"—an unobscure reference to Culloden. He wrote that his role model for the character Waverley (an English Hanoverian soldier who embraces Jacobitism and Highland culture through his experiences in Scotland) was a "noble specimen of the old Highlanders, gallant, courteous and brave, even to chivalry" (1814:xxix).

Coupled with the prominent role of Highland soldiers in the military, Scott's works transformed the villainous and murderous Highlander of the public imagination into courteous medieval knights. With such figures as heroes, his fiction redeemed Highlanders, and then Scots in general, from traitorous associations. These "noble" folk remained "savage" only in Scott's descriptions of their closeness to nature: "springing like a roebuck from a cliff of considerable height" (1828:208) and "couch[ing] like their own deer" (79).

While Scott described the Highlanders' appearance as wildly dramatic, he simultaneously emphasized their "innate manners" and graciousness. He describes an appropriately tartan-garbed Highlander in *The Fair Maid of Perth* as "a colossal person, clothed in a purple, red and green checked plaid, under which he wore a jacket of bull's hide" (1828:207). In the same scene, a monk meets a band of Highlanders and fears being carried off and tortured to death in "cruel ceremony," yet they befriend and aid him; this, and many like scenarios throughout Scott's literature, shows his well-intentioned mission to raise common British misconceptions about Highlanders and lay these notions to rest.[12]

I detail Scott's efforts here because his contemporary readers regarded his discussion of Highland customs as we might today regard a scholarly ethnography. Though his are fictional accounts, Scott claims a kind of "ethnographic authority" in relating his descriptions of Highland life—impressing upon his readers in his novels' introductions that

> I had been a good deal in the Highlands at a time when they were much less accessible and much less visited than they have been of late years and was acquainted with many of the old warriors of 1745, who were, like most veterans, easily induced to fight their battles over again for the benefit of a willing listener like myself. It naturally occurred to me that the ancient traditions and high spirit of a people who, living in a civilised age and country, retained so

strong a tincture of manners belonging to an early period of society, must afford a subject favorable for romance. (1817:xv)

Such authority allows him to dispel one stereotype of Highlanders and
replace it with one he considers more favorable. He certainly convinced
Victoria, who quoted Scott in her personal diaries and wrote of Scotland, "There is . . . no country where historical traditions are preserved
with such fidelity, or to the same extent. Every spot is connected with
some interesting historical fact, and with most of those Sir Walter
Scott's accurate descriptions have made us familiar" (Duff 1968:26). A
self-professed admirer of Scott, Victoria also wrote, "I think the Highlanders are the finest race in the world" (Cheape 1995:58).[13]

Although Scott may have consciously set out to vindicate the Highlanders, his romanticizations did so by creating a simulacra of Highland
life that came to symbolize "Scottish" culture.[14] His descriptions of
elaborate and ceremonious Highland rituals shaped the nineteenth-
century re-creation of Highland Games in Scotland and America and
continue to influence heritage revival today. Scott was essential to the
development of Highlandism. His works encouraged tourism in the
Highlands: an industry firmly established by the annual visits of his
admirer, Queen Victoria. Though Scott wrote that he never believed
Lowlanders to have worn plaids (tartan), he gave the tartan industry a
thrust by orchestrating George IV's visit to an Edinburgh draped in the
cloth and dotted with kilted bagpipers. By the middle of Victoria's reign
there were multitudinous tartans in "dress" or "hunting" styles with
specific clan or area designs. Her own husband, Albert, designed a
"Balmoral tartan" for their summer holidays. As Cheape notes, "'Highland dress' turned into 'tartan costume.' A practical dress with style
became in the nineteenth century a fashionable dress with little regard
for function" (1995:52). By 1938, the Countess of Erroll could introduce
a book on tartan thus: "One great love which all Scots share is their love
for the tartan. . . . I am happy to see a note on the correct way in which
tartan should be worn; there is nothing worse than seeing a girl dressed
as an imitation Highland man in kilt and sporran. Anyone who appreciates the tartan well enough to wear it should wear it correctly" (Bain
[1938] 1961:7). Today, clan and community literature frequently features articles on how to do just that.

Tartan and the Scottish-American Community

In the mid-1990s, a number of southern states beginning with Tennessee and North Carolina adopted an annual "Tartan Day." On March 20,

1998, upon the urgings of another southerner, Senator Trent Lott of Mississippi, the U.S. Senate adopted Resolution 155 making April 6 "National Tartan Day." Even Scotland does not have a day for its famous fabric—why have Americans so embraced its symbolism?[15]

For Scottish Americans, tartan is a badge of membership within the Scottish community and of clan affiliation. One's choice from a variety of styles of clan tartans signifies one's knowledge of clan and Scottish history. That the symbolic use of tartan in the celebration of identity is a legacy of Highlandism in no way discounts its present meanings and emotive power. Tartan is a very old fabric; Dio Cassius, Diodorus Siculus, Livy, Polybius, and Strabo all describe the ancient Celts throughout Europe as wearing speckled, checked, or striped clothing.[16] The fabric survived longest in the outliers of the Celtic world in those areas unconquered by the Romans, namely most of Scotland and the island of Ireland. Though its significance has evolved through the ages, what does seem clear from the classical and historical sources is that, as an article of material culture, it has always been an important reflection of identity; in this it does have continuity with the meaningful role tartan fulfills today.[17]

The Gaelic word for tartan is "breacan," meaning parti-colored or speckled. Over two thousand tartan patterns, called "setts," exist today. The original distinctiveness of setts related simply to local environments. Regional varieties of plants provided different colors, and early dyers simply used what they liked and what was available. Likewise, the design was up to the weaver's skill and fancy. Tartans were therefore linked with locality. Giving us an early account of western Highland life from his seventeenth-century travels, Martin Martin noted, "Every isle differs from each other in their fancy of making plaid as to the stripes in breadth and colours. This humour is as different through the mainland of the Highlands, in so far that they who have seen those places are able at first view of a man's plaid to guess the place of his residence" (Martin 1970 [1716]:247). Eventually local patterns evolved into standardized "setts" and the myriad of "ancient" distinctions used today.[18]

Individual tartans' connections to family names developed largely as a nineteenth-century innovation. Just as the tourist trade in Ireland claims the knot-work patterns in Aran sweaters identified drowned fishermen by family, the association of tartans with "family" identity has been a merchandising strategy for nearly two centuries. While some tartans may be connected with clans simply because that tartan was the product of the available dyes in the area and clans were regional, Highlanders before Culloden may have assembled a variety of tartans in one

Major Don O'Connor in late-nineteenth-century dress
and Ronald McLeod in eighteenth-century dress with
wooden shoes (McLeod's mother was from Belgium).

outfit; very few tartans can claim any documented historical connection
with clan names.[19]

Many clan societies have tartan origin stories. One I especially liked
is about the Morrison tartan. The tartan received a Letters Patent from
the Lyon Court in 1909, but (as so often happens in the reestablishment
of "ancient traditions" not forgotten, but out of practice) a discovery
was made that lends authentication to today's clan tartan. In the 1950s,
during the same time in which the first Morrison Clan Chief in three
hundred years was recognized, a bible was found on the Isle of Lewis

wrapped in a "300 year old piece of tartan" with a convenient note pinned to the cloth stating, "This is the Morrison tartan" and quite significantly dated 1745 (Morrison 1991:7). Notwithstanding that the bible was found "bricked up in the fireplace of a blackhouse"—when blackhouses were so-called because they generally did not have fire-places[20]—a new tartan was made accordingly. This serendipitous dis-covery, further authenticated by the biblical involvement, appears in clan society information leaflets and in explanations of the tartan by its wearers. It is a unique story and one of which clan members are espe-cially proud as it provides them, in their opinion, one of the few "legiti-mate," "genuine" tartans linked to a family name.

The quest for a historical record detailing a systematic association of tartans with individual family names became a craze among Lowland society circles following George IV's Scottish visit. Historian Hugh Trevor-Roper documents the amazing charade of the "brothers Allen" who published what they claimed to be a sixteenth-century manuscript illustrating all "authentic" clan tartans. Bonnie Prince Charlie sup-posedly gave the work, entitled *Vestiarium Scoticum*, to their father and accounting for this relationship led them to eventually intimate their own descent from Prince Charlie. They were hounded out of the country almost exactly one hundred years after their supposititious "grandfather."

Though discredited themselves, the Allen brothers' *Vestiarium* was nonetheless adopted by the Highland Society of London and the bur-geoning Scottish tartan industry (Trevor-Roper 1983:31–41). With the founding of Clan Societies from the 1880s on in Scotland, each claiming their own tartan, the tartan–clan connection brooked no further chal-lenge. Some clan societies now claim "authenticity" for their tartans through their appearance in the *Vestiarium Scoticum*.

The publication of a variety of reference books with illustrations of tartans alongside "family histories" gave the tartan industry established "tartan experts" and "scholarly" sources to cite in its promotions. Such books emphasize "the strength of emotion which seized upon the sym-bol of the tartan to express a sense of kinship" and the supposed antiq-uity of the tartan/clan connection "which has lasted in Scotland ever since the kindreds of the earliest Scots of Dalriada blossomed into clans" (Grimble 1973:11). This view of tartan's significance, developed through Highlandism and elaborated through the tourist industry, is that held today by many of the Scottish-American community. We may be able to trace the development of the clan/tartan association, but this does not make its contemporary expression "spurious" as Trevor-Roper describes it (1983:38). Today, tartans do identify Robertsons and Mac-

Wayne Cathey exhibits his tartan and clan identity wherever he goes. The Catheys are a sept of Clan Macfie. Macfie (Maca'phi) is thought to derive from "MacDhuibhshith," which means "son of the dark fairy." By tradition, the Macfies descend from a selkie.

Leods, Campbells and Grahams, within the international Scottish community. The wearing of tartan further symbolizes a love of Scottish heritage, whatever one's particular perspective of it may be. Current clan / tartan setts may not be ancient themselves, but the belief that they are instills them with an almost sacred quality as heritage.

Approaching Scottish Americans about the authenticity of clan setts, I encountered many levels of belief in the meaning and value of tartan. Several informants became quite angry and defensive (unfortunately at me) when the antiquity of their tartan was challenged. However, others involved in clan societies and heritage groups did say that tartans were "created." Among those who acknowledge this, there is a division between those who would then rank tartans from "most to least authentic" and those who think a tartan designed yesterday is as authentic as one from the eighteenth century, since the invention of new tartans "just carries on Scottish traditions."

Anyone can have a tartan designed for them today, whether or not their name is Highland or even Scottish. One informant, Doug Ikleman, designed a tartan for his German surname from the colors of the German flag, which he explains "literally weaves the two traditions together." He could wear the Fraser tartan, as Fraser was his mother's name, but wanted to "contribute something" to the celebration of Scottish heritage for his family and suggests that the tartan may be worn by those of German descent who participate in Scottish events.

Another twentieth-century innovation is the distinction between ancient and modern color schemes.[21] A "weathered" or "muted" color scheme was put out around the 1950s by the Dalgleish Weavers, supposedly after a piece of tartan was found at Culloden (the colors leached by the peaty acid at the moor).[22] Appealing to both aesthetics and feeling for the Jacobites, the different color schemes are yet another way to sell the same item in three variations. Tartans are also created today to commemorate historic events, for Scottish-related organizations, and even for businesses such as television corporations and the *Encyclopedia Britannica*. For those who prefer a tartan worn by the ancient Gaels, reproductions are available of the ninth-century tartan of Kenneth MacAlpin, the first king of both the Picts and the Scots. If that is not ancient enough, some of my informants and I have encountered those who claim their tartan was worn by Celts who fought the Romans.

The "best" tartan is imported from Scotland, mostly through the major players of the tartan industry, the large woolen mills of the Borders and Highlands (though there are a few weavers who supply the community from within North Carolina). One is recognized as an authority and "in the know" when one personally orders tartan through Scotland rather than buying from an importer. Knowing the weaver is even better, and many members of the North Carolina Scottish community obtain their tartan from one of the only full-time handloom tartan weavers in Scotland—Peter MacDonald, who is also the sole supplier of tartan to one of the community's favorite kilt-makers, Bob Martin.

Both MacDonald and Martin are unique in their trade in actively researching the history and "invented histories" of tartan. They see the invention of new tartans as part of the continual evolution of the cloth and its meaning. However, both disagree with the legalistic dress code practiced in the Scottish-American community (see appendix). In a series of articles about the kilt, Martin notes that to wear "*only* a certain jacket, shoes, belts, etc., with the kilt makes the outfit into either a costume or a uniform—neither of which it is" (1994:1). He also suggests wearing the kilt often, outside of heritage events, but cautions that "to talk about one's heritage is one thing; to live it is quite another. If you wear the kilt . . . be prepared to talk to some extent on the subject of what you are wearing. . . . Study as much as you can—your clans, your area of ancestry, your interest in your personal heritage and on the heritage of Highland dress" (1994:2).

Wearing the kilt, or wearing any form of tartan, is, for many, a commitment to "discover" and "live" their heritage. Whether one believes that the tartan/clan name connection is of recent or ancient origin, most accept that it is now "traditional." Cheape writes of the tartan that "today it is . . . a mark of genealogy and descent, since it is now an established tradition that we distinguish the different 'setts' with the names of chieftains, families and clans. Yet, while individuals and groups can claim a tartan to wear to proclaim their pedigree and descent, they are also wearing a badge of nationhood and proclaiming a firm sense of belonging" (1995:72).

Among Scottish Americans, one's tartan is a source of pride and a further identity marker beyond "being a Scot." The Clan Henderson ceilidh songbook includes a song entitled "The Tartan," which emphasizes pride in its antiquity; its emotive power over those of Scottish descent; the diaspora of the clans; and attachment to the "homeland." I reproduce the first and last verses here from *An Canach*:

> There are hundreds of tartans so lovely to see,
> And many a famous has graced the bare knee;
> And the sett I wear is both ancient and braw,
> It's the pride o' my heart and the dearest of a'
> Aye! The children of Scotia may roam the whole world o'er
> But their thoughts aye return to the land they adore,
> And the skirl of the pipes send the heart beating high,
> And the Tartans of home bring a tear to the eye. (1990:8)

One of the first interests of many on entering the Scottish-American community is to "see" and "find out about" their tartan. The quickest way to discover a "family" tartan is simply to attend a Highland Games and wander about the clan tents until finding a name that belonged to at least one known family member, and then having volunteers at the tent explain "the heritage" and the tartan.[23] As the investment in proper Highland attire is considerable, those planning to research their genealogy are cautioned against investing in too much tartan at once.[24] After research, some find they are actually entitled to wear an "older" tartan or perhaps wear one "of their own" rather than wear that of another clan, of which they believe their own family name to be a sept (a minor family or division within a clan). As many of the septs have been under several different clans over the years, a sept member is sometimes entitled to choose among numerous clan tartans.

It is therefore best to know the full range of choices before buying. Some informants found that they later regretted their original choice of tartan, purchased in the first flush of enthusiasm; but because switching clans involves a certain amount of lost face, and because the expense of reoutfitting in the proper tartan is formidable, they stayed with their original "alliance." Tartan has become for them not only a symbol of Scottishness or clan identity, but also a symbol of their bonds established with new "kinfolk."

Once adopted, a tartan shapes community members' further experience of the Scottish-American community through their participation in clan-focused events and in their perception of their own identity (which grows with their knowledge of clan history). Wearing a tartan also means that other community members may then identify the wearer as "one of those Buchannans, MacLachlans," or other clan. While to the world, tartan means "Scottish," within the Scottish-American community the distinctions between tartans can actually mean more than in Scotland. Heritage celebrants use their knowledge of tartan at heritage events in classifying community members and in seeking out other clan members; they do so without respect to class, which generally correlates with enthusiasm for tartan in Scotland. The Highlandist interpretation of tartan is further elaborated in the construction of another identity, that of Scottish Americans. Tartan works on two levels in America: as both the symbolic standard uniting Scottish Americans into a community and as mechanisms for expressing a more distinct identity within that community.

Highlandism Today

Tartan is obviously a central element of today's Highlandism, one for which North Carolina appears famous. An Edinburgh journalist has counted "the star-spangled clansmen of North Carolina" among "the most ardent tartaneers" (Rosie 1991:7). Despite the difference in climate and flora of the Cape Fear Valley, many community members assert that ancestral settlers wore tartan and that it was in fact other Colonials' reaction to their dress that caused them to settle in the less desirable inland "sand hills" of North Carolina. Stories suggest that the Scots settled the Cape Fear Valley, not because of land grants in the area, but because they were mocked on arrival in Wilmington for their "peculiar costumes and unusual language" (Lefler and Talmage 1954:79). These are interesting rationales if they point to post-proscription retention of Highland dress, but more because they point to present assumptions about the distinctiveness of the Highland identity in America. The historical and contemporary importance of tartan in North Carolina (the first state to have its own tartan) is now enshrined with the 1994 opening of the Scottish Tartans Museum and Heritage Center in Franklin.[25]

The Highlandist perspective of Scottish heritage has acquired many new dimensions and celebratory rituals in the last few decades of Scottish heritage revival. American innovations, such as the "Kirkin' o' the Tartan" (in which clan tartan banners are carried forward during a church service, usually Presbyterian) and the "christening" of a new kilt with a small splash of whisky, are widely practiced in North Carolina. Highlandism was rooted in the militarism of British empire-building and the romanticization of the old clan military system. Celebrations of the Scottish-American identity employ military traditions, marches, and dress in rituals emulating contemporary Scottish events. Although some Lowland regiments were not required to wear tartan until 1881, every Scottish regiment today has its "pipes and drums," and all band-members wear full Victorian-Highland costumes of dress tartan, silver-buttoned doublets, feather headpieces, and horse-hair sporrans. Heritage events in North Carolina frequently feature military color guards and massed-bands in dress modeled after that of Scottish regiments.

Clan societies and associations are also a further manifestation of Highlandism. Like tartan, the rituals and traditions of clan societies provide a distinctive identity within the community. Clan associations provide another layer of rules and symbols, and another set of songs and stories (all specifically regarding clan history) to one's Scottish heritage. Tartan serves as the primary marker of clan membership today, but historically, several other documented emblems distinguished Highland clans.

Most common seem to have been the "plant badges," sprigs of a certain plant associated with a clan. The well-researched MacDonald appears at a Highland Games with a bit of heather on his or her cap or lapel; a Grant displays a twig of pine; a Macmillan brings a sprig of holly. Each clan also has its own motto: the Haldane motto is "Suffer," Clan Carmichael's is "Always Ready." These are vaguely, but not always distinct from the clan slogan or war cry; that of Clan MacNaughten is "I hope in God"; the MacDowalls' is "To Conquer or Die." In addition, clan societies now research and revive or claim arms, a military bagpipe march, a clan pipe tune, and a crest badge.

Most clan societies acquaint their new members with its particular fetishes in society leaflets and other literature. In America, this goes unquestioned and is perhaps historically more amenable to documentation than are clan tartans. However, the Lord Lyon, the final authority on heraldry and pedigree in Scotland, denies the existence of a "clan crest" or a "clan coat of arms." These belong to the chief alone; a clansperson may wear the crest badge only if it is encircled by a belt and buckle. To wear the crest alone is actually to claim the chief's position; to use the crest on one's property marks it as the chief's. Visiting Clan Chiefs enjoy pointing this out to the many games vendors who sell crest cap and blazer badges, crest cups and steins, and crested wall plaques and tea towels.[26]

The crest has become a further, yet contentious, marker of identity within the American community. Debate within the American community about this new innovation centers less on whether Americans should wear it on their person, thus indicating themselves to be the possession of their chief, and more on whether those who claim membership in several clan societies may simultaneously wear one clan tartan with the crest pin of another clan on their cap or lapel. Interestingly, the debate stems from Scottish reprimands. The meaning and use of heritage continues to respond to transnational developments and "authorities" from the "homeland." I provide these lengthy examples to demonstrate the continuing evolution, if not involution, of Highlandism in Scottish heritage celebration. The Highlandist interpretation of ancestral experience is perhaps most evident in the continuing focus on Culloden as the reason for the Cape Fear settler's immigration.

Exiled Ancestors and a Highlandized
Heritage Set before Culloden

Heritage celebration focuses on Highland life prior to Culloden, employing symbols of "Scottish" identity developed one hundred years after Culloden. Clan Gunn's information booklet explains that the clan system "ended with the defeat of Bonnie Prince Charlie's Highlanders on the Moors of Culloden, near Inverness on April 16, 1746" (Swann 1994:4). An essential tenet of today's Highlandism is that after Culloden, all was different. Within a few years, Highland society had "broken down" and the clan system abruptly ceased to function. This is an often repeated theme in clan society literature and in the clan tartan reference books popular in the community. In *The Clans and Tartans of Scotland*, Bain writes, "The clan system ended the afternoon of 16th of April 1746" (1961 [1938]:24). The Highlanders suffered tremendous hardships following the Rising, which did spur immigration, but ships full of Jacobite refugees did not immediately flood North Carolina's shores (as is so often portrayed in heritage literature and celebration). The focus on what informants call the genocide of Highlanders following Culloden denies other factors at work in the dismemberment of clan society.

Hanoverian repression following the Jacobite defeat accelerated changes already in process. The Hanoverians' Acts were not the first to take a toll on Highland culture or society. Ironically, the Stuarts, to whom the Highlanders proved so loyal, had never shown great tolerance toward the political, cultural, and linguistic traditions of clan society. James VI imposed the Statutes of Iona in 1609 on the most powerful of the clan chiefs in the Highlands and Islands in an attempt to break their power. The Statutes called for a significant reduction in the size of a chief's household (to reduce the chief's bodyguard and retinue) and in the type of hospitality given to a chief by their clansfolk (to break down clanspeople's relationship with their chief). They required the leaders of clan society to send their children to be educated in English in the Lowlands and forbade their ownership of firearms. They also targeted Gaelic customs by forbidding the performance of bards (poet-musicians who traditionally maintained clan lore and praised the chief through song and story) and by prohibiting such practices as temporary marriages.

Historian Alan MacInnes notes that commercial relations between the chief and his clanspeople had been developing for nearly a century before 1746, and that the period following Culloden merely formalized the chief's position as landowner. To MacInnes, the demise of clanship as "the essential significance of the Jacobite defeat at Culloden" was the result not of the Proscription Act, but of clan elite "wholeheartedly embracing the Whig concept of progress and deliberately subordinating . . . their personal obligations as patrons and protectors. . . . The picture of a contented society broken up by alien forces wholly underestimates the cultural tensions within the clans prior to the Forty-Five provoked by the commercialising of customary relations by chiefs and leading gentry" (1989:72–73).

Cheape and Grant also note that improvements in communication and transportation helped to dismantle the clan social and military system (1997:60). While this is the historian's interpretation, my informants take a different view: they base much of their respect and interest in Highland tradition on the belief that their ancestors were bereft of their cultural expression and independence by Hanoverian persecution and legislation.

Though as many Lowlanders as Highlanders emigrated between 1763 and 1775, heritage lore describes forced expatriation of Highlanders as a diaspora. Many community members ascribe to what Meyer called "the exile theory," the belief that the majority if not all of Scottish emigrants were Highlanders driven to leave Scotland solely because of the Battle of Culloden. Many of those who settled in the Cape Fear Valley came from Argyllshire and had fought against the Jacobites. Historian Ian Graham cautions, "It is an exaggeration to describe Jacobite settlers as a 'wave' of emigration" (1956:45). Jacobites were transported immediately after the "Forty-Five," but according to David Dobson's compilation of emigration records, more people were banished to the plantations as a result of the Covenanter Risings in the seventeenth century (1984).[27] The Highlanders' mass emigrations over several decades of the eighteenth century had a number of causes, chief among them the changes in land tenure, the advent of "rack" rents, and the breakdown of clan society and of the chief's role as protector. However, as MacInnes notes, the period of repression following the Battle of Culloden merely accelerated forces of change that had already been making the clan social and economic system less viable. From the many historical reasons for immigration, a romanticized few provide an image of noble, persecuted Highlanders involuntarily leaving their beloved homeland because of their steadfastness for "a cause." This is not a recent heritage invention, but a story that itself has a history.

The inaccuracies of the exile myth are long-lived and seem to have developed shortly after the Revolutionary War, in nostalgia for home and in attempts to redress the Highlanders' association with Loyalism. Tales of banishment are supported by post–Civil War accounts of the Cape Fear Scots' descendants that are now revived as oral tradition in the Scottish-American community. In 1868 David MacRae began a travelogue-style interpretation of Americans for the British public called *The Americans at Home: Pen and Ink Sketches of American Men, Manners and Institutions.* In his travels across the country, MacRae spent time in the Cape Fear region and devoted three chapters to its description. Collecting histories from those he interviewed, he reported that North Carolina was a refuge not only for Jacobites from Culloden (1746), but also for those persecuted in an earlier Jacobite period incident, the 1692 Massacre at Glencoe.[28] MacRae interviewed a Hector MacNeill, who described the Scottish settlers' arrival to the area: "Most of them exiles from Scotland consequent on the troubles which followed the downfall of the Stuarts . . . some of them MacDonalds who had been fugitives from Glencoe" (1868:187). In heritage lore today, political persecution has come to figure as the largest, if not the sole, reason for the ancestral departure from Scotland. It is beyond doubt that the Highlanders suffered tremendously for their support of the Jacobites, but those in America had to be reminded of that suffering during the Revolutionary War.

Highlanders were so closely associated with Loyalism that just prior to the war an "Appeal to the Highlanders lately arrived from Scotland" appeared in Williamsburg, signed by a fictitious patriot called *"Scotus Americanus."* I quote from J. P. MacLean: "Let us view this Continent as a country marked out by the great God of nature as a receptacle for distress, and where the industrious and virtuous may range in the fields of freedom, happy under their own fig trees, freed from a swarm of petty tyrants, who disgrace countries the most polished and civilized, and who more particularly infest the region from whence you came" (1919:423). The preeminence of Culloden in Scottish-American mythology continues a similar forgetfulness about the multiple reasons ancestors immigrated. A focus on the dramatic and immediate demise of Highland society in 1746 detracts from the role the clan chiefs later played as landlords in removing clansfolk from their land. Descendants of the same "petty tyrants" in the Appeal of *Scotus Americanus* are honored guests at today's Scottish-American functions.

Today's Highlandism is a blend of historical documentation with emotive stories and songs of massacre and deprivation. In North Carolina, as in Victorian Scotland, it ignores the nineteenth-century Highland Clearances. This is so in North Carolina because the original settlement was before Clearance times.[29] In Victorian Scotland, acknowledgment of actual political and economic practices could not have coexisted with the myth and romance of Highlandism. Small groups of Highlanders did come to the Cape Fear Valley in the nineteenth century, but their memory is overshadowed today by that of their eighteenth-century predecessors.

The temporal gap between the immigrant Scots community and the contemporary Scottish-American community condenses at heritage events and in community literature so that the nineteenth-century Scottish Americans forming the actual bridge fade from view. The period during which the Scots assimilated, handed down new American traditions, and even attempted to downplay a Highland Scots origin (as they did immediately after the American Revolution) is seldom referenced in celebratory events. Beyond the new cultural, economic, and political losses of Scots-turned-southerners after the Civil War, I heard comparatively few mentions of the nineteenth-century "keepers of the flame" in conversation, presentations, or song at heritage events. Yet continuity through this period is assumed and accepted (if glossed over) as a validation of present activities and is implicit in participants' explanations of "the Scottish-American community." Any vague reference to a tradition carried on in the nineteenth century (such as "Scotch Fairs" and Scottish-style Presbyterian catechisms) may be used to connect the practices of today's community with the Colonial community rather than to nineteenth-century ancestors. The use of the Gaelic language and the survival of many Scottish customs in North Carolina are historically referenced well into the nineteenth century, but today's revivals—which emphasize continuity through these references—are nevertheless based on notions of what eighteenth-century practices were like.

The Scottish-American community's Highlandism recalls the deeds and experiences of Scots who were touched by Culloden and celebrates their legacy through events and dress developed in a nostalgic nineteenth-century Britain. The deeds of bonny, kilted soldiers frame images of the auld country—never the writers of the Glasgow "Kailyard School," the industrial heritage of Scotland, or its great artists in the Celtic revival of the late nineteenth century. Those nineteenth-century Scots uninvolved in Highlandism are also excluded in the celebration of a heritage focused on the "death" of Scottish Gaelic society.

What may begin as selective choosing and enhancement of traditions takes on the significance of heritage with time. As John MacKenzie notes: "Myths gain their power from repetition and demonstrate their strength through their continuing acceptability. . . . Their popular influence is also secured through an iconography of simple, but potent visual references to the main themes and messages of the story" (1990:30–31). Tartan provides an automatic reference to the experience of the Jacobite Highlanders, as remembered in nineteenth-century Scotland—well after their "exile." Symbolizing the clan system and its demise, tartan's adoption by Americans of Highland, Lowland, and Ulster-Scots ancestry affirms, not only the continuing appeal of Highlandism, but enduring transnational links between "a home across the water" and descendants of immigrants who crossed that water centuries ago. The following chapter will address the development of the heritage movement in North Carolina and the North Carolina community's uniqueness within America.

Scottish Heritage and Revival
in North Carolina

Sunny afternoons spent wandering through rural church cemeteries as a child with my great-aunt Edna taught me what can be learned by pondering the epitaphs of departed saints. Gravestones outline individual and family histories, and their placement within a cemetery relates still more. Who rests beside whom, and how central a location they occupy in the grounds, communicates something about their lives and relation to their community. Most revealing for Aunt Edna was the condition of the plot and the stone. Tokens of recent visits, wilting flowers and well-tended spaces, quietly eulogize those whose remembrance remains fond. In contrast, once beautiful—or even pompous—markers now obscured by weeds and lichen no longer memorialize a person, but the analogous mortality of human memory. Those still visited are those who continue to play a role in community or family life. Their faithfully maintained graves represent more than their own lives; they provide a sense of place and roots for relatives or descendants in the area. Aunt Edna aptly concluded that only neglected graves make a cemetery sad.

I kept her words in mind when another guide showed me the cemeteries of the Cape Fear Scots. Having taken many heritage pilgrims on the cemetery tour before, Mr. McGugan's reminiscences knowingly centered on the hazards of poison ivy and snakes at our first destination, the secluded "Old Scotch Burying Ground" on Widow Bethune's Hill. Purposely situated on high ground near the town of Carthage, this final resting place of immigrant Highlanders was overgrown, but not uncared for.

Among the leaning and broken stones, and the trees that have grown between them since their placement, were several newly erected marble markers, not for new residents, but for MacGillivrays, MacCaskills, and other "Macs" who settled in the sand hills in the 1700s. In fact, all of the oldest sand hill cemeteries, such as "Stewartsville" outside of Laurinburg, or the burial grounds at the earliest Presbyterian churches (Longstreet, Barbecue, Bluff, and Old Bethesda), host new stones for the long-dead.

Erected by individuals and clan societies to commemorate eighteenth-century ancestors, the new stones tell of immigration from places in the Scottish Highlands and Islands; they often note occupation or nick-names, and they may express clan affiliation with carved clan crests. These monuments also tell another story about the continued impor-tance of immigrant ancestors for contemporary Scottish Americans' sense of self, place, and community. As Mr. McGugan kindly pointed out the ivy and the highlights of these hallowed grounds that mark Scottish territory, my interest in the older, original stones diminished with re-gard to the continued devotion evidenced by new memorials. These were not sad places. Their monuments relate identity-shaping memories and collectively serve as tangible reminders of a heritage.

Why these particular Scottish ancestors shape that heritage and how varied Scottish traditions have blended in North Carolina are the sub-jects of this chapter, which explores both Carolina's unique settlers and unique heritage revival.

Lowland, Highland, and Scots-Irish
Roots of North Carolina's Scots

Three groups of Scottish immigrants came to North Carolina, each with different cultural backgrounds and reasons for immigrating, and each settled in different areas of the state. Lowland Scots tended to settle more as individuals along the coast with the English. For reasons previously discussed, Highlanders tended to settle together in the Cape Fear Valley. The Scots-Irish settled primarily in the western backcoun-try, the mountains, and in the Piedmont along the Eno and the Haw Rivers. Considering their wider dispersal, their much greater numbers, and their favored status after supporting the Patriots in the Revolution-ary War, it would seem that Scots-Irish imagery should have predomi-nated in any heritage revival—especially as an identity forged in this country.

The Scots-Irish so named themselves to convey their distinctiveness from the Scots-Highlanders, whose Loyalist reputation survived long after the Revolution; later the name served to distinguish them from the

"Celtic" or native Catholic Irish, who came to America with the famines of the 1840s and 1860s.[1] But unlike the Gaelic-speaking Highlanders who kept alive cultural ties with their homeland (even sending for ministers and educators from their home areas), the English-speaking Scots-Irish who arrived before the Revolution more readily relinquished cultural links with Northern Ireland, where they had always been an ethnic minority.[2]

The Scots-Irish were Lowland Scots Presbyterians who, in the early seventeenth century, began settling the area of Ireland most problematic for British rule: the province of Ulster, where they are known as Ulster Scots. Sometimes unwillingly induced to play a part in James VI's "plantation" scheme, they maintained what Fitzpatrick (1989) has called a "frontiersman-mentality" for a century and a half before emigrating for the colonies. Those who left Northern Ireland went because of repressive trade laws, famine, and a decline in the important linen industry (Ramsey 1964:140). Once in America, they remained distinct from both Highland and Lowland Scots and received government land grants to do what they were known for: to live on the frontier as a buffer between what was considered civilized/government-protected areas and so-called hostile, native territory.

Despite the history of self-segregation among the various Scottish immigrants to America, it is the kilted Highlander image that has emerged in twentieth-century celebrations of "the auld country" and that has been adopted by descendants of Lowland Scots and Scots-Irish. A blending of traditions that ancestors would find anathema is not uncommon in heritage celebrations generally. Especially in the age of multiculturalism, we gloss gaps and fuzzy edges of our cultural knowledge in a willingness to embrace an inclusive heritage. In 1996, Radford University in Virginia adopted the MacFarlane as its "official tartan," began a Highlander Festival and adopted a new mascot, "the Highlander," "in celebration of" its Scots-Irish roots. As today's image of the Highlander evolved from the Jacobite period, it is interesting to consider that the ancestors of today's Scots-Irish fought for William of Orange against the Jacobites in Ireland. Imagery of the Jacobite period remains powerful fuel in Ireland's "Troubles," as Protestant Ulster Scots' annual July 12 and August 12 parades still commemorate James II's defeat at the 1690 Battle of the Boyne and the Siege of Derry. Jacobite themes do not seem to have shaped the immigrant experience, folklore, or group identity of Scots-Irish immigrants in the American South the way they have those of the Highland Scots defeated in the cause.[3] Yet many of today's Scots-Irish involved in "Scottish" celebrations now adopt cultural artifacts associated with Jacobite Highlanders as heritage. Perhaps this is best explained by the fact that the Scots-Irish lacked dramatic ethnic boundary markers.

Historians Tyler Blethen and Curtis Wood refer to the Scots-Irish as "a people practiced in abandoning their past" (1983:20). While they famously brought folklore and musical and architectural traditions, they did not bring a material culture as distinctly representative of their identity as the Highlanders'unique fabrics and style of dress. What crossed the Atlantic and became part of their new identity related more to worldview, subsistence strategies, and farming techniques—not the artifactual material culture of the Highlander that has become emblematic as "Scottish" in heritage celebration today.

However, the Scots-Irish, Scots-Highlanders, and Lowlanders maintained discrete identities and settlement strategies in Colonial America. The Highlanders retained their Gaelic language and, while prominent members of the Cross Creek community also spoke English, many employed translators when dealing with Scots-Irish, German, and English merchants (Meyer 1961:112–18). Even the Lowlands dialect, "Scots," is considered a separate language by many speakers. Little record exists of intermarriage between the different Scottish groups—even long after their political antagonism over the Revolutionary War. What all three largely shared was, and is, the Presbyterian faith. The Presbyterianism of North Carolina, and the South in general, has its roots in the Scottish Lowland Covenanting tradition. Today, Lowland perspectives of religious faith blend easily with the Highland identity embraced by Scottish Americans, but this was not always so.

"Covenanters" were mostly Lowland Scots who formed a 1638 "Covenant" with God in rejection of Episcopalianism. Outlawed by the Crown, they held their religious "conventicle" services outdoors. They followed John Knox's advocacy of militant opposition to irreligious or immoral government leaders and considered the Stuarts (for whom the Jacobites fought) "anti-Christs." Worshippers came to the illegal conventicles armed against the government forces who often disbanded them.[4] Many Covenanters were transported to the Carolinas, and churches there still incorporate "Covenant" in their names. Lowlanders who later settled in North Carolina brought a pride in their seventeenth-century Covenanter ancestors that was still alien to the eighteenth-century Highlanders around whom heritage lore has formed.

Highlanders generally fought with the Royalist troops *against* the Covenanters—not so much from religious conviction, but out of spite for the Covenanting Campbell Clan. The events of the Covenanting period reflect the centuries-old cultural differences within Scotland, especially across the Highland/Lowland divide, but also between clans.

It was the faith of the Covenanters that many of the later Lowland immigrants took with them to Northern Ireland and, as the majority of Northern Irish Scots who left for America were of these later arrivals, to the Colonies as well.

While the Scots-Irish kept themselves apart from the Highlanders in America, Scots-Irish missionaries did not, so that both groups of settlers (divided by culture, politics, and economic strategies) came to share a faith. Most of the Highlanders settling in North Carolina were already Presbyterians of various perspectives.[5] (Catholic Highlanders mainly immigrated to Canada and those who came to North Carolina generally became Presbyterians.) Few educated clergy traveled the frontier often, so predominantly Gaelic-speaking Highlanders had to take what they could get: English-speaking Scots-Irish missionaries. Only in 1758 with the simultaneous founding of Barbecue, Longstreet, and Bluff Presbyterian Churches did the first Gaelic-speaking minister, Rev. James Campbell, arrive—and he was forced to leave because of his pro-Independence sympathies and his Highland congregations' Loyalist leanings. From their initial settlement on, Highlanders were exposed to the Covenanting Presbyterianism of Scots-Irish missionaries and subsequent ministers. Today the blending of Highland culture and Lowland faith (oppositional in ancestral Scotland) is a striking aspect of southern Scottish heritage celebrations.[6]

Blended Traditions in Heritage Celebration

Religious aspects of Scottish heritage celebration most evince the merged traditions of North Carolina's Scots. Emphases at Scottish events in the Cape Fear region and elsewhere in the state include not only Scottish heritage, but Christian heritage as influenced by the Covenanters. At heritage events, Covenanter-style Presbyterianism incorporates the new rituals of Highlandism. Today, a Presbyterian worship service honoring Scottish ancestors and called a "Kirkin' o' the Tartan" often takes place in an open field to emulate conventicles.[7] At the annual Loch Norman Games in Charlotte, the twentieth-century Kirkin' occurs outdoors like a seventeenth-century Covenanter service and is "defended" by the 78th Fraser Highlanders—a reenactment group wearing the eighteenth-century attire of Highlanders (who would have fought in opposition to the Covenanters and attacked their conventicles). The Kirkin' concludes with a "blessing of the tartan"—though Lowland Covenanters associated the fabric with enmity, and though endorsing the blessing and iconization of a material product is unusual in itself for Presbyterians.

Dr. Peter Marshall, chaplain of the U.S. Senate, a Presbyterian, and native Scot, originated the Kirkin' as a service of prayer for all Britons during World War II. Kirkin's became an annual event for the Washington St. Andrew's Society and are now exceptionally popular and considered traditional in the South. Appealing stories have already emerged that provide eighteenth-century origins for this new custom. Again, explanations begin with Culloden and merge distinct religious and cultural perspectives. During the years of tartan's illegality, defeated Jacobites are said to have brought to church swatches of their clan tartans, over which their pastor would secretly invoke God's blessing.[8] Documentation shows that Kirkin's are of recent origin, yet their acquisition of more emotive historical roots that reconciles those roots with current faith and practice is a fascinating and revealing cultural process.

We adopt from the past what serves us in the present. The solemn procession of tartan banners at a Kirkin' is all the more solemn and meaningful when perceived as an expression of freedom—the revision of an illegal tradition practiced by a desperate people in defeat and at their peril. The rapid evolution of myth is in keeping with Highlandist themes and importantly invests simple ceremony with richly layered meanings. As an act of remembering ancestral fortitude through persecution, whether one's ancestors actually experienced it or not, the Kirkin' has become a truly hyphenated celebration of a generalized Scottish heritage and present American liberties.

Such an alluring blend of Lowland and Highland traditions also characterizes Scottish-American innovations in rituals marking life transitions, or rites of passage. Infant baptisms may involve the use of water brought from the Scottish Highlands (even though the family may be of Lowland or Scots-Irish origin), and weddings in the Scottish community are always "Highland weddings." Every Highland Games, most Scottish-oriented religious services, and sections within community literature pay tribute to the "Flowers of the Forest"—those who have passed on during the year. Highland pipe-players perform the same Lowland lament (written to commemorate townsmen of Selkirk who fell at the 1513 Battle of Flodden Field), as community members place stones on a memorial cairn after the Highland tradition. Performers also play and occasionally sing this tune at funerals of Scottish Americans deeply involved in the heritage movement.

Two standard events for North Carolina heritage associations that also combine Lowland and Highland expressive culture are St. Andrew's Day Dinners (November 30) and Burns's Night Suppers (January 25). Lowlanders revered relics of St. Andrew when Celtic Christianity still predominated in the Highlands, yet his day is celebrated in Highland style. Robert Burns (1759–96) was a Lowland poet famous both for writing in his native "Lallan" (Lowland) Scots dialect, and composing romantic, after-the-fact Jacobite songs. Like Sir Walter Scott, he contributed to what is called the "shortbread-tin-version" of the Scottish identity.[9]

Celebration of St. Andrew's Day and Burns's birthday are Lowland traditions. Dinner on the day of Scotland's patron saint is now the main annual social function of St. Andrew's Societies across the world, although it is not a public holiday in officially Presbyterian Scotland. The Lowland Scots development of Burns's Night was later adopted by Ulster Scots so that some Scots-Irish abroad also celebrate January 25. However, this is not a tradition passed down through families and never has been. It began in men's literary and social associations. There are now Robert Burns Societies around the world. The most active in North Carolina is the oldest, begun in Charlotte following a Burns's Night Supper in 1955. All of North Carolina's Scottish interest groups hold events honoring the poet's birthday—even Franklin's Scottish Tartans Museum sponsors a Burns's Night Celebration featuring bagpipes and the "Museum's Own Scottish Country Dancers."

These Lowland traditions are today celebrated in Highland dress and with Highland music. The featured fare at both is haggis: a sheep's paunch stuffed with liver, heart, and other organs mixed with suet and oatmeal, and at one time flavored with blood. (In view of the ingredients it is somewhat comforting that the meal is generally blessed with Burns's "Selkirk Grace.")[10] The haggis is boiled and ceremoniously cut open at both dinners—with a Highland broadsword or a reproduction of a basket-hilted sword from the Jacobite Period when available. On Burns's Night, his own "Address to the Haggis" in the Lowland Scots dialect is read or recited as the dish is "piped" into the dining area.[11] After-dinner entertainment by pipers and Highland dancers generally figures at both events in North Carolina.[12] Programs for the dinner often note "Ceud Mile Failte" (100,000 Welcomes), though Burns did not speak Gaelic.

Heritage events not only combine Highland/Lowland influences, but also combine time periods and unrelated themes in a dynamic pastiche of "Scottish" celebration. Event dinner menus add Scottish names to entrees, Scot-ifying American, or English, foods: what is considered traditional English fare, roast beef, becomes Bannockburn Roast Beef (Bannockburn being the best-known Scottish victory over the English); chicken becomes Chicken Stornoway or Pitlochry Boneless Poulet (French terms commonly invoke the "Auld Alliance" between Scotland

and France against England); salad becomes Highland Salad (though salad was not an option in the celebrated, eighteenth-century Highlands); even basic vegetables acquire Highland place names such as Barra Green Beans and Callanish Carrots. Dinners are followed by toasts, to honor Queen Elizabeth II and the American president, the order being occasionally reversed.[13]

As occasions for "remembering," heritage events incorporate any symbolism and historical motifs that celebrants literally "re-collect." All heritage revivals generalize and combine partially recalled meanings for greater appeal. Just as Burns's Night in America becomes a celebration of "Scottish heritage" in general, most Robbie Burns Societies today focus less specifically on Burns than on "the preservation and promotion of the customs and traditions of Scotland." Combining traditions in the celebration of a heritage only partially remembered, many Scottish societies define Scottish heritage in terms of "Scottish dress," Highland and country dancing, Burns and bagpipes. Though stereotyped, today's expression of Highlandism in heritage celebration provides a sense of solidarity among the diverse Scottish-American community and a sense of continuity between today's celebrants and equally diverse "ancestral Scots" for whom that unity never existed.

While North Carolina heritage groups draw on several traditions to evoke a unified "Scottish heritage" amenable to those of varying descent, their celebrations are considered by many participants, and by "outsiders" from other states, to be the most "legitimate" celebration of "Scottish roots" in the United States (their words, not mine). Descendants of Scots-Irish and Lowland and Highland Scots in North Carolina all locate the historical heart of the state's Scottish-American community in the original Highland settlement in the Cape Fear Valley.

North Carolina's Unique Scottish Heritage
and the Legacy of Flora MacDonald

Beyond having the largest concentration of Highlanders anywhere in America, the eighteenth-century Cape Fear settlement is remarkable for drawing the largest number of any Scots directly from their home territory in Scotland. Not only did Highlanders first travel to the place they intended to settle, they stayed there—an unusual occurrence for Colonial Scottish immigrants. Lowland Scots eventually moved inland, decades after their coastal settlement, and Scots-Irish incomers to North Carolina generally traveled down the Great Wagon Road from Pennsylvania. Because of the original and purposeful settlement in the Cape Fear, the Valley's Highland community features in heritage lore as

The McArthur family still lives on land in Pinehurst, North Carolina, settled by their fifth great-grandfather, who emigrated from Scotland.

the homeland of Scots in America. However, it is not where the heritage movement began, in terms of "Scottish events." The first Burns's Night Suppers and Scottish Country Dances were in the mostly Scots-Irish-settled Charlotte, and the state's first twentieth-century Highland Games commenced in the Scots-Irish-settled mountains.

These events began, however, with reference to the Cape Fear settlers, and today's statewide organizations all draw upon Cape Fear connections. The Cape Fear Highlanders made North Carolina the most Scottish of states, which somehow confers authenticity on events throughout the state "beyond the pale" of Highlander settlement. Today, those with roots in the Scots-Irish areas who attend heritage events, unless they are

Flora MacDonald, as painted in 1747 by Richard Wilson. Born on
South Uist, she returned to her husband's native Skye after the
American Revolution. (Courtesy Scottish National Portrait Gallery)

interested in genealogy, never suspect that their ancestors might disapprove. Even many involved in clan society activities do not distinguish between Scots-Irish and Highlanders, but may distinguish themselves as North Carolina Scots.

Another major factor in North Carolina Scots' particular pride in their heritage, often evoked in celebrations, is the brief Cape Fear residence of the Jacobite heroine Flora MacDonald. Flora MacDonald is a central figure in Jacobite mythology in Scotland as well, so North Carolina's claim on her is indeed prestigious within the Scottish-American community. Flora's fame comes from helping Bonnie Prince Charlie escape his Hanoverian pursuers by dressing him as her maid and traveling with him to the Isle of Skye. Flora was in her fifties when she, her husband, and two of their sons immigrated to North Carolina in 1774. Though they left as persecuted Loyalists just a few years later, no other state can claim such an association with such a famous Jacobite immigrant.[14]

The romantic drama of her connection with Prince Charlie is repeated over and over at heritage conferences and events in the state as it is at interpretation centers and tourist shops across Scotland. The "Flora MacDonald Highland Games" in Red Springs is an annual commemoration of her North Carolina legacy. Heritage events and symposiums have included the performance of an opera about Flora.[15] Writing about the Highland settlement in his "The Highland Call," North Carolina playwright Paul Green featured Flora and her family. First performed in 1939 and again in 1976 Bicentennial celebrations, the play is well known to community members. Participants at every North Carolina ceilidh (an evening of song, dance, and Scottish music) sing "The Skye Boat Song," which relates the tale of Flora's heroism:

> Loud the winds howl, loud the waves roar,
> Thunderclaps rend the air;
> Baffled our foes stand on the shore,
> Follow they will not dare.
>
> *Refrain:*
> Speed bonnie boat, like a bird on the wing,
> "Onward," the sailors cry!
> Carry the lad who's born to be king,
> Over the sea to Skye
>
> Though the waves leap, soft shall ye sleep,
> Ocean's a royal bed:
> Rocked in the deep, young Flora will keep
> Watch by your weary head
>
> (Refrain)
>
> Many's the lad fought on that day;
> Well the claymore could wield,
> When the night came, silently lay
> Dead on Culloden's field
>
> (Refrain)
>
> Burned are our homes; exile and death
> Scatter the loyal men;
> Yet e'er the sword cool in the sheath,
> Charlie will come again (Donaldson 1988:3)

In today's North Carolina Scottish community, Flora MacDonald is still a popular given name. Many people in the Cape Fear area also claim to be descended from Flora MacDonald. In view of Flora's age and the fact that Flora, her husband, and two sons returned to Scotland, this is doubtful, but illustrates how half-remembered histories become heritage and the continuing strength of Flora's mystique. In 1976, the British Broadcasting Corporation did a series of programs on "America at 200." One of the programs was *The Valley of the Scots*, filmed partly at the first of a short-lived Highland Games at Ellerbe, North Carolina. One participant states, "I am Flora MacDonald, a descendant of the original Flora MacDonald," in a strong accent of the area. The clip's repetition throughout the program is meant to be humorous. Many of the older members of the Harnett County Historical Society, with whom I viewed the video, did not appreciate the humor, not because it seemed to mock her accent, but because, as one man told me, "It was probably true, you know."

A little over one hundred years before the BBC, another Brit came to interpret Americans to the British and encountered Flora's descendants. David MacRae makes several mentions of the legacy of Flora MacDonald, including a man who claimed to be Flora's grandson. He "always wore ruffles and wouldn't do manual labor because of his high connections," as a result of which he was "so often poor and went without shoes, but not without his ruffles" (1868:199).

It is interesting that this man thought of Flora as a "high connection," as if her brush with royalty made her such. She is regarded as a kind of North Carolina royalty today. MacRae relates what he was told of her arrival to North Carolina: "The heroine was received at Wilmington and various points along her route with Highland honours; the martial airs of her own native land greeted her as she approached Cross Creek; the little capitol of the Highland Settlement" (1868:187). This story may be fabulous, but if a true representation of accounts he heard, it reveals nineteenth-century perceptions of the Cape Fear community and the continuing power of legends about Flora's presence within it.

Of these legends, the people I interviewed remember only snatches in which she is portrayed much like a queen or imperial personage. Because the predominant stories about her stem from her week-and-a-half acquaintance with Bonnie Prince Charlie, it is as if through that experience she retained his aura. She and the prince are described with the same words: "brave," "gallant," and "noble" (though not "bonny"). On a slab monument at the former Flora MacDonald College in Red Springs, an inscription reads: "The Preserver of Prince Charles Edward Stuart will be mentioned in history and, if courage and fidelity be virtues, mentioned with honor."[16] As a dominant symbol of Jacobitism and of Highland identity in the Cape Fear Valley, her image is even stronger than Prince Charlie's. She did "come back again" to Scotland (as so many Jacobite songs implored Charles to do), having had other adventures abroad, while Charlie merely drank abroad.

One story reverently retold at heritage events relates to Flora's involvement in the Revolutionary War. Her husband was a Loyalist captain, and Flora is said to have traveled with the Loyalist Highland troops from the Cape Fear settlement before the Battle of Moore's Creek Bridge, slept the first night at camp, and reviewed the troops from the back of a large white horse. Though her husband had fought for the Hanoverians in the "Forty-Five," Flora's Jacobite fame was a significant factor in raising the Highland forces. While she helped Charlie away from the disaster of Culloden, her celebrity for this helped lead many Highlanders to death in what has been called the "American Culloden." For many of those who survived Moore's Creek and subsequent battles, emigration once again became inevitable.[17]

Flora's experiences are a continual source of interest for heritage enthusiasts, and of research by community historians. When I initially considered an archaeological survey of the Cape Fear Valley, everyone I met wanted me to locate Flora MacDonald's "plantation" and each person had a different, and somewhat passionate, conviction about where it might have been. Flora's mobility during her brief stay in North Carolina has caused much contention about where her main house was located and whether it was or was not called "Killiegray."[18] (Similarly, there is such a controversy on the Isle of Skye over which house Flora had lived in, that Historic Scotland—the national body responsible for the research and upkeep of many historic sites—has removed the structure long claimed to be her home from its list of historic properties.) Members of the Scottish-American community from all over the country come to search for Flora's house.

Without an undisputed home site, Flora's connection with the Cape Fear is perhaps best enshrined through the renaming of the Red Springs Seminary for Women as Flora MacDonald College. The area's association with Flora was so well known that an out-of-state commencement speaker in 1916 suggested the name change.[19] Flora MacDonald College gave new life to the former spa town of Red Springs and provided a focus for the eventual development of heritage events that are still held at the college buildings. (In 1961, the Presbyterian synod of North Carolina merged Flora MacDonald College with the male Presbyterian Junior College of Maxton to create St. Andrew's College in Laurinburg.)

Few of the Flora MacDonald alumnae with whom I spoke knew much about Flora before attending the college; an interest in things Scottish was not a prime factor in their choice of schools. From their days at the college they recall requirements to learn the "Highland Fling" (and to dance it in a kilt), the Presbyterian services on Sundays, and the portrayal of Flora as exemplary of the high ideals of womanhood to which students should aspire. The Flora MacDonald alumnae who are involved in Scottish heritage are still referred to as "Flora girls." At several events that I attended they have been asked to stand and be recognized as a living symbol of yet something else now in the past.[20']

Since 1991, St. Andrew's College has given an annual Flora Mac-Donald Award for those active in promoting awareness of things Scottish. What award recipients have promoted generally fits with the heritage movement's conception of "Scottish." Sloan notes that "the tradition of the Presbyterian academy can be traced most directly to policies followed by the church in Ulster" and that the earliest known Presbyterian academies in North Carolina were founded at Wilmington and at Crowfield, by ministers who had come over directly from Ulster (1971:39, 42). However, the Presbyterian St. Andrew's College and its parent academies have celebrated a Highland heritage. The St. Andrew's Scottish Heritage Center, "established to highlight and preserve the Scottish traditions of the Carolinas and beyond," displays several Jacobite relics, including a lock of Bonnie Prince Charlie's hair.

The St. Andrew's Bagpipe Band tours the circuit of heritage events, drawing recognition and community support for "America's only Scottish-American University." North Carolina's heritage movement has many unique aspects when considered within the wider Scottish community (a Presbyterian academic tradition, the eighteenth-century Highland community, and a connection to an actual Jacobite heroine— even if she was hounded away). North Carolina also claims a unique process of heritage revival, significantly influenced by the efforts of one man, Donald MacDonald.

Heritage Revival and Donald MacDonald

Associations of Scottish descendants were formed across America just prior to the Civil War and mostly in the North and West following the war. Coinciding with the arrival of "the famine Irish" and large numbers of non-northern European immigrants, these associations blurred the hitherto distinct Lowland, Highland, and Scots-Irish identities in commemoration of collectively "Scottish" origins. North Carolina did not have the influx of Irish or southern and eastern European immigrants that the northern cities and Midwest experienced, and Scottish developments in the state related specifically to Carolina's southern context and unique history. A succession of short-lived "Scottish patriotic" societies formed in North Carolina between the 1880s and 1920s, perhaps beginning in the 1880s because the South was just awakening from the shock of war, or perhaps because of a new influx of Scots Highlanders in 1884 to the Cape Fear Valley.

This new immigration was the British Napier Commission's answer to the hardships Highlanders endured as a result of "The Clearances." Set up to study and alleviate the Highlanders' distress, the commission invited over forty families to emigrate to Carolina with the promise of shelter and employment for a year after their arrival. Immigrants came mostly from the Isle of Skye to the Valley and many, not finding the "Highland," predominantly Gaelic-speaking community they had expected, or the prosperity that the commission had promised, returned to Scotland.[21] Their experience is not well documented, so any association between their presence and the simultaneous founding of Scottish societies could be completely in error.

Following the Great Depression, a second attempt at reviving the Scottish community came in 1939 when a bicentennial celebration of the Highland settlement took place in Fayetteville. The event was intended to be annual, but World War II intervened. In the two years of its existence, a thousand people signed their names in the visitor book. Many noted their ancestry back to Scotland, adding beside their names that of an ancestor five generations earlier. Interest and awareness was certainly there, but a heritage movement with staying power would have to wait until after the war, and for an energetic leader.

The current revival began, as it did across the country, in the 1950s. In North Carolina, it was led by Donald MacDonald, a charismatic news reporter who, as such, was perfectly placed to promote events and an interest in Scottish heritage. He attended a gathering of MacLeods in eastern North Carolina in 1953, which inspired him to organize the MacDonalds into a clan society. He went to Scotland in 1954, met the chief of Clan MacDonald, visited the Edinburgh Festival, and attended the Braemar Highland Gathering. Back in North Carolina he gave talks about his trip wearing the kilt he had bought in Scotland. He hosted a Burns's Night Supper in 1955 in Charlotte, as a result of which the Robert Burns Society of Charlotte was formed. He afterward became cofounder of Clan Donald U.S.A. and its first North Carolina commissioner.

In 1956, he met Agnes MacRae Morton of Linville, who was interested in MacDonald's activities and the prospect of a Highland Games to draw tourists to the area. They settled on "MacRae Meadows" for the site of the first Grandfather Mountain Highland Games and chose August 19 for the date—the anniversary of the 1745 raising of Prince Charlie's standard at Glenfinnan. MacDonald noted, "No other setting could compare with it and I believe that this is the main reason that it has become the premier Games in America" (Mitchell 1992:3). The first games attracted a few thousand people; MacDonald never expected them to grow to the current crowds of over 30,000 (MacDonald 1993).

As his guide for organizing the games, he used his Braemar Souvenir Program. He also performed a variety of roles to ensure the success of the first games. The Highland dancing competition drew only as many contestants as there were prizes and took place only because Mac-Donald himself performed a "Highland Fling." A religious service was required to open the Sunday games, so in lieu of a Scottish minister, MacDonald also preached a short sermon.

Braemar is Scotland's most prestigious games, attended by the queen, and Grandfather is America's most renowned, so that MacDonald is often referred to as "the father of America's Braemar." He is certainly the author of North Carolina's Scottish heritage revival, orchestrating the first games, Burns's Nights, clan society events, and Scottish country dancing. He researched both Scottish history and the history of Scots in North Carolina and lectured across the state, as he is still invited to do, to awaken interest in Scottish heritage. The shape of many now "traditional" events within the community was conceived by Mac-Donald, and his activities in the western part of the state still leave their mark—in one case, literally.

MacDonald thought the Scotland-like landscape of MacRae Meadows in Scots-Irish territory was the best setting for a Highland Games. He also managed to "improve" the un-Scottish feel of at least one "sacred place" in the sand hills homeland of the Carolina Scots. He felt the Stewartsville Cemetery was not a romantic enough setting for the graves of several immigrant Jacobites said to be buried there, so he brought Spanish moss, not indigenous to the spot, to hang from its trees and "add to its appeal." A 1988 BBC production on Scots abroad, entitled *The Blood Is Strong*, opens with a shot of the what are now moss-laden trees over reputed-Jacobite tombstones.

The camera crew was taken there by MacDonald's nephew, James MacDonald, who has become a fluent Gaelic speaker and has won Gaelic singing competitions in Scotland. All of MacDonald's family have become involved in the heritage movement: his sister and her daughter, Flora MacDonald and "Flora MacDonald the younger," are the music directors at the Grandfather Games, and a brother-in-law organized Grandfather's sporting events for over twenty years.

MacDonald also brought music back with him from his tour of Scotland. He introduced North Carolina to the romantic songs celebrating Jacobitism by Lady Caroline Oliphant Nairne, as well as to clan songs. One which he mentions as particularly popular in the early days of the revival was called "My ain folk." It was the type of song over which he notes "exiles would weep copiously, but we do it because of romantic notions over what [Scotland] was supposed to be like and never was" (MacDonald 1995). Four decades later in 1997, he and his nephew organized the first Gaelic Mod (a singing and drama competition) at the Grandfather Games. The first Mod in Scotland took place in 1891, also in an attempt to revive interest in the language. Its inclusion at the Grandfather Games, with Scottish judges and some competitors flown in for the event, is just one of the latest transnational developments in North Carolina's unique heritage revival and another MacDonald contribution.

Donald MacDonald married a native Gaelic speaker and singer, the late Marietta MacLeod, and has lived in Scotland since the 1960s, where he has been involved in activities at Highland Games and became the first American to be elected president of a Burns Society in Scotland. He has an active interest in the heritage movement as it has developed since he left, and is amused by what he calls the "sometimes over-serious" attitudes which many community members carry into events. (While taking his heritage seriously, MacDonald appreciates the selection of tradition—especially as a well-known selector—and emphasizes the importance of fun.) He enjoys returning for events and maintains links with their organizers. He was warmly received as the Grandfather Mountain Games' honored guest in 1995 and is invited to speak at North Carolina events whenever he is stateside. His enthusiasm and hard work significantly shaped the tone and structure of Scottish heritage celebration and contributed to the North Carolina community's prominence in America.

Singing the Heritage: The Importance of Song in the Claiming of Identity

Donald MacDonald's use of song to reintroduce people to their past and to their heritage is still a part of new members' education in learning about Scottish History and the Scottish community. Song is a featured part of any "Scottish" evening; its importance in heritage revival is like

Donald MacDonald, Honored Guest at the
1995 Grandfather Mountain Highland Games.

the well-tended grave—it reveals carefully maintained memories. Song reminds us to remember and gives the long dead a role again in current affairs. To conclude this chapter I single out the expressive form of song as an important vehicle for communicating "the heritage."

Song reiterates and reinforces central paradigms of heritage lore. Song lyrics thereby intensely and immediately summon the emotions that unite participants in celebration. Turner calls celebration "meta-experience" because it "distills all other kinds of experience to draw out the part that is essential to each of them. . . . Language is, no doubt, only the tip of the intersubjective iceberg, the dead husk of the living celebratory fruit, but it remains the most efficient means of expressing and communicating thoughts and feelings of a community" (1982:19). Through song, community members express and reaffirm their beliefs. Song communicates knowledge, and knowledge of songs communicates a sense of belonging within the community.

Part of the standard entertainment at any ceilidh or heritage dinner is the singing of "traditional" songs of Scotland—mostly those songs born of Highlandism and Jacobite romanticism. They are also standard for such Highland Games singers as Alex Beaton and Colin Grant-Adams, two of the best-known singers who cover the games circuit. Songs are a particular, and poetic, form of storytelling, the retelling (or resinging) of which functions to express beliefs in common origins and history, and to emphasize an identity shaped by suffering. Laments about the Jacobite period are favorites in North Carolina. Such tunes as the "Skye Boat Song" and "Will Ye No Come Back Again?" (addressed to Prince Charlie) are sung at every event.

The stock tunes also include the Jacobite-themed "Loch Lomond," the Burns's "Auld Lang Syne" (at the close of every event), and the more recent and happier "Scotland the Brave." "Amazing Grace" is sung and piped at most events (the St. Andrew's University pipe-band members moan when it is requested—"Oh no, not the 'A' word"). While members of heritage societies know the words to these most popular tunes, lyric sheets are generally available. Songs such as "It Was All for Our Rightful King" and "The Yellow-Haired Laddie" send people to their notes, as well as the "unofficial Scottish national anthem," "Flower of Scotland."[22]

Sung again and again at heritage events, these familiar tunes unfailingly evoke a solemn reverence and often emotional responses. Perhaps a speaker gave a particularly moving talk, or conversation over dinner evoked a strong sense of "what was past" and "what was lost," or talk of travel in Scotland brought on nostalgia; but it is rare to attend a "Scottish evening" and not see someone get teary-eyed as the event concludes in song. Informants explain the continual power of these songs to evoke an emotional response simply through their familiarity and association with good times. While informants say they are often moved by listening to recordings about "what they love" at home, singing or hearing a familiar ballad or lament in a space where those present share your feelings and understand the meaning makes the experience more intense.

Songs provide easily remembered and repeated versions of myths. The tune sets the tone and reinforces the emotive power of the story. As Eliade notes, myth "is an account of events which took place . . . 'in the beginning'" (1961:57). Heritage songs locate "the beginning" in the hardships of the ancestors that eventually brought them to America. Singing about their experience allows participants to access that experience, to feel its enduring potency and the bond with each other that it provides them. Eliade writes, "In narrating [singing] a myth, one reactualises, in some sort, the sacred time in which the events narrated took place. . . . From the mere fact of the narration of a myth, profane time is—at least symbolically—abolished: the narrator and his hearers are rapt into sacred and mythical time" (58). Group singing, or performed song, creates a distance from everyday concerns and strengthens community spirit as song evokes the events that make up "the heritage," and so the group identity.

Perhaps most affecting are the songs specific to clan history. Clan ceilidhs occupy the evenings after the larger Highland Games, and there tales relating to a specific sense of Scottish-American identity lead to bowed heads and clouded eyes. Songs through which Donald MacDonald introduced many North Carolinians to the history of Clan Donald still bring an emotional climax to Clan Donald ceilidhs—especially those songs commemorating events at Glencoe, one of the most tragic moments of the clan's history. Set in 1692, these songs relate the story of a sept of MacDonalds living at a dramatically beautiful mountainous area called Glencoe, whose chief's tardy oath of allegiance to King William III resulted in the massacre of his clansfolk. Government soldiers led by a Campbell, the MacDonalds' ancient rivals, descended on Glencoe, where they were nonetheless fed and entertained in the homes of the Glencoe MacDonalds for ten days before receiving orders to kill all their hosts under the age of seventy-five. Campbell's atrocity and flouting of the Highland hospitality ethic makes Glencoe a particularly notorious part of the Jacobite period.

> They came in a blizzard, we offered them heat.
> A roof for their heads, dry shoes for their feet.
> We wined 'em and dined 'em, they ate all our meat.
> And they slept in the house of MacDonald.
>
> *Refrain:*
> Oh, cruel is the snow that sweeps Glencoe,
> And covers the grave o' Donald.
> And cruel was the foe that raped Glencoe,
> And murdered the house of MacDonald.

They came from Fort William with murder in mind.
The Campbell had orders, King William had signed.
"Put all to the sword," these words underlined.
"Leave no one alive called 'MacDonald.' "

(Refrain)

They came in the night, while our men were asleep.
This band of Argylls, through snow soft and deep.
Like murdering foxes among helpless sheep,
They slaughtered the house of MacDonald.

(Refrain)

Some died in their beds, at the hands of the foe.
Some fled in the night and were lost in the snow.
Some left to accusin', who struck the first blow.
But gone was the house of MacDonald.[23]

The song, "The Massacre of Glencoe," communicates information about history, clan rivalries, Highland life and culture, persecution, and a clan's attachment to place. The memory of those Glencoe Mac-Donalds' experience is instilled, through the singing, as a part of the heritage of all MacDonalds. Associations and feelings for a place that many heritage celebrants may never see is cultivated through the retelling of this story through song. Part of experiencing the heritage is to recall, intersubjectively, the ancestors' most powerful and memorable (usually tragic) experiences, and the most common way to do so as a group is to sing about them.

William Donaldson notes the characteristics of the later Jacobite song as including "wild landscapes, the preoccupation with defeat, and the pervasive ambience of exile and loss" (1988:79). The Jacobite songs sung today by those of Scottish descent around the world were written well after the Jacobite period. Donaldson notes that "most Jacobite songs died with the events that gave them birth" and that later Jacobite songs were only passed off as originals by James Hogg and Robert Burns, among others (1988:4). Those sung today were written in the environment of Highlandism in the nineteenth century. Even the "Skye Boat Song," the favorite at North Carolina community events, was written by an Englishman, Harold Boulton, in 1885.

Yet for most participants, the assumption that songs were written by lamenting Jacobites continues to add to their appeal, as Hogg and Burns intended. A constant topic of conversation concerns how the song-writer must have been feeling "to set down those words." When I brought up discussion of any song, informants' typical responses included "Can you imagine what it must have been like?" and "It makes you wonder how they must have felt." For many, the songs are a link with their (real or imagined) Jacobite ancestors' feelings. They sing them with a somber respect for the message and for the experience of "their ancestors"—the experience that is theirs by inheritance. Singing songs is more than an activity to fill time at events. Songs are sung or performed not simply because they are Scottish, but as an act of remembering. The singing of these tunes is like the repetition of a creed; it reaffirms concepts of the past and of one's own family history.

In Scotland, ceilidhs are known for boisterous fun and spontaneity. Scottish-American ceilidhs, in contrast, may be carefully planned with moments of striking solemnity. Participants do not laugh, talk, or even smile during the singing. When I tried chatting on a few occasions where I thought it might go unnoticed, I was quickly hushed. The atmosphere must be right to evoke the proper emotions conducive to remembering and reverencing the Jacobites' sacrifices and losses. Those not "in the mood" told me they keep quiet anyway "in respect to other peoples' feelings," including the song-leader's, of course. Song-singing sessions elicit a certain deference and sobriety similar to a religious service. Indeed, explanations for the general lack of conversation and conviviality during singing sessions express a wish not to "hinder the Spirit."

Looking around during song sessions, participants' demeanor seemed to me very similar to hymn-singing behavior. I knew many of the participants had grown up in churches, mostly Presbyterian; in my own experience of Presbyterian churches, few songs are sung smiling and eye contact is avoided. As in the singing of hymns, the singing at heritage events seemed to be as much for an unseen audience as for those participating. As opposed to the singing of drinking or working songs, or the more militant or bawdy Jacobite tunes sung in pubs and at ceilidhs in Scotland, the focus of one's thoughts in Scottish-American ceilidh singings are (supposed to be) on the "literal" meaning of the words and on the ancestors who are their subjects. Singing becomes almost like that at a memorial service for the dead, so present are the dead in the words and in thoughts. Song invokes the presence of the dead ancestors and, as it is they who legitimize the group identity, enhances the sense of unity and connectedness among the living.

The one song during which people do meet eyes and hold hands around the room is generally the last, "Auld Lang Syne." The singing of this well-known Burnsian tune to conclude North Carolina events celebrates those "Scots" present now—both forming a group whose members identify with each other, and "being" the present embodiment of a group identity that has a past and an anticipated future. The specifics of that identity depend upon whether the song is sung in the company of fellow clan members, fellow "North Carolina Scots," or at community-wide events. The intensity of meaning will vary with singers' knowledge or perceptions of each other, but through the sharing of song, participants acknowledge one another as inheritors of "the tradition" and as its present caretakers. During this particular song, a look is passed that communicates each person's responsibility and value in maintaining the group and that, after a night of fellowship, signifies belonging and acceptance.

The *communitas* experienced through shared knowledge of song affirms group membership and the idea of a Scottish-American community. Song has enabled heritage revival in North Carolina by communicating, in a moving way, chosen memories of ancestral Scots that intervening generations forgot to share. Highlandism has directly influenced the selection of these memories that smooth the blend of Lowland Scot, Scots-Irish, and Highland traditions within North Carolina's unique Scottish community. The following chapter will examine the shape and various interests of that community.

Kith and Clan in the Scottish-American Community

O Heavenly Father, Who has established the Human Race in Families; send Your
Blessings of Familial Joy and Grace upon our Clan; Grant that as You have
bestowed upon us a Place in History, we may bestow upon our Children a True
Understanding of that Place; May we ascend unto You from Earthly Labors
of Honor and Honesty, ever worthy of our Name. Amen and Gardez Bein!
—The Montgomery Family Prayer, by David C. Montgomery

The Montgomery Family Prayer succinctly captures many aspects of
the Scottish-American community's celebrated worldview: the clan as
family with earthly patriarchs; the singular Human Race divided only
into clans—divinely fathered; heritage as an honorable history and example for living that older generations are responsible for teaching to
the young.

The old Highland clan system now has a new "place" in history
through its international rebirth in clan societies. On the national and
local scales, an appreciation of that place binds Americans of varying
interests by gender and generation, within a Scottish-American community. A confederation of clans abroad, the Scottish-American community evidences an ethnically "Scottish" identity in the American context
and a unity that clansfolk lacked in the Scottish homeland. Clan rivalries
still surface, but to different ends: as heritage (and in fun). Uniting
Americans of all clans, of all socioeconomic backgrounds, with different
interests and from different geographic regions, the Scottish-American
community exists in the minds of those who nonetheless share a sense
of kinship through their common emphasis on familial "places in history"—on heritage.

"Imagining" the Scottish-American Community

In his classic work, *Culture and Community*, anthropologist Conrad Arensberg defined communities primarily as population aggregates (1965:16). Our conceptions of communities have since changed as anthropologists increasingly study our own and other industrialized societies. The meaning and importance of community also evolves in these societies with changes in living patterns (the proliferation of suburbs and growth of one-person households), and with increasing personal and familial mobility to meet employment demands. A particular sense of community as a feeling of trustful interdependency with "good neighbors" has become part of what many Americans, emerging from postmodern self-reflection, feel is lacking in contemporary American life. It is partly this bonded sense of community that many try to recapture in ethnic organizations and national and international voluntary associations such as Scottish heritage societies. Our concept of community has expanded to refer to cities, even nations, and, in this case, those who share a particular ancestry or history. The term now implies a sense of belonging and identity on various scales that crosses geographical boundaries and unifies members mentally more than physically—in what have been called "imagined communities."

Benedict Anderson writes that "all communities larger than primordial villages of face-to-face contact are imagined." They are imagined, because members "will never know most of their fellow-members, meet them, or even hear of them, yet in the minds of each lives the image of their communion" (1983:6). Communities of the imagination are not distinguished by greater or lesser authenticity, but by the style in which they are imagined. The Scottish-American community is imagined through a unified sense of "Scottish" identity that members feel ancestral emigration deprived them for generations. Promotional materials for *The Highlander Magazine* describe the community thus: "The Scots are an unusual ethnic group . . . because they are first Americans, Canadians, Australians, etc. They are totally assimilated and are citizens of the country they live in. They don't all go to the same church or live in the same neighborhood, but scratch a Scot and underneath there is a fierce pride in his or her Scottish heritage—and rightfully so."

Distinguishing the Scottish-American community from other imagined communities is an emphasis on presumed kinship. Especially in the South, members may extend a sense of shared identity to genealogies. Many families hold their reunions at Scottish heritage events, and these events themselves have become reunions of the larger "cousinhood" of Highland, Lowland, and Scots-Irish "Scots." Discovery of a shared surname in the family tree, or ancestors from the same areas of Scotland, is enough to establish the familial feeling between community members that pervades events generally. The emphasis on kin is a part of what makes Scottish events such friendly, welcoming, public gatherings where one "never meets a stranger." The Scottish-American community's imagining links people not just mentally across space, but across time and socioeconomic class through ancestry; sometimes verifiable, sometimes also imagined, but generally defined to include rather than exclude.

Substantive Imaginings: Community Literature

Anderson has emphasized the importance of printing for transmission of cultural traditions across space and generations within imagined communities (1983). Literature in the Scottish-American community (including national and international newspapers and magazines, clan society information leaflets and newsletters, and internet sites) forms a major link and communication network for community members. As the Scottish-American forum and bulletin board, such literature is a tangible link to the idea of community. Literature provides directories to local or special-interest Scottish organizations and vendors of Scottish goods. Community publications are also a significant source of information about upcoming events and how to properly dress for them. Literature introduces newcomers to community beliefs and rituals; affirms the value of Scottish traditions; and reiterates the generally agreed upon premises and histories that underlie the Scottish-American identity. As *The Highlander* promotional further explains, "That's why *The Highlander* exists, to fulfill this pride all Scots have—to recount the history of our people and to help the scions of Scotland know something of their beginnings, to spin the tales of heroism, bravery and clan loyalty, or even, on occasion, give the details of abject treachery that make the stories of Scotland so fascinating" (1994).

The Highlander notes on its cover that "over 100,000 Scots in the US and Canada read each issue." The transnational *Scotland Now* is "written, edited and published by Scots in Scotland for Scots in North America." *The Scottish Banner* claims to be "the largest Scottish newspaper in the world outside Scotland." *Scottish Memories* advertises itself as "The Magazine for *Bravehearts* with Real Scottish Blood." Specifically related to the Cape Fear Settlement is the periodical publication of the North Carolina Scottish Heritage Society, *Argyll Colony Plus*. This journal features genealogical and historic research about the Cape Fear Highlanders and finds subscribers among their descendants across the nation.

Also focused on the Cape Fear settlers, but concentrating on immigrants from the Inner Hebridean Island of Jura, the on-line Jura Research Newsletter draws contributors from around the United States and from Scotland.[1] Further, each clan society issues newsletters to members explaining clan traditions and Scottish history and dress.[2]

As Scottish and Scots-Irish Presbyterians have always placed a premium on literacy for individual interpretation of "The Word," Scottish Americans are expected to do their own research on their heritage, and the literature provides references to the sanctioned sources. Oral tradition within the Scottish-American community leans on the literate traditions and emphases of complex societies. In general conversation about dress, history, and so forth, participants often cite printed sources "chapter and verse" rather than assert a position on their own authority. Orally relating clan histories is an important part of heritage activities, yet most tellers' performances reflect an unspoken distrust of oral tradition, as they continually reference published works. Whenever uncertainty about a genealogical link or historical incident emerges, speakers often solicit collaboration from one or two bystanders who just as often defer to a text by a local historian. Though these sources were once oral histories, their accessibility in printed form invests them with a definitive authority.

Being an authority on some aspect of Scottish heritage provides prestige within a group. Each clan society or heritage group has at least one "expert" on various topics, often the editor of the clan newsletter or someone who "has written on that." Knowing (about the heritage) *is* belonging within the community, and written knowledge defines and anchors an identity that it may never be lost again. While different opinions surface on the origins of events or tartans, argument over these differences combines written with oral traditions. In a sense, literature now restores oral histories to those whose great-great-great-grandparents stopped telling them.

In describing the imagined Scottish-American community, I make frequent reference to the literature—as community members do themselves. To say that the community is "imagined" is meant in no way as disparaging, or to insinuate that it is not also very real. Though the community is not characterized by face-to-face interactions or communal living on a daily basis, and though most members will never meet or know of each other, community events do draw members into face-to-face, and even (temporarily) communal living relationships. This imagined community operates as a *Gemeinschaft* during the events specifically designed for its expression as such.

Community members demonstrate an interdependency in the organization of local, state, national, and international events, and in public rituals that confirm their shared sense of identity (a group identity). During "regular time," between such events, a sense of community is experienced through the literature that enables communication and exchange of cultural knowledge between geographic locales and generations. Through both literate links and event gatherings, the Scottish-American community is conceived in cosmic terms as a unity between all those of Scottish descent, known and unknowable—an imagined community. The primary form of its imagining relates to spiritual *and* genealogical kinship through the once local and regional Scottish clan system—now reborn as national and international clan societies.

Scottish Clans and Scottish-American Clan Societies

Ethnohistorian Robert Carmack notes that "folk histories of tribal societ[ies] . . . seem to function more as supportive charters for present structural conditions than as factual accounts of the past" (1972:241). Today's international clan societies have readapted the folk histories of the semi-feudal Scottish clan system as both justification and frame for current activities and beliefs.

"Clan," Gaelic for "children," has come to mean "family" in the heritage revival. This present conception of "clan" makes those sharing a surname "kin" to each other and to all descendants of the apical, or founding, ancestor first associated with the name centuries or even millennia ago. Many clan societies appoint a clan genealogist or even a genealogical committee to trace their origins back to an "Angus Mor," or whichever woolly warrior is thought to be the first bearer of the name or the sometimes-mythological progenitor of those who first claimed it. Some in Scotland argue that clan membership is agnatic, that is, membership may be reckoned through the male line only (Campbell 1994a; Cory 1991). However, in America, descent and membership in a clan is most often reckoned cognatically (through either male or female lines) to the apical ancestor.

Literature on clan origins begins with "Tradition has it . . ." or "Tradition says . . ." followed by the story of "the first" ancestor and, generally, his military exploits. The information leaflet for Clan Mac-Laine of Lochbuie asks: "Who are We? . . . We are descended from Gillean-na-Tuaighe, or Gillean of the Battle-ax, a fierce warrior born about 1210" (Clan Maclaine 1992:2). When the apical ancestor's name is a distinctively Scandinavian "Magnus" or "Thorfin," clan literature briefly summarizes the history of the Norse in Scotland, thereby extending the clan's own history and, in some cases, backing a further claim to "Viking heritage." If little is known of the clan ancestor, an explanation of the name itself is given, especially when an origin story is connected to the name. For example, the Borders region name Turnbull originated, by tradition, in the early 1300s when William Rule saved the life of King Robert the Bruce by "turning" a ferocious bull from his path. Thereafter, Rule was called Turn-e-Bull. When the same king died in 1329, the Lockharts acquired their name by taking his heart on crusade in a locked box.

Explanations of names with Gaelic origins follow standardized conventions. Gaelic names frequently referenced an area of residence or an individual's distinctive physical attributes (e.g., Rory Rua [Rory of the red hair], Malcolm Ceann Mor [Malcolm of the big head], and Fergus Og [the younger Fergus]). The name "cam beul" (crooked mouth) evolved into the last name Campbell.[3] A person known as Iain Bain (or, the John that is blond) now has descendants with the last name Bain or Bean. Other distinctions in Gaelic names concern prefixes. The prefix "Mac" (son of) appears variously as Mc and M'; therefore, MacDougall is "son of Dougall" and clan members with that name are considered "sons of Dougall." "Nic" (daughter of) appears less commonly in some surnames.

As the successor to "the first" ancestor, the chief of a clan or of a family may be directly called by the surname (for example, the head of the Bruce family is called "The Bruce"). The chief is the "father" of the clan, generally inheriting his position for life by descent from the apical ancestor. Many of the Scottish clans have been chiefless for centuries, making them "broken clans."[4] Numerous chiefs' positions have only been restored in this century with the revival of Scottish heritage interests abroad and the development of clan societies (of which one of the oft-stated objectives is the reestablishment of the chiefship).

Clan Morrison, originally from the Outer Hebridean Islands of Lewis and Harris, lacked a chief in 1900 when the clan society first formed in Scotland (the last chief lost his head in the 1600s). Only in 1967 did the Lyon Court (the legal court of heraldry in Scotland) select, from among several claims, a candidate who could trace his family thirteen generations to the Morrisons of Harris, the hereditary keepers of a clan possession. Morrison then became a legal clan, which required a new coat of arms, badges, crests, and, of course, a new tartan. The Lord Lyon recognized a chief of Clan Hannay only in 1983. Clan Henderson acquired a chief in 1985 after one hundred and fifty years as a broken clan and, prompted by American Skenes' petitions to the Lyon Court, Clan Skene regained a chiefship in 1994 after 167 years of being "heidless" (head-less). Both Clan Moffat and Clan Shaw waited four centuries for the restoration of their chiefs in 1983 and 1970, respectively.[5]

In some cases a branch of a clan has established itself as sufficiently independent to warrant a "Chief of the Branch." Chiefs of branches are not called chief of the name, but "chief of the clan X of Y," with the "Y" denoting a location and signifying the chief's ultimate subordination to the clan chief. North Carolina purists claim that although improper titling occurs in the North Carolina community, it is more a problem outside the state—especially "in the West," where "even" elected heads of Scottish societies with no clan affiliation will be called chieftain.[6]

Upon joining a clan society, one must pledge loyalty to the chief when one exists. Certificates demonstrating entitlement to wear a particular tartan (issued by tartan centers in Scotland and from "traveling computer archives" at Highland Games) include an oath of loyalty (which the owner will presumably sign before framing). Such certificates read: "I solemnly declare myself to be loyal to the aims and traditions of that Clan or Family and to its Chief or Head from now and hereafter." Upon joining Clan Wallace, the new member pays dues and receives a "Bond of Manrent," whereby he or she swears allegiance to the chief.

Although chiefs ultimately owe their allegiance to the monarch, and Queen Elizabeth is toasted at heritage events today, at the time of the actual clan system, loyalty to the chief was always above loyalty to the monarch. Holding land in the name of his clansfolk for communal (corporate) use, the chief was the absolute patriarch and arbitrator; his word was law and he could expect abiding loyalty. However, he was not distant from his clansfolk. Reporting on the Highlands in 1724, General Wade remarked that though clansmen paid a "servile and Abject Obedience to the Commands of their Chieftains . . . they are treated by their Chiefs with great Familiarity, they partake with them in their Diversions, and shake them by the Hand whenever they meet them" (Grant 1997:46). A chief's activities were at the center of Highland life and they continue to be a major focus in Scottish heritage celebration.

Many clan society members relate a deep regard for their chief. As "father figures," today's clan chiefs travel the world making public appearances, wearing the three feathers that distinguish a chief and parading with their clansfolk at heritage events. Clan society members often celebrate the chief's birthday. Many comment on how much more cohesive their clan society seems after a visit from the chief, or following society members' group trips to visit the chief and clan lands.[7] In speeches at games and other events, clan chiefs remind their clanspeople of their traditional relationship from generations past and affirm current "bonds of kinship, trust and respect." In his remarks as honored guest at the first annual Culloden Games in Georgia in 1995, Lord MacDonald—High Chief of Clan MacDonald—said he felt "the special bond of clanship, stronger than even twenty or thirty years ago" and that he had "the feeling of being a father looking down on my children." When the chief lacks an heir, or "tainistear," a commander may be appointed to act in place of a chief, as in the case of Clan Currie.[8] The thirtieth and last clan chief of the Curries died in 1992, having chosen an American as his successor and making him clan commander in recognition of his efforts to "rally the clan" in North America. Clan society members consider him "the present-day patriarch of the clan." When a chief exists in Scotland, he or she may also appoint a commissioner for the U.S. organization, or the organization itself may elect officials.

Large clans may have various positions (commissioners, deputy commissioners, lieutenants, commanders, standard bearers, and conveners), all of which are representative liaisons for the chief in America. Clan Lindsay, for example, has a clan chairperson elected for a five-year term and a president. The largest and most highly structured clan society, Clan Donald U.S.A., has state and deputy state commissioners, and, in some places, local conveners. Besides the clan society, the nine branches of MacDonalds and its various commissioners are also a part of the Glencoe Foundation, the Clan Donald Lands Trust, and the Clan Donald Foundation.

I use "clan" and "clan society" interchangeably here, as do my informants when speaking of "clan activities," "clan gatherings," "clan newsletters," and so on. This is just a matter of convenience, however. The Clan Fergusson Society information leaflet explains the important distinction as follows: "A Clan Society is the modern day counterpart of a Scottish Clan. However, it is not a clan or a branch of one. It is a social organization, a voluntary association of individuals who share a common history and heritage and who are under the spell that Old Scotia casts upon her sons and daughters" (1993:4). One may unknowingly be a member of a clan by descent, but membership in the clan society requires actively claiming one's "inheritance" and pledging to pass it on. Though his separation of the terms is commonly lost in community practice and celebration, Tom Shaw, vice president of the Clan Shaw Society, explained, "You can't join a clan—you are either in it or you aren't, but if they are liberal you can join their clan society without being in the clan" (Shaw 1994).

The North Carolina heritage revival has played an important role in the foundation of national clan societies. Donald MacDonald cofounded one of the first post–World War II Scottish clan societies in the nation,

Clan Donald U.S.A., and many Scottish Americans following his example did so at the Grandfather Mountain Scottish Highland Games,
which MacDonald also cofounded. When the American Branch of Clan
Cameron received approval from the chief, Cameron of Lochiel, in 1967,
it took the name "the Grandfather Mountain Branch of the Cameron
Clan in North America." Both the Clan Gunn and Clan Rose Societies
began in 1969 on the Grandfather Mountain Games field. The Clan
Buchanan Society in America and the Clan MacKay Society of the
U.S.A. followed the next year. The Clan Fergusson Society (1972), The
Clan Lindsay Association U.S.A. (1974), the Clan MacLachlan Association (1977), the Clan MacNachtan Association of North America
(1978), and the Clan Henderson Society (1985) are just a few of the
many national clan societies that continue to be conceived and inaugu-
rated at the Grandfather Games in Linville, North Carolina—the most
prestigious "gathering of the clans" stateside.

Clan societies have international, national, and branch memberships
and activities. Some clans have two or more competitive, and occasionally fractious, societies in America (which might be viewed as echoing
the spirit of the original clan system). Clan Urquhart Association notes
in its newsletters that it "is the only publication of Clan Urquhart and
the Urquhart Family in North America which is sanctioned by our
Chief" (1994:1). Of the two Boyd societies, one claims to be "the only
society sanctioned by the Lord Kilmarnock, Hereditary Chief of all
Boyds." Of the two Clan Armstrong societies, one notes that it was
awarded Arms by the Lord Lyon in 1985 and the other advertises itself
as the preeminent purveyor of "correct clan information."

As proof of "legitimacy" (again, their word, not mine), the literature
of many societies emphasizes societal membership in the Council of
Scottish Clans and Associations (COSCA). Founded in 1974, COSCA is an
educational and charitable organization for "the preservation and promotion of the customs, traditions and heritage of the Scottish people
though support of Scottish-oriented organizations" (1994:1). Modeled
after the Scottish Standing Council of Scottish Chiefs (founded 1952),
COSCA originally comprised only family and clan organizations, but now
includes the many heritage, dance, and reenactment groups that have
emerged in the past fifteen years. The development of COSCA is quite interesting, as it reflects the relatively recent and widespread growth of
clan societies in the United States.

Like other British colonies where Scots settled, the United States had
early sprinklings of Scottish associations, mainly "friendly societies"
such as the St. Andrew's Societies, which acted both as social organizations and as charities to "relieve the distress" of new immigrants. The

idea of a clan emphasis came only in the late nineteenth century with the founding of a national fraternity, vaguely analogous to the Elks or Lions Clubs, called "The Order of Scottish Clans." These clans were local male social clubs that took various clan tartans without regard to the member's "actual" clan heritage. They developed elaborate rituals and titles loosely based on what members had learned from sources such as Sir Walter Scott. Clan societies as we know them today did not become popular in the United States until after World War II. Unique and particularly American interpretations of "clan" have developed since.

Community Interpretation of Clan, Family, and Kinship

Most Scottish Americans join clan societies that share their surname or are part of their family history; and, as clan has come to mean "family," clan history becomes their family heritage. Claiming surname as an indicator of kinship throughout history assumes that all MacDougalls, or septs of Dougall, are biologically related.[9] Community members often assume that even those sharing names derived from occupation, such as "Smith" or "Forrester," are necessarily kin. Actually the large numbers of MacDonalds or MacNeils stem, not from remarkable ancestral fecundity, but from the progenitors of today's MacDonalds or MacNeils allying themselves with a clan chief of that name at a time when most people did not need last names. However, the structure of societies today would make it appear that everyone of a region with a shared surname shares ancestry.[10]

Though biological kinship was an essential part of reckoning membership and position within a clan, membership also stemmed from semi-feudal alliances with chiefs and their immediate underlings. Individuals or groups could choose to join a clan with which they lacked any marital or biological ties. Residential unity also shaped clan membership. Attachment to specific ecological niches for livelihood and defense became the prime identifier for many clans: The MacLeods of Lewis, the Frasers of Lovat, the Glencoe MacDonalds, the Shaws of Tordarroch, the Robertsons of Rannoch. Smaller groups and families might ally themselves with powerful clans in their area for defense and other reasons without any regard for common ancestry.

The allegiance of these "septs" (allied families within a clan) to the larger clan might last months *or* centuries, so that current alliance with clan societies is an interesting matter of preference for those with regional/district or "sept" rather than clan surnames. Present-day clan societies grant membership to those whose surnames are those of fam-

ilies once considered septs of the clan. Several clans, such as Farquharson, claim over a hundred septs. Many clans claim the same septs: both
Clan MacBean and Clan MacKay claim the Bains/MacBains (as at some
point the Bains were probably allied with each).

For today's geographically dispersed imagined community, an assumption of biological kinship among clan society members overrides
the regional, political, and social motivations for alliance in the late
medieval and early modern period. Clan Gunn's newsletter, entitled
"The Gunn Salute: Good News about a Great Family," notes that the
Highland clan spirit lies in the belief that the clan is one family. Clans
Gunn, MacIntyre, Urquhart, and others list in their clan objectives
"promoting the spirit of kinship among members." Clan MacBean defines itself as "an association of families for the promotion of brother-
hood and cousinship." In its literature, Clan Carmichael claims that
their chief "has re-established the traditional unity of Scottish families
by scheduling international gatherings of the clan," the aim of which is
"to develop a unified family of Carmichaels worldwide." Not only do
distinctions between clan and clan society commonly blur in celebration, but historical distinctions between kin and non-kin clan members
now fade in favor of familial appeal. Clan Moffat's society leaflet lists
several variations of the name and states, "It doesn't matter how you
spell it, we're still kin" (1995:3).

Notions of the clan as a family reflect current and nineteenth-century
perceptions and evaluations of "family." The chief as father was more
like the Tsar or Tsarina of Russia being "the little father" or "little
mother" of their people. We know from early Irish law tracts that chiefs
and minor kings protected their people (tuaths) in times of danger and
that his "honor price" could be used by any of his underlings in negotiat-
ing disputes (in which the higher honor price generally won the case).
The Scottish Highland clan system functioned in a similar fashion.
Those residing in the territories under the power of a particular chief
were members of his clan, not in terms of kinship, but in terms of
obligations. Clansfolk were obliged to give the chief military aid and
food supplies, and he, in turn, was responsible for their protection.
In disputes, clan members used his name (like an honor price). Even
though clan loyalties were strong and were more than military alliances, people could ally themselves with other clans, and political alliances switched frequently, meaning that people might take the names
of different chiefs in succession.

Confusion between biological and sociopolitical dimensions of clans
stems from nineteenth-century Highlandism and its later perpetuation
in the myriad of books celebrating tartanry (such as Robert Bain's *The*

Clans and Tartans of Scotland, originally published in 1938). Reedited through the years, Bain's text is still a staple of heritage enthusiasts' libraries and still states that blood relationship was the "important fundamental in the clan system" (1961:15). Biological kinship was important for the clan elite, from whom a chief would come, but not for all clansfolk. Clans were variably composed of a minority of immediate kin and a majority of non-kin inhabiting the clan's territorial base. Bain divides the clan between "broken men" (those without a chief who join a clan for protection and thereafter claim the chief's name), and "native men" (whom Bain interpreted as a small core group of the chief's "blood" relatives).[11] Yet, this distinction is overwhelmed by his and other authors' discussions of cultural "inheritance," and of hereditary "natural rights" to certain tartans. Historically, the importance of kinship varied with the extent and power of the clan in question. In celebratory practice today, the historical extent and power of a clan has become "family history."

Alastair Campbell of Airds, Unicorn Pursuivant of Arms of the Lord Lyon's Court, has attempted to educate the Scottish-American community on what he considers "a distressing" confusion through lectures at North Carolina events and in national community literature. In a series of articles in *The Highlander*, Campbell notes that one of the sources of confusion is the translation of the word "clan." As noted above, "clan" means "children" in Gaelic, but Campbell points out that it can apply to a single lineage "right up to the major power-groups which could put several thousand men in to the field" (1993:54).

New claims for clan status are now often received at the Lyon's court—the final and legal authority in recognizing or denying the existence of a clan. So many claims are made that Campbell fears "the whole system will become swamped and lose any real meaning" and that "not enough consideration is given to our ancestors' thoughts on being combined into a new grouping which might well have been anathema to them during their lifetime" (1994:55). Campbell argues that, instead of creating new clans or drawing rigid lines around which names can belong to clan associations, the policy of his own chief, the Duke of Argyll, is most appropriate and "entirely in the spirit of what actually happened in the past." Argyll announced that "he would accept anyone as a clansman of Scottish descent who wished to acknowledge and follow him as Chief" (1994:54). However much some may consider clan societies contrived, especially because of the belief in kinship, the establishment of "new" clans is also in the spirit of the original system and might be seen as part of the continual renegotiation of identity and meaning.

The American, and especially southern, emphasis on "blood" kinship within the clan could also be seen as an American cultural influence on conceptions of Scottish heritage and/or an American elaboration of Highlandism. Now, not only does each clan have a specific tartan, but the wearer of tartan becomes the bearer of clan reputation. By donning a tartan one claims the aristocrats of the clan as one's own "cousins" and the heroic deeds of clansfolk as one's own heritage. One's choice of tartan expresses one's knowledge of the heritage and tells its own story of one's lineage and family background. Those who are members of several clan societies simultaneously select a tartan that represents the clan whose history and ancestral members they deem most admirable. If clan members have kilts of several tartans, the prestige and relevance of particular family histories may decide which tartan is worn to particular events.

Those wearing tartan like to volunteer stories about the origins of their clan tartans with brief (and sometimes not so brief) clan histories. Such discussion dominates the basic "getting to know you" chat and gap-filling conversation at heritage gatherings. Everyone has a name, so everyone has at least that story to tell; the story of the clan with which one feels an inherited affinity through family tradition or through surname alone. Though clan does not necessarily mean kin, the emphasis on family and kinship in Scottish heritage revival reflects other contemporary American interests in genealogy and origins.

Genealogy and the Quest for Ancestors

Reawakening interests in ethnic identities after World War II were further galvanized by the American bicentennial celebration and Alex Haley's book (later television miniseries) *Roots*. Celebrations of America's coming of age stirred many Americans to explore their ancestors' place in history—in America's history and abroad. In the last three decades, genealogy has become one of the nation's most popular hobbies.

Ancestor-hunting is understandably a major interest among community members. Even among those with a transgenerational awareness of Scottish roots, locating ancestral quarry with clan names confirms beliefs in one's kinship within the community and integrates clan history within one's own perceptions of self and identity. My informants and community literature continually refer to "revelations" and "discovery" through genealogical research. Discovering ancestral experiences becomes, in a heritage sense, a discovery of one's own "past lives." The perils and challenges, joys and sorrows encountered by one's predecessors are, in direct and indirect ways, part of what makes one oneself;

John Burnett displays his family tree at the Burnett tent.

discovering them is self-discovery. To quote a genealogical author popular with community members: "Discovering your heritage is a homecoming in the truest sense. The entity that we call 'me' is the most
recent chapter in a long line of stories—the stories belonging to those
who make up our pedigree. Our ancestors have met life's challenges in
their own particular ways, and in doing so have bequeathed to . . . us a
unique . . . heritage" (Vandagriff 1993:xi–xii).

In pursuit of heritage the genealogist collects lives with a mission:
restoring the legacies of forgotten or half-remembered generations es-
tablishes one's own legacy. Informants say that providing those in the
future with some of the past gives a satisfying completeness to one's
own life and secures one's own place in history. Reenactor Margaret

McKinney explains her interest in genealogical research as being "a link in the chain"—"contributing to the threads that bind the past with the future generations" (McKinney 1997).

"Thread" is a common metaphor within the Scottish community: "threads of fate," "threads of hope," "threads of history" are all references to a belief that we are simultaneously tethered to, and liberated by, our heritage. Community members speak allegorically about the threads that compose clan tartans' distinguishing designs, or setts, as "lines of descent." It is in tracing these figurative threads that Scottish Americans shape and explain the "fabric of heritage." Genealogical research documents that heritage in written form for future generations.

The cross-generational transmission of ancestral information is a central theme of community events and literature. Newcomers to the Scottish community often say their Scottish ancestry was "revealed" to them only when they began genealogy, and that they wish to secure "the life-enhancing" sense of Scottish identity (which they "missed out on for so many years") in the minds of their children and grandchildren. For those who have recently joined the genealogical search, community members who relate tales of their Cape Fear ties evoke pure ancestor-envy and inspire a desire to ensure that one's children and grand-children not forget it "again."

Many clan societies list among their aims and objectives to encourage participation of members' children in Scottish activities and games competitions. Clan Montgomery newsletters and leaflets note, "We are concerned that there are many Montgomeries who would like to pass on to their children the Inspiration, Strength and Stimulation that lie waiting in the Montgomery history and family traditions, but who may not be familiar with the wealth of ACTUAL DETAILS" (Clan Montgomery 1993).

What we know of kinship and inheritance reckoning practices among the Celts of Ireland and Scotland is a four-generation system beginning with the *fine* (the immediate nuclear family), the *gilfine* (descendants of a grandfather), and extending to the *derb fine* (those with whom one has a common great-grandfather). Clan kinship beyond the "native men" of the premodern clan, and as celebrated today, was and is what anthropologists call fictive kinship: socially recognized rather than biological kin. Few community members acknowledge this, which is why the tartan and tourism industries thrive on name associations with clans and places. Some merchants, and community authorities on tartan such as Philip Smith, a prominent member of TECA (the Tartan Educational and Cultural Association), connect names with tartan by reading the current phone books of an area and linking all the included names with district tartans.

Few clan societies in Scotland or abroad have adopted Argyll's suggestion that individuals may ally themselves with any clan of their preference. Though (to a limited and regional extent in the premodern period) this was Highland practice, it is the genealogical discovery of Scottish surnames and therefore clan identity that adds meaning to clan membership and heritage for today's "American Scots." In a Clan MacFarlane newsletter, a new member expressed her happiness at having "found" the clan, noting that as a member of the Scottish community, she had always participated with Clan Leslie (her grandmother's name) or with the Robertson Clan (her great-grandmother's name). Discovering that her name was a sept of the MacLarens, she wrote: "This year I proudly marched with the MacLarens and met the Clan Chief. . . . My pride in being of Scottish ancestry has increased 10 fold and I thank all the MacLarens who welcomed us into the fold" (Swangren 1994:9).

The genealogical research that reveals these unknown or lost connections is a primary element in Scottish-American community activities, conversation, and literature. Some clan societies require detailed documentation of one's family for membership and many request the name of at least one Scottish ancestor for their genealogical records. Few clans require documentation very far back, unless, like several families from the Scottish Borders, the roots of the clan or name are in the past few centuries. The largely Lowland Clan Hamilton requires demonstrated descent directly from the one male founder of the clan.

Excepting Clan Donald, many larger clan societies average under two thousand members, and most others under one thousand members nationwide. The Clan Lindsay Society admits those with the surname Lindsay or one of the following sept names: Byer, Cobb, Crawford, Deuchar, Downie, Fotheringham, Summers, or Rhind. Lindsay literature notes that only "by allowing recognized septs could enough members be found to form such an organization" (1994:1). Clan Currie offers regular memberships based on surname, and associate memberships for those "whether Scot or not, kinsfolk or just curious" (1994:4). Clan Gunn has an honorary membership that "may be conferred upon an individual who has substantially contributed to the betterment of the society, but who would not otherwise be eligible for membership" (1994:3).[12]

The Family of Bruce Society opens membership to all Bruces and their descendants within three generations, but specifies those "in direct line from King Robert the Bruce, his brothers and sisters, and his Bruce forebears." Given that this king died in 1329, linking applicants to his forebears would require extensive research. Since so much research is generated by members, the society annually publishes a member roster listing their qualifying ancestors. As in many clan societies, the first duty of Clan Moffat's new members is to provide the society genealogist with their family history for the society archives.

Some clan societies have separate newsletters or quarterly publications devoted to genealogical research and "the importance of charting and documentation." The McClain Exchange publishes research relating to the name in America up to the late 1800s, including land, military, census, and marriage records; probate files; cemetery surveys; and family bible histories. Many clan members publish their own research through one of the specialists in custom genealogical publishing. Community literature is filled with queries and answers about lost ancestors and individuals offering their own published research for sale.

Genealogical research on Scottish ancestors in their homeland is somewhat easier for ancestors from the Lowlands, where written records were more extensively kept. Ironically, documentation in support of one's clan identity and Highlander image is then easier in the areas that were predominantly anti-Highlander and anti-Jacobite. Like "Latter Day Saints" who research non-Mormon ancestors to pray them into paradise, clan society members may use genealogical research to redeem their clan's historical reputation (especially when that reputation unfavorably alludes to Hanoverian sympathies).

As community members explore their family history, they generally continue to rely on Highlandist themes to "flesh out the bones." Lowland ancestors become clansfolk, but they may be distinguished from "Jacobite cattle thieves."[13] Among Scottish-American genealogists, playful clan-bashing carries the Scottish Highland/Lowland divide into heritage celebration.

Lowland "Clans"

Because the clan system was part of Gaelic society, and Lowlanders were not, there is some debate about whether Lowlanders can really belong to clans. Several Lowland "clans" explain that they lack septs because they were a "closed clan," never having merged with other Scottish clans. This basically means that they never took part in the actual clan system of alliances, and that membership today is based solely on surname. Rather than "chief of the clan," chiefly titles in the Lowlands include "chief of the Name and Arms" or "of that Ilk" (a head of a landed family having the same name as her or his property).

Surname and family societies of Lowland origin do call themselves clan societies. A few of these Lowland societies that have Norman or Anglo-Danish apical ancestors, like Clan Armstrong, also have more

Map 3. Clan and Family Territories of Scotland

liberal membership policies welcoming "Irish and English members."
Clan Forrester, a surname derived from occupation, admits that "after
much research, no connection to a tartan could be established" (1993:1).
The Dunlop/Dunlap Family Society does not call itself a clan, but has
acquired a tartan and participates fully in Highlandism. Both Clan Davidson and Clan Henderson (with Borders and Highland connections)
note that their respective clan roots are from several families from
several different time periods, all "perhaps of quite independent origin."

Several Lowland groups now calling themselves clans playfully contrast their ancestors' "clans" with the "oat-eating" Highlanders "who slept in the heather." "Clan" Hamilton not only claims its Lowland origins and descent from an English adventurer, but calls Highland clans such as Clan Donnachaidh "a bunch of wild Highlanders." (Clan Hamilton society members nevertheless cheerfully sport tartan kilts and bagpipes.) Members of Highland clan societies still express indignation at historical references to their ancestors as savages and cattle thieves (especially as community lore describes a materially poor, but Arcadian existence).[14]

Cattle rustling was an important enough strategy in Highland subsistence that Gaelic had a specific term for a rustling event. Like an Irish "tain," or cattle raid, the "creach" was a "lifting" of cows. In addition to providing needed livestock, creachs were also a rite of passage for young males to prove their "manhood." Creachs most often involved Lowlanders' cattle, as Lowlanders were "foreigners" and did not carry out the reprisals that could be expected within the clan system. However, clans did conduct violent creachs in other clans' territory that could initiate clan battles. These were not small affairs: Cheape and Grant tell us that, in 1545, a MacDonald of Glengarry "carried off about two thousand head" from the Grants at Glemoriston (1997:157). Disputes over stolen cows could become transgenerational "cold" feuds likely to break into something "hot" at the slightest offense to any clan member's honor. Occasionally at Highland Games, one particularly notorious cattle-thieving clan will "return" a cow (a cardboard cutout or ceramic figurine of a cow) to a Lowland "clan" offended centuries ago.

Though descendants of Scottish Lowlanders may jest at their fellow community members' cattle-thieving ancestors, they do not shun their dress—as their own ancestors would have. Many Highland clan societies that take pride in their "turbulent pasts" (such as the MacFarlanes) also list in their aims and objectives "to have a presence at Highland Games in full Scottish regalia as well as at local social affairs for better public awareness of *our* way of life" (emphasis added) (MacFarlane 1995:2).[15] Many descendants of Lowlanders, including those with the surname of the great Borders families the Douglases, Scotts, and Kerrs, also consider "full Scottish regalia" as part of their ancestors' "way of life." I once slipped and asked a Lowlander Livingston (whose cattle the MacFarlanes raided) to explain his costume and was quickly reprimanded not to call it a costume: "It is our national dress and people take it very seriously. . . . We are very proud of our tartans."

Lowland "clans" all encourage uniform Highland dress. Clan Hender-son includes in its objectives the "perpetuation of Scottish dress." Clan Elliot includes a sheet entitled "Wear it with pride" in their new mem-bers' information packets. Clan Lindsay also promotes the "honoring" of Scottish heritage by "the wearing of our clan tartans along with various accoutrements" (none of which were a Lowland heritage).

Jacobitism, which many Lowlanders opposed, has also become a taken-for-granted part of Lowland clan lore. Stories explaining clan traditions often place their origins in the Jacobite period, rather than in earlier times that may be historically documented for some surnames. Consider current lore about the Cunninghams, whose name originated as that of a district of the Scottish Lowlands and who were historically pro-Hanoverian. One symbol of the clan adapts the shakefork (a farming implement to shake grain from straw) and the motto "Over Fork Over" from the Chief's crest—thought to allude to the office of "Master of the King's Stables" (Way 1994:377). More romantically, an old Scottish legend printed in clan literature says the apical ancestor received the lands of Cunningham in the eleventh century for hiding the English-supported Malcolm (later Malcolm III) from pursuing troops of the Celtic king Macbeth. Yet at Highland Games clan tents in several southern states, I have heard this story told with Bonnie Prince Charlie replacing Malcolm under the hay and fleeing "English" troops—though Charles was pursued by as many Lowland Scots and sheltered during his flight in the Highlands and Islands. This oral divergence from clan literature demonstrates the pervasiveness of Jacobitism and Highland-ism in heritage lore.

Through the veneer of Highlandism, differences between Highland and Lowland heritage are not always obvious at events. However, as heritage becomes more specialized, as it will with the growing number of enthusiasts of different ages and interests, the Highland/Lowland divide (invisibly bridged for most Americans by Highlandism) may be-come more important in claiming a Scottish identity. Nineteen ninety-seven saw the North Carolina creation of the Scottish District Families Association, designed, according to founder Jeff McDavis, to "address the growing numbers of people attending Scottish festivals and Games without connections to the Clans or Clan Associations." McDavis as-serts, "Approximately seventy percent of all the families of Scotland were not associated with the Clans, yet we are all equal in our pride and support of our heritage" (McDavis 1998:2). In the years of my fieldwork (1991–99) I witnessed an increasing awareness of Lowland identities (though few "conversions" from the Highlandist creed.)

Clan Pride and Famous Forefolks

Stories of the Scottish diaspora buttress the reclamation of a "Scottish" identity. The dismemberment and dispersal of various clans is a common theme in clan newsletter articles, in clan songs, and in event speeches and conversation. The MacLaines of Lochbuie claim their clan base shattered when, under coercion, seventeenth-century MacLaines settled the plantations in Ulster. Describing the death of a sixteenth-century chief that left Clan Moffat nonexistent in Scots law for centuries, clan literature laments, "This was to be the fate of Clan Moffat for four centuries—headless, broken, scattered throughout the known world, its place in history forgotten, sometimes purposely ignored" (1995:3). Many informants told me similar stories about their clans; the more dramatic the demise, the more emotive the call to reestablish the clan to its "proper place in history."

Most diaspora narratives are of course linked to Jacobitism. Accounts of clan history after 1746 play on several motifs: Hanoverian-appointed tyrants; the proscriptions against tartan and the pipes; the loss of greatness and independence; forfeited lands and clan strongholds; emigration and eviction. Discussion of the constructive impact the Scottish diaspora has made on the world generally provides a positive denouement to these sad tales. Stories of famous Scots (who might not have found renown had their ancestors not left Scotland "after the 'Forty-five'") follow many recitations of Jacobite grievances.

Such cathartic narratives of ethnic success are common to many Americans who acknowledge an emigrant background and ancestral hard times. Jacobitism and the fame of later Scots abroad form the bookends of Scottish-American heritage and balance the commemoration of ancestral grievances with a pride in ancestral achievements. An emphasis of clan tent displays at Highland Games and at other heritage events is the documentation of distinguished clan descendants who have succeeded in the professions, in the military, or as members of Parliament or Congress. Every clan has its trophy ancestors: Clan Buchanan claims James Buchanan, fifteenth president of the United States, and the founder of the United Naval Academy, Franklin Buchanan; the Hepburns claim actresses Audrey and Katharine; Clan MacGregor claims World War strategists and the Confederate general James Longstreet.[16]

Famous owners of the shared surname enhance the prestige of the clan. Members identify these famous people with the "potential of the clan" and even genetic "tendencies." Clan X might be "known for its musical talent," while the Macwhatevers are considered "natural soldiers." Identifying themselves with the famous who share their surname is something individuals would probably not do without exposure to the present-day clan system, in which the same name translates to the same family. The random person named Armstrong is not as likely to feel a connection with the astronaut Neil Armstrong as would a Clan Armstrong member. Clan society members have seen Neil Armstrong featured in clan literature as a "cousin" and as an example of "their family's" success and inherent capacities.

Membership in the clan society enables one to share the successes of those with a common name; it separates the deeds of other generations from ordinary history as one's peculiar heritage. In many countries, Clan MacNachtan notes, "the great historic families were separated from the mass of the people, not so in Scotland. The pride of the Name has never depended on wealth or rank, and all bearers of great Scottish names share alike in their ancient traditions" (MacNaughton 1994:1). In games displays and leaflets, the Clan Leslie Society asks, "Why should you become a member?" The answer is the common theme in all clan literature:

> Those of Scottish ancestry are blessed by a special bond of kinship and common heritage embracing hundreds of years. Our aim is to help you learn more about that heritage with a sense of pride and a spirit of enjoyment in that knowledge. We invite you to join with us in this adventure and realize your own sense of history in being an active part of a truly distinctive people. Everyone benefits as we contribute our individual pieces to the puzzle in an effort to preserve a heritage that is worth the endeavor. (Leslie 1995:1)

It is with a spirit of enjoyment that clan members identify each other by the colors of their clothing as sharing the same roots, and then immediately launch into an intimate discussion of family trees—often without even an introduction. Frances Nantista of Clan Hay explained the community this way: "There is a sense of family, beyond family. . . . If you say you're Scottish, people you don't know will hug your neck." She added that she had always heard about Irish and Italian ethnic groups, but "didn't know I had an identity until I found the Scots" (Nantista 1995). "Finding" an identity ascribed simply by surname is becoming increasingly popular among what Lieberson would call America's unhyphenated whites (1989:159–80).

As the most common form of introduction to the Scottish-American community, clan societies are at the heart of today's Scottish heritage revival. In the past few decades, they have surpassed the centuries-old, and exclusive, St. Andrew's Societies as the representatives and shapers of a Scottish-American identity.[17] Clan membership and even the clan societies themselves as organizations have become a "family" inheritance. Promotion of clan events and society membership plays on family pride and the current American emphasis on family values.

Clan societies are celebrating kinship at a time when actual kin links seem to be breaking down. Employment demands and divorce not only separate the nuclear family, but also contribute to geographical distance between grandparents and grandchildren. After the 1960s, when it is now practically expected for the young to openly flout their parents' beliefs, heritage revival offers a kind of counter-counterculture. Heritage celebration not only revives a definite sense of identity (one which is willingly accepted from one's ancestors), but through experience at events and through the imagined sense of community also creates a realm in which those of different interests and generations mingle.

Gender and Generation in Community Interests

Though a section on "women's roles" is now generally considered obligatory in cultural analysis, the overwhelmingly male orientation of the Scottish-American community seems an important subject of inquiry. Such an orientation should not be surprising considering the military emphasis embedded in "Scottish heritage." In subsequent chapters I consider male visions of the heritage and masculinity "on the pedestal." Here, I wish to discuss the organization of community groups by gender and generation.

The clan society model is the early-eighteenth-century patriarchal clan system. Heritage imagery of the clan remains that of a family grouping, headed by a warrior chief who could demand absolute loyalty and obedience. At a time when gender roles are undergoing dramatic change, this focus within Scottish heritage celebrates the *un*sensitive male. Clan societies themselves are hierarchical with a predominance of male figureheads. The emphasis on family events and kinship helps cover the exclusion of women in many events and at the organizational level.

Excluded from North Carolina's St. Andrew's Society, women also carry few elected positions in nationwide clan societies. In mid-1990s Directory Issues of *The Highlander*, of 207 clan societies and 66 society branches recorded, listings included only 19 women with titles such as commissioner, president, or convener. Out of the total 273 clan societies and branch societies, 120 (or 44 percent) were based (by contact address) in the South, with 17 based in North Carolina. However, only five of the women with positions were southerners. This is not to say women do not perform much of the work in organizing community publications and mailings, or planning and hosting society events, but they are less commonly recognized for their efforts with titled positions.

Eighteenth-century clan members took their chief's name; women in the Scottish community today may have the chief's name, but in community literature it is still preceded by "Miss" or listed as, for example, "Mrs. Roger MacMeeken." These naming traditions show both the age of those involved in the society organization and the editing preference of community publications. In North Carolina, they may also show a regional conservatism. The use of a husband's name, or a prefix indicating marital status, in a realm in which names have such value in the claiming of identity, speaks volumes about the role of women's identity within the community.

Married women in the community often give precedence to their husband's clan interests. When both partners in a marriage have Scottish ancestry, the woman may be a member of her own clan society, but still reports sitting with her husband at his clan tent and attending his society's events more often than her own. Many women with no Scottish ancestry spend a great amount of time researching that of their husbands and participating in their clan organizations. A button seen occasionally on retirement-age women says, "Happiness is being married to a Scot."

As mentioned elsewhere, men's attire is far more elaborate than women's. Watching a group of men being photographed in their kilts, I asked a nearby MacLean woman what she made of their display. She told me, "This is basically a male thing." At many events it has been kept that way by "ritual" and "tradition": only in 1994 were women allowed to march in the Parade of Tartans at the Grandfather Mountain Games (the oldest in North Carolina and most prestigious in the South).

Though the military aspect of the Scottish community will be addressed in another chapter, it is perhaps worth noting here that the presence of military bands, as well as of mostly male, civilian pipe bands and the male-only Scottish athletics, make the games, in some ways, a very male environment. Many of the women with whom I spoke did not perceive the games' environment in that way, but they had plenty to say about their exclusion from St. Andrew's Societies, various rituals, and the rather patronizing female competitions at some games (e.g., "tossing the broomstick"). However, the "Bonniest knees contest" (in which a blindfolded woman feels the knees of kilted men to pick her favorite) drew no objections. Undoubtedly, further consideration of women in the community would yield rich material, but I focus instead on the disproportionate male imagery and ritual.

Further considerations before launching into analysis of community

Karen Becker of the Scottish Spinning and Weaving Society.

events relate to generational and special interest divisions within the community. Within the mainstream community there are basically three main generational divisions. These categories overlap and their boundaries blur at many events, but I describe the community's generational groupings to provide a better picture of the events and trends I discuss in the rest of the text. What I will for convenience call the "first-generation heritage revivalists" are largely retiree, clan society enthusiasts who toast Bonnie Prince Charlie and whose activities are defined by Highlandism and tartanry. The second generation, those from their twenties to their early fifties, generally have more specialized interests in weaving, reenacting, athletics, and country dancing.

The third generation community members—such as dancers, ath-

Award-winning contestants in the Grandfather Highland dancing
competitions are "piped" around the games field with their trophies.

letes, and bagpipers of college age or younger—are more concerned
with their interests as a competitive art form than they are in genealogy
(though the inheritance theme is prominent in their activities, too).
Their interests are most transnational, in that they strictly abide by
rules and regulations from Scotland, and regard the ultimate Scottish
experience as competing, not traveling, in Scotland. Those whose parents are not involved in the community may become so because of their
child's interest, but often stop attending events when the children stop
competing. They may speak of themselves as part of the dancing or
piping community (in which they have consistent face-to-face interactions) within the wider Scottish-American community.

Suggesting such broad generational differences might mistakenly
imply that heritage celebration will utterly change as community members age. Many of the dancers and pipers I spoke with whose parents
were in the heritage movement said they would continue to come to
events and sit in the clan tents at games with their parents even after
they stopped competing because it was "a family thing." Several young
pipers said they would "always want to play the pipes," even if they had
to switch or drop out of bands. The general structure of the community
and its basic themes and perspective will endure—as it centers on her-

itage and preserving a vision of a Scottish cultural inheritance. Yet as we have already seen in the American elaboration of Highlandism, community traditions do, and will, acquire new meanings and practices. As a conclusion to this chapter, I consider fringe aspects of the imagined community and new directions in the further specialization of heritage interests.

Room for Celts and Vikings

I consider the St. Andrew's society members as the Balmoral Fringe—being more interested in and of the same age range of those who celebrate Highlandism; but not as devoted to its research and exploration as the mainstream community. At the opposite end of the spectrum is the Celtic Fringe, those old enough to have been "hippies," or young enough to feel they missed out on that counterculture. The Celtic Fringe focuses on pan-Celtic interests rather than Highlandism and is the counter-culture of the Scottish-American community.

David Lowenthal writes that "those who detach from themselves some part of their past commonly substitute another. Disavowing materialist values, many young Americans who forsook middle-class parental milieux for radical lifestyles in the 1960s also flocked to prehistoric archaeological digs, finding an alternative heritage in remote antiquity" (1985:38). Though participants in the Celtic Fringe most correspond in age to the second generation, their interests do not coincide. These fringers are distinguished from mainstreamers by their lack of exposure to, or interest in, Jacobitism and Highlandism. Celtic Fringe interests lie broadly in the more ancient traditions of Scotland, Ireland, Wales, and Brittany, covering the Celtic folk music revival; Scottish rock groups; "Celtic" artwork in the style of medieval illuminated manuscripts; Celtic folklore; and archaeology.

Finding their interests in the centuries prior to those the mainstream community is celebrating, fringers do not attend Burns's Night Suppers or genealogy events. They are involved in a whole different realm of literary interests regarding paganism, not Presbyterianism. They are interested in a wider range of music, preferring the smaller elbow pipes to the Highland bagpipes. They will attend Scottish Games, but they visit the vendors of Celtic music and paraphernalia, not the clan tents, explaining, "The games are not really what [they] are into," but the games are "as close as [they] can get over here." While the clan society members want their heritage documented to the real and last McCoy, the fringers explain their "quest" for a heritage that is a little mysterious

"First generation" Lt. Col. David Cone in a Crimean
War–period piper's uniform, with Charlotte Patterson dressed
as an ancient Celt, at the Loch Norman Highland Games.

and perhaps even more romanticized, but not romanticized in a formalized way. Many fringers are in groups such as the Society for Creative Anachronisms, and unlike reenactors, the participants I spoke with
expressed more concern for imagination than authenticity in their
heritage play. Some of the second generation Scottish heritage enthusiasts crossover in musical interests and know such Scottish bands as
Ceol Beag, Altan, Battlefield Band, and RunRig, but they are unlikely to
know even the most renowned Irish musicians playing Celtic music.
They tend not to buy recordings by Irish groups, or if they do, they
usually choose the well-known Chieftains (not the politically vocal Wolf

Tones) or recent Clannad releases (not the group's early 1970s Gaelic songs). They do not explore Irish culture or the history behind Irish music as the fringers do, and as they themselves do with Scottish music.

While such "Celtic" as opposed to "Scottish" interests may still be marginal within the community, appreciation is rapidly growing for the "Jacobite" ancestors' even more remote pasts. Nationwide, Celtic interests have grown phenomenally during the years of my fieldwork. The number of Celtic festivals across the country (some connected to Scottish events, some not) have quadrupled. The idea of a Celtic-American identity is becoming more popular as a self-proclaimed category for Scottish, Irish, Welsh, and Cornish Americans—in other words, non–Anglo Americans from the North Isles. As the heritage movement grows it becomes increasingly specialized and other romanticized Scottish "traditions" combine in celebration and in Scottish Americans' sense of identity.

Only a few clans highlight a pan-Celtic identity in their literature. Clan Gregor, or MacGregor, claims to be one of the "oldest and purely Celtic Scottish Clans"—claiming descent from Kenneth Alpin, who united the Picts and the Scots in the ninth century. Clan MacDuff members explain that, by tradition, the family name was that of the Celtic Earls of Fife. The MacNeills of Barra note that their bardic tradition is shared by relatives in all the Celtic lands. Clan Currie claims an Irish poet from the second-century court of the King of Connaught as their founder. While Clan Currie is deeply proud of its ancient Celtic roots, Clan Gordon (from the northeast, "Doric-speaking" region of Scotland) freely admits its roots are not Celtic but Norman, and still other clans emphasize Viking connections.

In North Carolina, the Scottish-Viking heritage is celebrated in a loose association referred to as "The Kingdom of Raknar." The late Robert "Hagar" Swanson, himself a member of three clans with Viking links: Gunn, MacFarlane, and MacKay, founded the group at the Grandfather Mountain Games. (Swanson styled himself "Hagar the Horrible"—with the cartoonist Mort Walker's permission.) Meeting annually at the Grandfather Games, the group is an assembly of some of the most involved members in the Scottish network hierarchy, including the presidents, commissioners, or deputy commissioners of clan societies, and dancing groups.

Membership in the Kingdom of Raknar is established by invitation and an initiation akin to fraternity hazing. (New members inducted at Grandfather crawl on their hands and knees to kiss the "king's ring.") Members, identifiable by their blue- and white-horned helmet lapel pins, tell me they are celebrating their "Viking-Scottish and American heritage" (American is included as part of the claim that the Vikings discovered America). The group's rituals are meant as a spoof, though I spoke with older couples who considered their initiation ceremonies an honor: it means being included in the inner circle of the Scottish-American community among clan society presidents and the organizers of the most prestigious Highland Games in the country.

Among the clans who play up Viking origins, Clan Gunn claims that "practically without exception the Highland Clans chiefly lines claim descent from the Norse Vikings, [and] Clan Gunn is no exception, tracing its beginning to King Olaf the Black of Norway" (Gunn 1994:1). Clan Montgomery traces its origins to a Norman Viking founder a thousand years ago. Clan Hamilton Society members remark on their first chieftain's "Gaelic and Norse blood." The MacDonalds also claim Scandinavian heritage, since clan founders were the "Lords of the Isles" (the Hebridean Islands) where the Vikings were most active. While the chiefly lines may have been of Norse descent, the people were Celts, but this does not stop today's celebrants from claiming Viking heritage, just as they claim their chief's name as their own "blood inheritance."

Though these clans point out other aspects of their Scottish heritage, these are not seen as alternative to the celebration of Highlandism—at least not yet. The emphasis on diaspora and exile stories reveals that the community's perspective of heritage is still heavily weighted to one main period. Emphasizing this period of loss demonstrates that there is still a sense of bereavement and a need for reclaiming.

The construction of heritage is an ongoing process. The clan societies of today developed a hundred years after Highlandism romanticized the clan system of one hundred years before. The Scottish-American community, as an imagined community, has grown through the development of clan societies, aided by community literature. Through this literature also, the community has maintained somewhat standardized images of Scottish identity and Scottish heritage. Desktop publishing and the internet will continue to impact the way in which the community is structured and imagined.

The activities of the Scottish community remain those of a revival— meaning that a performance aspect flows through much of the singing, dancing, poetry-reciting, and storytelling at events. Much of celebration seems a reenactment of ancestral traditions as perceived from the eighteenth century. Newly created traditions celebrate the present sense of community (the experience of each other as sharers of an identity), but focus mostly on past ways of life. The next chapter will consider the nature of tradition by examining the community's most "substantial" reenactment of romanticized Highland life: the Highland Games. Through a study of event and process, I discuss where and how a very real sense of *Gemeinschaft* may be experienced when an imagined community physically assembles in celebration of its identity through the celebration of the past.

The Brigadoon of the Scottish-American Community

Scottish Highland Games and Gatherings

> There's a fire on the mountain where the spiny thistle grows.
> And it's burning in the heart of every Highlander who knows
> For all that fate has offered there's endurance in the flame.
> When the fire's on the mountain we'll be coming home again.
>
> Through storms of chance and circumstance the thistle has
>   been spread
> We're a lifelong band of brothers it can truthfully be said.
> When the fire's on the mountain we'll be coming home again. . . .
> —"There's a Fire on the Mountain," lyrics by Keets F. Taylor

Written to capture the spirit of the Grandfather Mountain Highland Games, "Fire on the Mountain" has become the event's theme song. Its performance throughout the games evokes the heritage lore motifs about Highland identity, the Scottish diaspora, and group kinship that underscore community identity. For the Scottish community, Highland Games and Gatherings have become temporary physical expressions of an "imagined" unity. Through tartan parades, massed bagpipe-band performances, dancing, athletic competitions, and solemn rituals in honor of ancestors, the Highland Games are an enactment of the community's guiding beliefs and the central themes of Scottish heritage. The fire that opens the Grandfather Mountain Games symbolizes the gathering of now-dispersed clans at a place that has become home to heritage celebrations, and therefore to the assembled community. The selection and reformation of traditions producing today's Highland Games are a celebration of both Highlandism and of constantly evolving and unique community perspectives.

The Highland Games and Gatherings

By tradition, Highland Games grew from competitions held by a king or chief for the dual purpose of amusement and the selection of fit young men as bodyguards and laborers. The early-seventh-century Ulster Cycle of myths and sagas mentions such strength and endurance contests.[1] Northern Irish raiders, known to the Romans as "Scotti," began settling in Argyll during the late fourth century and may have brought such sporting traditions (along with their Gaelic language) to the land that eventually bore their name.[2] However, the first recorded athletic trial is that organized by King Malcolm Ceann Mor ("big head") on the Braes of Mar in the late eleventh century.

Through subsequent centuries, the games combined with the periodic meetings, or "Gatherings," of regional clansfolk and clan chiefs to make clan and marriage alliances, and to settle disputes. In addition to these social and political roles, the ancient Highland Gatherings had economic functions. Largely self-sufficient Highland communities, relying principally on cattle, oats, and barley, would also gather seasonally for harvest celebrations, for trade, or for a *creach*. Today, international Highland Games and Gatherings draw those with Highland, Lowland, and Scots-Irish ancestry to compete and spectate, to meet their clan chiefs and their "cousins," and to share knowledge and lore about the heritage. Historical clan reputations and rivalries reemerge in playful enactment of deeply held perceptions about "the Highland past" and Highland ancestors.

Highland Games and Gatherings, in the form we know them today, began with the Highlandism of Sir Walter Scott's era. One of the first Highlandized Highland Games, and that which set the example for events around the globe, was the Braemar Gathering—held where King Malcolm's subjects competed early in the millennium. The location and timing of this revival relates both to themes of Sir Walter's popular writings and the revalorization of "Scottish" manhood by Highland soldiers' publicly acclaimed performance in the Napoleonic wars.

The Braemar Highland Society first formed in 1817, and by 1826, four years after George IV's visit to a Highlandized Edinburgh, the society included in its aims the preservation of Highland culture ("specifically the kilt") and the promotion of sport. In the 1840s, the Braemar Gathering became an annual outing for Queen Victoria and the sporting landlords who emulated her. With their patronage, Highland Games sprang up across Scotland between the 1850s and 1880s. The revived games annually number nearly one hundred in Scotland today and close to three hundred in the United States and Canada. Highland Games and Gatherings may be found in all former British colonies, wherever Scots emigrated, and also in Indonesia and the United Arab Emirates, where professional Scottish athletes fly in to perform.

As tartan and the kilt took on new meanings (and new owners) after the Acts of Proscription, the revived games, likewise, became large performed pageants with brilliant costumes and ordered events quite in contrast to their smaller fairlike origins. Highlandized Games presented a festival picture of "Scottish" life in a romantic caricature of eighteenth-century Highland culture. Recognized as fantasy at the time, their form, like the clan/tartan connection, have become traditional and continually acquire new elaborations.

Sociologist Grant Jarvie illustrates how the redevelopment of the Highland Games tradition "paralleled much broader transformations within" Scottish society (1991:101). He notes that "divorced from their original social context," the Highland Gatherings between 1840 and 1920 were "inextricably linked" to Balmoralization, or Highlandism (itself inextricably linked to dependency and English cultural domination) (1991:102). During this period, rules became standardized and Highland dress became the "statutory mode of attire" with "accessories that would have struck the old Highland Clansfolk as amazing . . . incorporated into the outfit" (1991:103).

Considering the growth of the leisured middle class and international tourism, I view the twentieth-century development of the games in terms of an exchange between Scots abroad and the homeland.[3] Where Jarvie excludes the Jacobite emphasis in heritage celebration (a factor important both in Scotland and North Carolina) to focus on nineteenth-century Highlandism, I view Highlandism as an ongoing process—itself a continuing celebration of Jacobitism (depoliticized and kitchified)—and transnational in its impact. The standardization of games' rules in Scotland during Jarvie's period is now the work of the Scottish Games Association, whose rulings have international authority. In addition to judges for athletic, musical, and dancing competitions, even the clothes worn to games around the world are imports from Scotland.

Do Scottish Americans know the role of Jacobitism and Highlandism in shaping their celebrations and perceptions of heritage? Most do not. Does the convoluted development of meanings shaping today's Highland Games and the creation of rules and other events make them inauthentic today? Hardly. Rightfully considering the intentions and social contexts of predecessors, historical analysis tracing the genesis of traditions should not discount the intentions and context of those traditions' current inheritors and practitioners. Whatever their origins, today's Scottish-American Highland Games have deep meaning and significance that affirms a sense of community and group identity.

The last two decades have witnessed a scholarly frenzy to deconstruct invented traditions, after the seminal works of Edward Shils (*Tradition*, 1981) and Eric Hobsbawm and Terence Ranger (*The Invention of Tradition*, 1983). Merrily exposing the historical "realities" behind public myths and celebrations, many of these bubble-bursting studies conclude that by their invention, such traditions are laughable and invalid. Some of what is considered traditional at Scottish events could be called invented traditions, and when historical origins of some traditions are known, their contemporary form or practice can be amusing. This does not, however, invalidate the very real meaning that their practice now imparts. All traditions are invented at some point. Invented traditions are designed to be meaningful, and it is this function that makes them worthy of respectful study.

Traditional Inventions and the Process of Authenticity

In the twentieth-century American revival of "Scottish traditions," revived and revamped in nineteenth-century Scotland, new meanings and rituals coat the surviving threads of ancient customs. Often without historical documentation, or in opposition to it, these new meanings importantly attribute continuity from the past and a sense of authenticity to new practices. Why are these concepts of continuity and authenticity so important to how we value tradition that they are often invented?

Any inherited knowledge or procedure is "traditional." Traditions evolve with each generation, yet much of their authority and power comes from their reification as unchanging and ancient "things"—often quite detached from those who actually practice and perpetuate them. As invented traditions commonly derive from past practices or notions about what past practices were like, I prefer to discuss heritage rituals as selections from tradition, or innovations.

Authenticity lies in having a verifiable, or accepted, origin and/or presumed continuity of practice. I am not concerned with proving or disproving the authenticity of community traditions, but with understanding the process by which their form becomes perceived as ancient and how, through their annual or more frequent repetition, they become established as traditional with a conjectured continuity from "the past." Erik Cohen refers to this process as emerging authenticity in which new cultural developments may acquire the patina of authenticity over time (1988:379). Despite the relative newness of many "Scottish" traditions, they have become ritualized and rule-bound, and with each reenactment they become more authentic.

Whether authentic and continuous or not, a tradition's significance is linked to how and why participants perceive it as such. Many who critique inventions at heritage events and folk festivals ignore the emotions participants invest in old, presumed to be old, or overtly new traditions. Even first annual traditions may feel authentic when practitioners believe them to be "in the spirit" of what their ancestors once did. From the cultural studies' approach, John Dorst suggests that Americans attending folk festivals (apparently "mystified" by their own postmodernity) unquestioningly embrace the authenticity of festivals as an escape from their seemingly inauthentic lives (1989). From the anthropological perspective, I attended Scottish Highland Games as participant-observer and encountered those who celebrated their Scottish heritage as the foundation of, rather than an escape from, their lives. I contend that, while people at Scottish Highland Games are perhaps anti-reflexive about the authenticity of the whole event (with its "inauthentic" microphones, stages, and port-o-lets), they are reflexive in discussing their beliefs and in their apparel or performance preparation.

In reviving (reliving) the past through activities developed especially for its celebration, the space between "then" and "now" often disappears. Tempers flare at Confederate battle reenactments. Tears flow during retellings of the seventeenth-century massacre of the Glencoe Mac-Donalds. People want to remember the joy and the pain of the historical other (as a possible ancestor) in these events. They want to relive those events; they may even want to change their outcomes, and feel, through their reexperience, that these events are a part of what makes their heritage, and so makes them themselves.

Authenticity of spirit and assumed continuity with the past is especially important for imagined communities as the basis for their imagining. As Lowenthal notes, continuity implies "a living past bound up with the present, not one exotically different or obsolete" (1985:62). The reality of continuity is less important than how, and why, it is conceived. It is not always the original that seems authentic, but current views of what "the original" was like. We continually re-create the past to explain and give meaning to the present. Imagined communities select from history and from tradition what provides a feeling of connectedness with both those who went before and those present, those sepa-

rated by time and by space. The selection of tradition is an act of identification, by which we distill our many statuses and roles into those we
find most meaningful. Selected traditions efficiently accomplish what
traditions are meant to do—provide a quite coherent sense of self, community, and other—and this, rather than disputable origins, is what I
wish to consider by examining the Scottish Highland Games.

The games are one of the most important arenas in which to study
the community because they draw together all its varied elements and
visions of Scottish-Americanness. About the utility of events as data,
Moore notes "unlike many forms of dialogic interview material, the
most significant events are not generated by, nor elicited by, the inquiries of the anthropologist" (1994:365). The articulation of various
perspectives and interests at the games and the face-to-face meeting of
community members leads to the further creation of new groups and
the communication of knowledge and theories about "proper" attire,
clan life, genealogical research, and other Scottish subjects. Games allow one to see the recreation of traditions and the perpetuation of authenticating myths in process, as well as the questioning and debate
over the same. While the traditional authenticity of the reinvented
games is now unchallenged by most Scottish Americans, every event
witnesses their further evolution. Each gathering introduces new traditions and rituals, and their adoption and repetition at other games estab-
lishes their emergent authenticity. To examine the games is to see both
the celebration and the making of Scottish heritage.

North Carolina's Scottish Games and Gatherings

Central to the Scottish-American community's annual activities, Highland Games and Gatherings draw together people of varying Scottish
descent with the common purpose of remembering the ancestors. The
ritual role-playing of those presiding over the games, the wearing of
certain dress, the precise scheduling of highly structured events, and the
continuous flow of pipe music produce a setting in which participants
may achieve a sense of connectedness and intersubjectivity with both
the ancestral past and the present "cousinhood."

Highland Games came to America in the wake of nineteenth-century
Highlandism. Developing mostly in the North and West after the Civil
War, all but two games terminated with the Great Depression (Don-
aldson 1986:40). The post–World War II development of Scottish
Games has been greatest in the South (Berthoff 1982). North Carolina
is currently home to four annual Highland Games and multitudinous
Scottish festivals.

Founded in 1956, the oldest and best known are, of course, the July Grandfather Mountain Highland Games. The four days of events in Linville draw crowds of over 30,000. Grandfather is the site for the annual meetings of many national clan societies, and the model for the explosion of new Scottish Games from the 1970s to the present. The North Carolina games of most recent origin (1994) are the April "Loch" Norman Highland Games near Charlotte. These two-day Highland Games in a Scots-Irish-settled area drew approximately 10,000 people in their first year. Also near Charlotte and supported by the Charlotte Robert Burns's Society is the late October Waxhaw Gathering of the Clans. The late Don Gallamore (a close friend of Donald MacDonald) organized the first Waxhaw Gathering in 1979. Through limited advertising, the one-day Waxhaw Gathering is deliberately kept smaller than the big games, partly for financial and locational reasons, and partly to maintain the atmosphere of a local event.

Preceding the Waxhaw Gathering at the beginning of October are the one-day Flora MacDonald Highland Games. Held in Red Springs, near the heart of the eighteenth-century Highland settlement, these games involve many descendants of the Highlander immigrants.[4] As part of the 1976 Bicentennial celebrations, the Red Springs events began in combination with a reenactment of a Revolutionary War battle (which is still a games event). Each of the North Carolina games share the same basic format, but offer somewhat different emphases and have distinct reputations for their size, length, and the types of musical performers, clan societies, and athletes each draws. The Flora MacDonald Games emphasize local history and community and their heroine namesake, while the Grandfather Games draw upon a broader sense of community, and offer both a venue for specialized interests in Viking heritage (The Kingdom of Raknar) and the Celtic Fringe and more Highlandized pageantry.[5]

Heritage society members often say that, unlike other American games introduced in this century, North Carolina games are revivals because of the historical and authenticating existence of Scotch fairs in the state. Nineteenth-century Scotch fairs were largely agricultural fairs, as were the fairs in Scotland with which games occurred in conjunction. The Flora MacDonald Games and the short-lived Ellerbe Games (1976–77) have both stressed the old Scots fair tradition. Informant Jamie MacDonald explains that fairs took place at Ellerbe in upper Richmond County during the nineteenth century and, beginning in 1798, at Laurel Hill in the Highland settlement. At these fairs, "cattle, horses, chickens, butter, eggs, apple cider, brandy, cotton, and leather goods were brought to be sold or traded" (1993). From late-nineteenth-century accounts, David MacRae described the November Laurel Hill Scotch Fair as drawing eight to ten thousand men; women no longer attended by the time of his writing "because of the drinking" (1868:251).

The fairs took place on the second weeks of May and November from Tuesday until Saturday. The timing coincides with agricultural fairs still held biannually in Scotland at Whitsunday (May 15) and Martinmas (November 11). (These are not to be confused with the "Holy Fairs" of the communion season—a creation of Lowland Scottish Covenanter Presbyterianism [Schmidt 1989].) Though historical records make no mention of games occurring with the Scotch fairs in the North Carolina community, for many community members the existence of the fairs provides a unique link between North Carolina games (begun in the 1950s) and those harvest-time events held in Scotland when the clan system functioned.

The timing of games no longer concurs with the agricultural cycle. Originally an autumnal event in Scotland, they now extend through the tourist season from mid-May to mid-September. In Scotland, but especially in the former British colonies, games' dates significantly fall on anniversaries of historical events, most frequently Jacobite. The Braemar Gathering coincides with the date Jacobites rallied for the 1715 Battle of Sherriffmuir. Organizers held the first Grandfather Mountain Games on August 19, when the clans first raised Prince Charlie's standard in the "Forty-Five." The date served as a symbolic summons to dispersed clans to join in commemoration of a lifeway and a heritage that lore says ended with Charlie's defeat at Culloden. The first annual Loch Norman Games fell on the anniversary of the Battle at Culloden; though organizers said this was a serendipitous accident, many participants assumed it was intentional and the anniversary was a popular topic of discussion at the games.

Many clan societies plan functions and meetings on anniversaries of Jacobite or clan-specific events. (For example, at the 1993 Georgia Stone Mountain Games, the twenty-eighth chief of Clan Gillen held a clan congress to commemorate the one-hundreth anniversary of the twenty-sixth chief's visit to the 1893 Chicago World's Fair.) Most clan societies try to have their annual general meetings at games because many members travel long distances to attend and entertainment is readily available. The famous dates in Scottish history with which many games intentionally coincide provide a theme for emotive songs and toasts, and a topic about which an invited "expert" may speak at clan events.

In terms of Scottish holidays, New Year's festivities (or Hogmanay) have always taken preeminence over Christmas. Since the Grandfather

Games occur in July, the American "Christmas in July" becomes "Hogmanay in July." Its celebration at Grandfather, where the largest numbers of community members assemble from across the state and country, allows the community to celebrate this most important Scottish holiday together. The Saturday evening of the games features a "Hogmanay Nicht" of Scottish country dancing that, according to dancers from around the country, is *the* gala for country dancers in America. Its inclusion among the "traditional events" at Grandfather represents a further accretion in the pastiche of the games and the revival of holidays and historical anniversaries long forgotten by ancestors of Scottish community members, but viewed by their descendants as heritage.

Traditional Games of the Games Tradition

In Scotland, Highland Games are most often called "Gatherings"—the games being the understood purpose for the gathering. In the American South, events are more frequently called games—the gathering of clansfolk being the understood purpose (and occasional subtitle) for the games.[6] At American games, the sporting events provide continuity of tradition and often, though not always, take center stage, but in many ways are now peripheral to the actual goings-on. Many of my informants reported having attended games from 9 A.M. to 5 P.M. two days in a row, with scarcely a glance at the athletics area (something I have done myself). Other competitions (dancing, piping, fiddling, harp, and track and field events) and clan tents are positioned in reference to "the Heavies" (the heavy athletic competitions that give their name to the events), but in North Carolina, and at southern games in general, the clan tents and clan gatherings form the central focus. Though the timing and form of games and gatherings have changed, the athletic competitions continue to provide the raison d'être, if no longer the focus, for the larger American events, and evidence the consistent transnational links shaping Scottish-American heritage.

Competitors in "the Heavies" climb their way through local, regional, and national ranks to compete in World Championships held in Scotland. At multiday games, professional competitions may occupy the main day (Saturday) and amateur events occur on Sunday.[7] Covered "review" stands shelter the games organizers and guests of honor who, acting as chieftains of the games, receive salutes or other acknowledgments by athletes and performers on the field. On the games field itself, several events may be happening simultaneously as athletes banter with each other and discuss technique while awaiting their turns.

Heavy events usually begin with the clachneart (the stone of

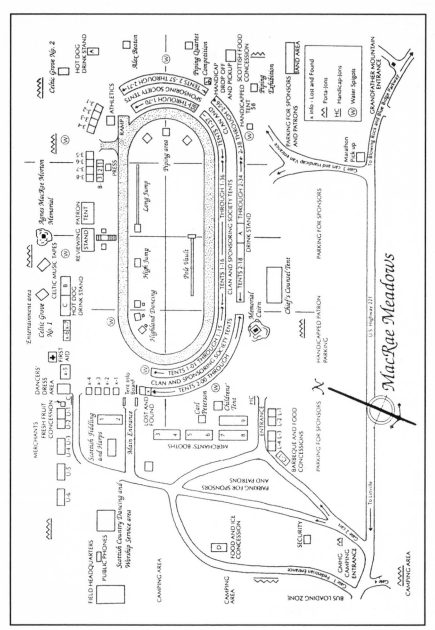

MacRae Meadows

strength), essentially a shotput. The stone used in Scottish games is traditionally taken from a local field or stream, the average weight used being about sixteen pounds. Discussing the limited exposure "Scottish" sports receive in the athletic world, many informants are quick to point out their belief that the modern Olympic shotput competition derived from the "manly art" of the Scottish stone throw. Another heavy event is the hammer throw. Swung in the air around the head three or more times, the four-foot hammer is then thrown behind the athlete for distance. A ball and chain called "the weight" (twenty-eight or fifty-six pounds) is thrown for distance and for height (up to fifty-six pounds). When thrown for height, the weight can also take the form of an agricultural weight with a ring mounted at the top. Holding the ring, the athlete swings the weight between his legs, over his head and, if successful, over a bar ten to fifteen feet high. Throwing a sixteen- to twenty-five-pound sack with a pitchfork—"tossing the sheaf"—is somewhat similar.

The most popular of the athletic events is "tossing the caber"—a pine-tree trunk with branches removed, between 100 and 120 pounds and usually about nineteen feet long and wider at one end. Holding the narrower end in his cupped hands and supporting the caber against his shoulder as it towers above him, the athlete attempts to run, comes to an abrupt stop, and throws the caber with all his momentum and an appropriate growl. If the caber is tossed end-over end, the athlete will receive the applause of onlookers, but not necessarily the winning title. Judges look for a perfect "12 o'clock throw"—meaning the caber lands directly in line with the athlete's feet as he stands at 6 o'clock on an imagined clock face.

Arnold Pope, who has participated in or judged Scottish athletics for thirty years, says one difference between American and Scottish games is that in Scotland an athlete would enter only a few events and in America one generally enters all of them, especially if given travel funds to attend. The North Carolina performance of a touring Scottish Pipe Band sparked Pope's own interest in Scottish events and, in addition to learning to play the pipes himself, he has since played an important role in teaching Scottish techniques to American athletes. Pope first went to Scotland to participate in the Aberdeen Games in the late 1960s and learned the "proper" form for tossing the caber. He became the first American ever to win in an Open Caber Championship in Scotland at Newburgh in 1971. He notes that though athletics at North Carolina games began in a small way with untrained athletes, they now conform to the standards of the International Scottish Highland Games Association (Pope 1995).

Larry Satchwell tosses the caber at Grandfather Mountain while athletic judge Ross Morrison follows close behind. (Photograph by Hugh Morton)

Even small games in America try to draw competitors in as many traditional categories as possible, and include a few events that are not standard in Scotland; for example, haggis hurling, "bonniest knees," and broom-toss contests are featured events at Waxhaw. (In addition to the track and field runs, these last three activities are those in which women take part.)[8] Rosie notes that the haggis hurl was devised in the 1970s by an Irish public relationist, Robin Dunseath, to be humorous. To Dunseath's "utter astonishment the 'ancient' sport of haggis-hurling took off" (1988:81). Dunseath now markets "How to run a haggis hurl" kits internationally. At the Aberlour and Strathspey Highland Games in Banffshire (in the northeast), haggis hurling is included in events, but is designated for "overseas visitors only."

New events and new games continue to appear in Scotland and around the world. Though many Highland Games in Scotland are as new as those in America, they still set the example to be followed. Some heritage event organizers in the United States even change "established" practices to conform more to what they have seen in Scotland. Beyond the athletic competitions, however, ideas and traditions travel both ways across the Atlantic. Some American innovations, such as the Kirkin' o' the Tartan, have also been adopted by Scots who visit American games. This raises interesting questions about the continual process of authentication, and about the role of tourism and tourist-oriented activities in perpetuating identity (see Chapter 5). Despite the transatlantic sharing of traditions, a comparison between Scottish and Scottish-American Highland Games reveals important differences between local traditions and the heritage celebrations of imagined communities.

Scottish Highland Games in Scotland

Who goes to Highland Games in Scotland? Mostly it is the locals. Unless competing, Scots do not travel to multiple games the way Scottish Americans "do the games circuit." Scottish sporting is a minority interest within Scotland as compared with football (soccer), rugby, golf, cricket, or even lawn bowling. Supporters of different caber tossers simply do not draw the crowds (or, thankfully, the pub fights) that the mere display of a football team's colors can evoke.

While I was a student at the University of Edinburgh and during subsequent stays in Scotland, Scottish friends found my interest in Highland Gatherings greatly amusing. Several students in the university's Highland Society told me they would never consider going to Highland Games because either they were "real Highlanders," or they considered games a tourist event "with no meaning anymore." Lowlanders with whom I spoke about games (who were not students, and not particularly concerned with Scottish studies) told me they would not be interested in going even if they lived nearby Braemar—but they would drive from Braemar to Glasgow or Edinburgh to see a football game. For many Scots, Highland and Lowland, the games represent a laughable stereotype of Scotland. Knowing of my plans to attend Braemar, friends with whom I was visiting in Aberdeenshire told me to have fun at the games and quickly imitated the "Highland fling" (a dance), waving their arms wildly above their heads. They would not accompany me—though they had never been—as they had "already seen the queen."

The most striking differences between the games and gatherings in Scotland and in America lie in the basic interaction of participants and observers relating to class structure, and in ideas about what is being celebrated. At American games, the organizers preside alongside a special guest (or guests) from Scotland, but the feeling is more demo-cratic—anyone may talk with them. In Scotland, organizers tend to be of the elite, or what one observer called "the plummy," "yah types" (a reference to their pronounciation of "yes/yeah"), and unspoken social rules still direct how they speak with whom. Not as likely as their American counterparts to beckon winning athletes off the field for a chat, they may only converse with games participants during the dis-tribution of trophies and awards. Members of local landed and titled families still present awards at several gatherings in Scotland, and at the grandest of all gatherings, Braemar, it is the queen and her family who preside and occasionally hand out prizes. Organizers at Victorian Games were required to be landowners. The very people partly respon-sible for the changes in Highland culture became its promoters—albeit in a form they found more palatable and flattering. Jarvie notes that "many [gatherings] have been affected by the equalizing process re-ferred to . . . as functional democratisation, yet residual groups of pow-erful landlords and descendants of the Victorian bourgeoisie still con-tribute to the modern Highland Gathering" (1991:87).

Jarvie also notes that today's Highland Gatherings are still "rela-tively dependent upon and have continued to perpetuate the cultural production and reproduction of symbols from the past in the person of the Highland chief" (1991:35). Though clan tents are not a presence at games in Scotland, many gatherings are associated with a particular clan (e.g., Clan MacPherson holds its annual rally and march simulta-neously with the Newtonmore Games in Inverness-shire) and the cur-rent clan chief presides over them (e.g., the chief of Clan Campbell presides over the Argyllshire Cowal Highland Gathering in addition to being chieftain for the Inverary Games held on his property).[9] Queen Elizabeth is of course considered chief to the Braemar Gathering. Being "chieftain" or "honored guest" at a games is akin to being chairperson for the day, though one is usually not involved in organizing the event. Many games in Scotland, especially in the Lowlands, opt for media or television celebrities as chieftains, rather than those titled by birth. In America, Scottish chiefs are often the "invited chieftain of the games"—though usually only the big games draw the "big names."

Grandfather Mountain, being America's Braemar, brings the most distinguished guests, such as Lord Elgin (a descendant of "the Elgin Marbles" family and "The Bruce"); Granville Charles Gordon, 13th Marquis of Huntly; and Rear Admiral Douglas Dow, director of the National Trust for Scotland. At American games, participants invest a fair amount of effort to impress the "honored visitor," rather than the other way round. The guest has already impressed the Scottish-

Chief David Menzies of Menzies, Honored Guest, visits with the
family of a child baptized at the Stone Mountain Highland Games.

American community by virtue of his or her being a live Scot and a
notable personage in Scotland. Depending on their status, health, and
inclination, and on the size of the games, honored guests from Scotland
may interact with the crowds in ways they do not in Scotland. Guests
may make brief statements at games and then circulate themselves
around the clan tents during events.

Clan tents are not part of gatherings in Scotland, and as seating (or
lack thereof) is determined by ticket price, there may be little space for
guests to mingle with the public. However, beyond these practical considerations, crowds at Scottish gatherings distinctly divide themselves
by socioeconomic class. The Scottish-American notion of "cousinhood"
among all of Scottish descent did not seem in evidence at the gatherings
I attended. For example, at the Lonach Gathering in the Scottish North

East, spectators on each side of the field seemed polarized by dress, accent, and interests. In the more expensive covered stands sat the local elite dressed as if for high tea, with hampers of pate and French bread. These participants spoke with "public school accents" (British public schools are what Americans call private schools), in contrast to other spectators' "Doric" and Aberdeenshire accents. None in the covered stands seemed to know the largely working-class athletes on the field or to show much interest in their performance beyond the occasional "well done." Again, by contrast, those across the field on chairs and blankets brought from home cheered throughout the events.

The "yah" crowd was more attentive to the arrival of the "Lonach Highlanders" (a social association of local men rather than a clan or regimental organization). Wearing kilts of the Gordon tartan with jackets and a plaid (in the August heat), "the Highlanders" had been "on the march" between well-known homes since dawn, stopping at each for a dram of whisky. (A horse-drawn wagon followed the marchers to carry any who succumbed to the morning draughts—though after twenty-two home visits in 1993 no one had!)

I attended the Lonach Gathering with Donald MacDonald, now an honorary member of the "Lonach Highlanders" and the only American invited to join their "march." Comparing the Lonach Gathering with American games, our discussion focused on the very different meaning of the public rituals involved in each. In America, games celebrate the past and the lifeways of eighteenth-century ancestors with a certain wistfulness and a relatively egalitarian sense of community. In Scotland, romanticization of the past is evident in costuming and the Victorian formalization of events through Highlandism, but the focus of contemporary gatherings is primarily on the community at present, with its various class divisions all participating in their own realm.[10]

Scottish participants with whom I spoke expressed less a sense of disruption and loss of tradition and simultaneously more a sense of its inventiveness than American informants. Whereas games programs and participants in North Carolina make frequent reference to the Scottish links of their areas and the "authentic Scotch fair" roots of the games tradition, gatherings programs and participants in Scotland express less concern with explaining origins. This difference would seem to stem from the greater importance of origin stories for ethnic identity. Scottish-American celebrations confirm and authenticate ethnicity, while Highland Gatherings in Scotland no longer reflect a regional ethnicity, but a Highlandized national identity. As the Highlander stereotype entails militaristic imagery, it is perhaps not so surprising to find various branches of the military setting up display and recruitment stands at the games in Scotland from Perth to Glasgow to Portree on the Isle of Skye. Many Scottish games also have carnival rides, "bouncy castles," cotton candy, and pay-and-win prize booths that readily integrate the new and the non-Scottish into the games tradition. Those with whom I spoke in Scotland attended gatherings as they would have attended a local fair, as indeed was the original spirit of the games in Scotland. Those who attend in America come to "remember their heritage" and meet their "cousin clanfolk" with the depth of feeling perhaps only geographic and temporal distance brings to recovered traditions.

Tartan Parades and Other American Innovations

As a symbol of ethnic identity, and restored traditions, tartan has a significant presence at American games. Though tartans and kilts are omnipresent at American games, at games in the Scottish Highlands and Lowlands, relatively few participants beyond bagpipe band members, games organizers, and competition judges attend kilted. Far less popular among Scots, kilts are sometimes required for specified American events and are mandatory for participation in "kilted mile" races and "tartan balls." The Grandfather Mountain and Loch Norman Highland Games are the first American games to have their own tartans—worn primarily by the games' own host bagpipe bands.[11] Clan tents at southern games generally have tables draped in clan tartan and often tartan awnings and banners. In both the Kirkin' o' the Tartan and the Parade of Tartans, clan representatives carry banners of the "clan cloth."

Murvan Maxwell began the Parade of Tartans at the Grandfather Mountain Games in 1965 to, in his words, "encourage audience participation" and to add a festive, colorful parade after his native New Orleans's traditions. Games programs and informants describe the parades as the ritual presentation of each clan to the honored guest of the games, and to the spectators and other participants. The Parade of Tartans exemplifies the American community's stress on the antiquity and continuity of the heritage and the idea of emergent authenticity. Since its institution at Grandfather, games across the country have adopted the parade. Most informants questioned at various games did not know when the parade developed, but many explained it was part of the original games in which the clans would parade past the high chief of an area to show their allegiance and would be identified to him by their "ancient" clan tartans.

Though only established in 1965, the Parade of Tartans has already

The 78th Highland Frasers stand at attention during a 1998 memorial
service at the Loch Norman Highland Games. The enclosure is
designated for the ashes of the community's "Flowers of the Forest."

undergone revisions and additions. In 1991, the Grandfather Games
Board of Directors introduced an "Award of Excellence" that recognizes
"pageantry, appearance, proper attire and accessories—keeping alive the
spirit and traditions of the Grandfather Mountain Highland Games," to
"encourage excellence" in clan presentations for the parade (Stewart
1992:32). The winning clan leads the parade the following year.

Other American innovations on the games tradition include the erection of a memorial cairn at each of the North Carolina Highland Games
sites in honor of Scottish ancestors and the "Flowers of the Forest"
(deceased members of the Scottish community), the "christening of a
new kilt," kilted clay shoots, and the inclusion of a military band tattoo
on evenings prior to games and other events. Life's rites of passage
such as funerals, christenings, and weddings are also shared with the
Scottish-American community at North Carolina's games fields.[12] With
the growing presence of vendors of "Scottish goods," the games might
be perceived as returning to their fairlike origins. A further innovation
now shared between Scotland and North America is the introduction of
Scottish Border Collie sheep-herding demonstrations that, as Donald
MacDonald notes, has a special irony since "nineteenth-century Highlanders were evicted because of the silly sheep" (MacDonald 1994). Still

Ward Weems of Weems and Sons offers a range of Scottish
goods from targes and swords to books and T-shirts.

nonexistent at Scottish games, but a vital innovation for games in the
American South, is the preeminence of clan tents.[13]

Southern Clan Tents: Fronts and Backs

The temporary face-to-face expression of an imagined community in
America, Highland Games renew group commitment, intensify friend-
ships, and unify individuals' research and perceptions into a coherent
vision of the heritage through discussion and ritual.[14] While celebrating
a Scottish-American identity, games around the country also respond to
regional American cultures and emphases, perhaps most strongly in the
South.

The southern fascination with kinship and lineage finds expression in
the numbers and importance of clan tents at southern Highland Games.
Elsewhere in America, clan tents are fewer in number and do not take
central stage as in the South. Visiting is the primary activity and draw
of southern games. Those who return again and again to Highland
Games come to visit with their "clan kinsfolk" and anyone who cares to
chat about Scottish, clan, or military history, genealogy, travel, or life
in general.

Many large southern games are now host to annual "family reunions" in the form of clan gatherings, and dispersed biological families are beginning to have annual reunions of two to four generations at the games. The games themselves seem like family reunions; given the southern belief in Scottish kinship, not only are those in the same clan society one's cousins, but also those in an allied sept or in a confederation of clans like Clan Chattan. After exhausting possible clan alliances and historical connections, southern Scottish Americans attempting to connect with each other may dismiss issues of specific kinship links in the satisfaction that their Scottish interests make them "spiritual kin." For many participants, finding common ground might also mean appealing to an ultimate kinship as "brothers and sisters in Christ."

The feeling of kinship (spiritual, ancestral, and familial) runs through games rituals, songs, emcee narrations, and most expressly in clan tent displays and conversation. Depending on the size of the clan society, a tent may have on average from two to ten volunteers setting up displays and speaking with visitors, as well as visiting other tents and event areas. Tent volunteers must be committed; they arrive early with tent hospitality and display supplies and leave late each day of the games, and they are often unable to attend evening events such as the tartan balls and sponsors' receptions. Very few younger couples set up and work the clan tents. Of those whom I met that did, most noted that—though they worked all week, had to bring school age children on a long drive to reach the games, could not attend evening events for lack of a babysitter, and often had to incur the expense of a hotel—they wanted their clan to have representation at the games and also felt the games to be a positive family experience for their children.

Having a representative tent at as many games as possible is a source of pride to all members; one of the features of clan society newsletters are the photos of clan tents at games across the country. Tent space varies in cost between games, but generally represents well over $100 of society funds. At many games, clan societies compete for a best clan tent award (judged on explanation of clan heritage within Scottish history, use of color/tartan, and demonstration of "clan pride" and "Scottish spirit"). Awards and recognition in future games programs are featured in clan society newsletters and displayed at subsequent games.

Clan tents offer an opportunity to further display, and discuss in detail, a distinct identity within one's Scottish identity. They also demonstrate community membership with what Erving Goffman has called "front" and "back" areas. Goffman defines front regions as areas "where a particular performance is or may be in progress," and back regions as areas "where action occurs that is related to the performance, but is inconsistent with the appearance fostered by the performance" (1959:134).

Members of the Lowland "Clan Kerr" pose before their winning tent at the Stone Mountain Highland Games.

The front areas of clan tents present a unified image of clan identity, while that identity and history may be hotly debated by members in the back areas.[15]

Occasionally framed with wood or painted cardboard to resemble a clan castle fortress, clan tent front areas exhibit the clan tartan with a photo of the chief (if one exists), a guest register, and new member information leaflets. Displays, and books set out for browsing, describe famous clan members, clan history, and clan lands. All are welcome to step up to the front area, look over displays, and ask questions. Usually two society representatives sit or stand behind the front area tables, encouraging passersby to stop and view exhibits, recruiting new members, and explaining clan history and activities to visitors. Only established members bring their chairs and ice coolers into the "back" area under and behind the tent; though friends from other clans and visitors especially interested in clan society membership may be invited back for a snack or a sit-down. As I became known at the games and found the same people setting up tents at many of the games I attended, I was invited back for sandwiches or shortbread, or to be introduced to an acknowledged authority on a certain topic.

In the back area, those clan members not engaged in answering questions sit and talk about genealogy, dress, new clan projects, and upcoming games. They also talk about politics, family events and a host of

The "back" area of Grandfather Mountain clan tents.

subjects not discussed with visitors to the front area. The back area is where socializing is most free, where meals are consumed, and where children and grandchildren play. While those in the front area present a united and harmonious "front" for the society, it is in the back area that disagreements over issues such as clan lore and dress codes surface in lively discussions. Though the tents are not large, general games bustle and noise keeps much of the back area activity out of visitors' earshot. Back/front distinctions are strongest at the beginning of events and tend to relax with the progress of the day or weekend games. This is especially true of tent arrangements in the games campgrounds at Grandfather—a gathering of the clans unique to the national Scottish-American community.[16]

Camping Out at Grandfather

Especially for southeasterners, but also nationally, the Grandfather Mountain Games are the chief annual event on the Scottish-American calendar. Participants begin arriving at the campgrounds a week before the games. Back/front distinctions are initially maintained among individual and family tents as community members adjust to the lack of privacy and as daily new arrivals crowd tents only a few feet apart. Back and front behaviors (in this case inside and outside the tent) merge rapidly as camp neighbors acquaint themselves. Everyone about is privy to all discussion, so after first settling into the campgrounds many withdraw behind tent walls to discuss even the simplest of decisions—what to cook, what events to attend, when to shower. As the days and even hours go by, people become more accustomed to their lack of personal space (conversations grow louder; answers to questions quietly asked at one tent site are shouted by campers several camp sites away; food, fires and toiletry supplies are shared; musical instruments come out and draw small crowds; those with RVs invite other campers in to visit). A sense of community develops within the campgrounds over and above that achieved through games events.

Those who camp out at Grandfather say it is the only way to really experience the games. Though a short walk from the games field, the campgrounds are where many participants say "everything happens" and the games spirit is strongest. Indeed, if these games are a physical expression of the imagined community, the campgrounds are where a sense of *communitas* is most obvious. Southern, Hogmanay, or clan-themed decorations adorn tents and motor homes throughout the camp and communicate perspectives of Scottish-American identity and of more specific identities within the community. As game attendees must walk through camp to the entrance gates, campground displays shape first-timers' initial impressions of what the games are about. Many displays become mini-clan exhibits that include lists of clan septs and perhaps banners or framed pictures / posters of clan castles and Scottish landscapes.

Participants may reserve several sites at the Grandfather Mountain campground to be near friends, family, and clan society members whom they may see but once a year. Often participants become somewhat territorial about the particular campsite they return to year after year. Others arrange camp next to people they have never met, but find that by the end of the weekend they are discussing family heritage, exchanging addresses, and planning to meet the following year.

A road divides the camping area into what are called the "McRowdy" and the "quiet" sides. Though noise and visitation continue throughout the night on both sides, the time to quiet down is signaled by a bagpipe parade from the nightly Clan MacNaughton ceilidh across the road to the McRowdy side. The McRowdies take pride in their reputation for sleepless nights and fun with McRowdy T-shirts and their own McRowdy "entrance gate." While individuals and families develop and alter decorative displays around their tents and RVs throughout the games, "the McRowdy side" has a unified "front." Reconstructed each year near a central tarp and fire pit, the display features Scottish, Confederate, and American flags, Highland battle targes, basket-hilted swords, wooden clubs, other reproduction, period weaponry, and occasionally a castle facade. The assembled artifacts come with individuals who return and contribute them each year. Seasoned McRowdies critique their collective display in terms of their group membership: "The display was better last year when so-and-so could make it" and because "this year so-and-so was afraid to leave his claymore in the rain."

Several McRowdy campers told me that they never leave their encampment during the games. They have seen the games before and return each year, many on their vacation time, they say, for the "fellowship" at camp. The McRowdies have established their own four- or five-day community within the annual camping community at the games. A physical enactment of the wider Scottish community, the "McRowdy Side" has its own rituals: an annual "sacrifice" (usually nothing livelier than a watermelon); a Saturday-night-after-midnight marshmallow war; and, more seriously reflective of their sense of microcosmic community, memorial services for anyone who was deceased since the last games.

In the campgrounds and on the games field, participants' behavior often follows a variety of front/back distinctions, demonstrate a range of interlocking identities, and, with years of participatory experience, reflect an accumulation of "insider" knowledge. Within the camps, certain "elders" emerge who have attended the games longer than others and who advise novices. Bonding through shared experience and interests is an expected part of the games experience, and my informants all agree that the purpose of the games is both to commemorate one's heritage and to have fun with spiritual kin who share it. Through the Scottish heritage revival of the last four decades, the games themselves have emerged as an authentic community "inheritance."

As Grandfather Mountain hosts what many consider the most prestigious games in the country, an excitement exists in just being there and the energy level in the campgrounds is tremendous. A great feeling of camaraderie attends the sharing of cooking fires, food, and the roasting of marshmallows. If the games represent the community coming face to face, the campgrounds are the greatest expression of mutual dependence not just for identity, but for the practical concerns of child care; protecting neighbors' gear from the rain in their absence; and attending to car trouble, occasional illnesses, and, in 1991, even a birth. Through displays and in participants' descriptions, the campgrounds symbolize the annual appearance of an otherwise imagined community, a community of diverse members from across the nation claiming a common identity and a shared heritage.

Emergent Heritage

Throughout my fieldwork I have been continually impressed by the speed with which new rituals acquire ancient roots—always in accord with Highlandist themes. At Waxhaw, I asked a member of Clan Lindsay how the haggis hurl began—and was surprised to receive the following answer:

> Well, a long time ago in the real old days . . . somewhere in the Highlands, by some stream . . . the men of the community were working on the other side of that stream from their homes and, instead of crossing over to get their lunch, or their wives crossing over to bring it to them . . . their wives sewed it up in a bit of tartan and threw their dinners to them across the stream . . . or river. . . . The men encouraged it as a sort of a game and that's how it got started.

I had never received any response beyond laughter when posing that question before, and was amazed to receive such an elaborate account. Nonetheless, I had to wonder if this older Lindsay woman simply wanted to be done with my questions. I asked if she was kidding me; she protested that it was what she had been told at Grandfather Mountain, "and so, it must be right."

Perceived continuity of tradition and authenticity of games events are important aspects to many community members' experience of the heritage, yet games have only occurred in North Carolina for the past few decades. What is said, performed, or practiced at Grandfather is now, for many of the Scottish-American community, "traditional." I found the groundwork for the first annual Loch Norman Games in 1994 (designed by Grandfather veterans) an interesting point from which to examine the process of authentication and traditions in the making.

In the Scots-Irish settled area of the Loch Norman Games, organizers involved local residents in an intense preparation to reenact their Highland "Scottish heritage." During the year and a half prior to the games, heritage enthusiasts gave lectures across North Mecklenberg County and the Charlotte area on proper dress, Scottish history, and meaning of a clan. At the games, the printed program and an announcer's continuous running commentaries described the origin stories behind almost every competitive and symbolic event, and related the saga of Culloden. Musical performers gave brief discourses on the history of their instruments and on each song played.

In any games' initial year the accent is on presenting and claiming a cultural heritage almost as justification for a fun event. The "goal of the games," as printed in the games program, is "to introduce people of the Carolinas to the rich pageantry of their Scottish heritage and encourage the growth, and develop support of, the extended clan families. We will showcase the work and dedication of those who practice Scottish arts, athletics and traditions as well as inspire our young people to keep those traditions alive" (Loch Norman Program 1994:5). Dick Taylor, the president of the games and master of ceremonies at Grandfather since 1983, relates that in "relearning" the heritage, "history books have been dusted off and reread. Family records have been dug out of the closet and shared" (1994:6).

Games are a reenactment of "Scottish heritage" as envisioned by various community members and a kind of theater, in which members of the community take on various roles in several arenas—each with their own scales of authenticity. They are an act of remembering through ritual, through dress, through song, and through the discussion of Scottish, clan, and family histories. An anonymous statement from the Loch Norman Games Program well expresses the sentiments of many of my informants:

An old Gaelic proverb says, "Remember the men from whence you came": We are a people to whom the past is forever speaking. . . . Far out of that dark nowhere, in the time before we were born, men who were flesh of our flesh and bone of our bone went through fire and storm to break a path to the future. We are a part of the future they died for. . . . What they did, the lives they lived, the sacrifices they made, the stories they told, the songs they sang and, finally, the deaths they died make up a part of our own experience. We will remember and set an example for those who will follow." (Loch Norman Program 1994:8)

This quotation expresses beliefs common to all ethnic/heritage revivals, that Scots' descendants as "a people" are somewhat unique in their relationship to the past and that as "a people," they have the responsibility to leave a legacy for "those who will follow." For many, that legacy is insured by strengthening the Scottish-American community.[17] Celebrating ancestral experiences as a common heritage among cousins, games events unify the current community. Explaining community perceptions about the meaning of games in the Highland past, a Flora MacDonald Games flyer notes: "These shared experiences of friendly competition and merriment tended to bond the people together to make them stronger, mentally and physically, to meet life's next adversity" (1995:2). Though today's games are a self-conscious reconstruction of community, the games experience does "bond" people and rejuvenate enthusiasm about the heritage through the exchange of knowledge about things Scottish, and through the simple sharing of time, food, and fun.

For all the elaborate ceremony and society hierarchy, games are anything but exclusive. While conversation may center upon genealogy and ancestral histories, that heritage is openly shared with anyone interested. As the emcee at the Grandfather Mountain Games announced in 1994: "There are three ways to become Scottish: be born into it; marry into it; or we will adopt you, so go to the 'What clan do you belong to tent' and figure out where you fit in."

Scottish celebrations in North Carolina are different from other European-American ethnic festivals in that participants are separated from the traditions that they practice, not by one, two, or three generations, but often by two hundred years. Similar to Kwanzaa's combined celebration of African Americans' varied roots, Scottish games draw those of varying Scottish backgrounds into the celebration of "all that is Scottish." Scottish games are also distinct from other Celtic Revivals in Britain and Ireland, such as the Welsh Eisteddfod, because they take place throughout the world and maintain transnational ties with the homeland—through the visits of clan chiefs and other honored guests, and compliance with athletic, dancing, and musical competitive standards.[18]

As the supreme community ritual of identification and of "remembering," the games cement conceptions about both a unified Scottish-American identity and a "Highlander" Scottish identity. Cultural revivals generally focus on expressive forms (art, dance, music, sports), and language, which come to represent the irretrievable cultural whole. Highland expressive culture coupled with an artifact of material culture—the tartan, which some call an art form—have come to represent Scottish heritage. Enactment of these expressive forms at annual games serves both to educate the young and new community members, and to intensify remembrance of the heritage beyond celebrations.

On the Sunday night after the games have ended and most attendees have left the mountain, those remaining gather to see the "spirit of their ancestors" in the form of a bagpiper-ghost. The "ghost"—a glowing bagpiper whose features are concealed in white light—floats across the games field at MacRae Meadows wagging its kilt and playing a mournful, melancholy air as it departs the games and the united community until the following year.[19] The ghost of Grandfather Mountain has recently been identified as Alexander MacRae, an immigrant Highlander who arrived in North Carolina in 1883 and for whom the meadows are named.[20] This event is clearly fun, but it also involves hushed and reverent reflection on the meaning of events of the past few days. Known as "the happening," the glowing apparition pipes his way across the meadows and into the evening mist, marking the conclusion of another four-day gathering of the clans abroad, a Brigadoon in Appalachia. Such new traditions instill community gathering places with heritage associations and make them points of pilgrimage as new "clan lands." The creation of "Scottish places" in North Carolina is the subject of the following chapter.

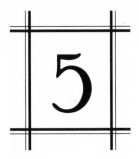

Heritage Pilgrimage and a
Sense for Scottish Places

Though pore-stinging humidity is inescapable almost anywhere in the South during late June, describing a breezeless summer morning in the Carolina sandhills as "sultry" is far too optimistic. Early on just such a sticky morning, members of the 18th Airborne Corps spill from camouflage trucks to unbolt anti-vandalism gates, throw open white-shuttered windows, and circulate light and air in the annual animation of one of the Cape Fear Valley's early historic sites. As they set up chairs and tables for the day's events, a kilted bagpiper tunes his instrument in the adjoining cemetery. Often traveling from several states away, and bearing casseroles and cakes whose layers rest uneasily in the heat, descendants of Cape Fear settlers assemble for a ceremonial service and "dinner on the grounds" at the church their ancestors established in 1756. Though encompassed by Fort Bragg since 1918, Longstreet Presbyterian Church remains a center of pilgrimage in the cognitive map of today's Scottish-American community.

Generations removed from Long Street's weekly religious community, participants belong to churches elsewhere, but still gather for the yearly congregational meeting that serves both as church homecoming and as the annual MacFayden family reunion. Infrequent or first-time participants introduce themselves and explain their genealogical connections to the church. Within the original congregation many families had close bonds through intermarriage, and first-timers are often surprised when regulars recognize them by, or comment on, their "family features." Families linked in friendship, but now dispersed, reacquaint themselves and form the next generation's bond. Hymn-singing and testimonials affirm a heritage of faith, while stories told over a shared meal strengthen a sense of common origins and identity. The multiple celebration of faith, kinship, and community coalesces in the power and meaning of place, making pilgrimage a significant aspect of heritage celebration.

For Scottish Americans, pilgrimage includes physically experiencing sites and heritage events in the original Cape Fear Highland settlement and in the homelands of the clans. Linking familial surname with clan membership, heritage tourists travel to Scottish landscapes particularly connected with historical and mythical clan happenings as "ancestral" clanscapes. An inherited sense of place for Scottish lands that were not inherited is all the more poignant and wistful because ancestors were deprived of them, often forcefully, and ancestral immigration was, for many, a last resort. Community members traveling to "the homeland" expect to see the places important in heritage lore and, as these places are so significant in lore, to see them preserved as they appeared at the departure of their emigrant ancestors, or at least as reminiscent of that appearance. The clanscapes visited by community members today are visited as the immutable scene of pre-Culloden life. Scotland becomes mapped, not by current economic or population centers, but by places of historical relevance to the heritage.

Scottish Americans' travel to Scotland and within North Carolina might be called heritage tourism, but it differs significantly from ordinary tourism. As heritage lore portrays the Cape Fear Scots as refugees from Culloden, travel to places with which they are associated somehow bridges the temporal and cultural gap between heritage celebration and Culloden. Visiting sites in which ancestral immigrants first dwelled after leaving the homeland is the next best thing to visiting the homeland itself. When they do visit the homeland, Scottish Americans see themselves as returned emigrants—albeit returning multiple generations later. As heritage pilgrims, the purpose of their journeys, both in Scotland and in Carolina, is a return to the source of their religious, secular, and familial traditions and values.[1]

Tourism and the Scottish Clanscapes

Travel specifically to Scotland by Americans of varied socioeconomic backgrounds began largely after World War II, in the wake of America's growing international importance. A cooperative feeling between Britain and America, exposure to the "old countries" acquired in Americans' wartime tours of duty, and increasing ease of transportation interested many Americans in touring the "auld sod." Travel promotions and touristic literature of the 1950s and 1960s focused on ancestral origins.

However, the major impetus for heritage tourism came with America's bicentennial celebrations and the inspiration Americans drew from Alex Haley's 1977 book, *Roots*. Interests in genealogy and ethnicity exploded through the seventies and eighties, sending many to explore and rediscover their own roots. When Americans began seeking their heritage in Scotland, they found a fully developed tourist industry nurtured by Highlandism.

The late eighteenth century's changing ideas about nature and "the moral value of landscape" coincided with the beginnings of tourism to Scotland as "the land of mountain and stream." As Highland identity came to be national identity in Scotland, mountainous Highland landscapes once considered wild and ungodly became not only sublime and picturesque, but the epitome of Scotland. In conjunction with romantic literature and Highland soldiers' roles in British empire-building, tourism helped transform Highland culture into Scottish culture and Highland landscapes into "Scotland." Often traveling the roads built by General Wade's Hanoverian troops to subdue Highland Jacobites, tourists came to the Highlands to view a way of life they had learned about from Sir Walter Scott—and an industry grew providing it for them.[2] Just as the Victorian ideal of the Highlander is that which survives in heritage celebration today, specific landscapes altered and idealized in Victoria's time have become representative of the pre-Culloden homeland of the clans.[3] The tourism industry in Scotland now draws visitors on the basis of heritage and homeland—appealing to dispersed Scots, generations removed, to come and see "how little has changed." It was once the sublime landscapes and their romanticized inhabitants that attracted tourists; now descendants of those inhabitants come to see landscapes representative of where their presumed ancestors dwelled.

Though heritage celebration focuses on "the complete destruction" of the Highland way of life after Culloden, heritage pilgrims frequently interpret Scottish landscapes of today (and the subsistence strategies they evidence) as traditional. Pre-1746 subsistence and settlement patterns in the Highlands (developed over centuries) changed forever with changes in Highland social organization during the second half of the eighteenth century. The Disarming Acts following Culloden outlawed clan military organization, and the strategic positioning of new British fortresses diminished the importance of clan seats at the chiefs' strongholds. The 1747 Heritable Jurisdictions Act abolished communal clan lands, one of the main integrative aspects of Highland society. Chiefs retaining some of these lands (who could no longer reckon wealth in fighting men) began to demand rent from their former military leaders, the tacksmen. These tacksmen then either demanded rent from their

Reconstruction of a Blackhouse at the Kingussie Highland Folk
Museum, Scotland. The model demonstrates a hipped, thatched roof
springing from double walls and anchored by stones and heather rope.

subtenants or emigrated with them. Subsistence had been based on an
agricultural-pastoral economy relying on the integration of grazing
and arable lands.[4] Farming practices of the nineteenth century and
today, known as crofting (not a term of Gaelic origin), were a Victorian
development involving the division of land into small rentable parcels
away from those areas best for sheep farming. What recent folklore has
construed as the traditional Highland subsistence—the crofter with a
small two-hectare farm—was the result of formidable taxes on larger
pieces of land (meant to encourage a breakdown of Highland communal
cooperation).

As the Highlands experienced political, economic, and social restruc-
turing, the romantic literature, landscape painting, and tourism that
shaped Highlandism made Highland landscapes symbolic of a national
Scottish culture, and heritage tourism further develops this theme to
make the whole of Scotland (Highland and Lowland) clan lands. Descendants of Highland, Lowland, or Scots-Irish immigrants come to see
the places imbued with clan connections through song and heritage
lore. Once symbolic of treacherous Jacobites, then symbolic of the Scottish nation, Highland landscapes (for heritage tourists) have now become clanscapes as palimpsests of ancestral experience.

Tour guides' running commentaries describe the landscapes of
eighteenth-century battles and clan feuds. Radical alterations in the

landscape that accompanied changes in agriculture and land tenure, and the wide expanses uninhabited since "The Clearances," may go unnoticed. Generally, heritage tourists come to see, or are shown, the land of heather and swirling mists, the land of Bonnie Prince Charlie and legendary warriors. They visit the Loch Ness Monster Center at Drumnodrochit, the Rob Roy Heritage Center and/or clan centers, battlefields, whisky distilleries, and tourist shops. Expectations about Scotland as the unchanged land of the forebears can go unchallenged in the pursuit of heritage.

Heritage Tourism and Pilgrimage

The cultural tourism of the Victorian seeking vanishing lifestyles and picturesque settings continues today in a similar form, but with quite altered meanings. Within a few generations, Highlandism's systemic impact bestowed the authenticity of continuous tradition upon the Highland entertainments embellished for tourists and sporting landlords. Such traditions compose much of what Scottish-American travelers experience in Scotland as heritage. Between hosts and guests, cultural tourism implies a power imbalance favoring the guests' essentialization and consumption of the host culture.[5] I call community travel in Scotland heritage tourism rather than cultural tourism. Although Scottish Americans go to have what they consider "authentic old style fare," enjoy "traditional music," and see "traditional" costume and dance performances, they are not distanced from it; they claim these traditions as their own heritage. Though the tourism industry targets Scottish Americans through heritage, I view community travelers not as tourists from a world superpower consuming another culture, but as pilgrims seeking to experience a culture they feel is theirs to partake.[6]

Heritage tourists and cultural tourists may attend the same events and tour many of the same locations, yet they perceive the value and authenticity of what they experience in different ways. Consequential to Highlandism and the way in which Scottish tourism developed, authenticity in heritage experience is often "staged" (MacCannell 1976), but the staging is an accepted part of the tradition and authenticity is in the mind of the beholder.[7] The hotel-sponsored "Scottish evenings," popular with Scottish Americans traveling in the homeland, are staged performances of "Scottish entertainments," including pipe and drum bands, Highland sword dances, or reenactments of a Burns's Night Supper out of season. While recognizing such as their heritage (and as the model for heritage events in the United States), heritage tourists fully appreciate the performance context. The performance itself has become traditional, and in both Scotland and America, dancing or musical demonstrations are not spontaneously joined by those standing about who may "know how"—they are performed by those trained to perform.

Transnational standards for training and judging Scottish athletes, pipers, and dancers means that Americans performing for heritage societies and at Highland Games will have similar repertoires to those performed at touristic presentations in Scotland. The American tourist no more interested in Scottish than in Japanese or Hungarian culture will interpret "traditional evenings" differently than the initiated Scottish-American community member, for whom such performances are familiar and their authenticity, or value, lies in viewing them *in* Scotland.

As with the pairing of tartan setts and clan names, such performances, along with Victorian-styled Highland Games and "heritage trails," all designed for the paying outsider, have become authentic traditions.[8] Tourism impacts how both hosts and guests perceive culture and tradition. In the 1950s, organized Scottish heritage celebration in North Carolina began with events modeled after performances Donald MacDonald experienced on his first trip to Scotland. Many heritage groups begin or alter their activities when members return from Scotland with accounts of unknown events or different procedures. The shape of tradition in Scotland also responds to external factors, as we have seen with the Jacobiting of the national identity. The North American interest in clan heritage has become a considerable factor in promoting today's Scottish tourism and historic preservation. While the "traditional performances" of Scottish entertainments are the model for heritage events and banquets in North Carolina, the demand for such performances in Scotland is significantly linked to Scottish-American tourism. When heritage pilgrims seek out native authorities, they also have something to share: Scottish and American dancers and athletes trade techniques, while pipers and other musicians exchange tunes and genealogists exchange research. Such transnational and mutually influential relationships continue to refine visions of a Highland past and heritage.[9]

Travel in Scotland by community members is about a visit to the past rather than to "another country"; it is not the Scottish culture of today that heritage tourists come to experience, but the culture of their ancestors. When heritage tourists go to the homeland they go to see the places and the landscapes that their ancestors saw—not the new housing areas or industrial buildings that may now intrude upon that landscape. Tourists do not come to see the latest Italian-style shopping center in Glasgow, chic French restaurants, or Scottish people dressed like Americans. They come to see the Scotland of more than two hundred years ago. They come to travel back in time rather than space.

Scottish Americans shop at tourist shops and woolen mills to purchase symbols of their heritage, yet perceive their devotion to this heritage as setting them apart from ordinary tourists, in their own view and in that of their hosts and guides. They visit museums and interpretation centers that focus on the places in lore with which they are familiar, and if they are on a package tour, they may see little in between. Their journey is a purposeful learning expedition for those with developed interests and a set of expectations and referents already in place. Tourism has proven one of the most rapidly developing and specializing industries of the nineties. Though tourism has long been a significant part of local economies, the specialization into family history and name-specific heritage lends the "never done before" feeling of early-nineteenth-century Scottish tourism (when the Highlands were still an "exotic" locale). This relatively new focus in tourism has developed to reach a market of "Scots abroad."

Scottish Americans refer to their own journeys to Scotland as "pilgrimages"—not the individualistic pilgrimage of finding oneself, but that of finding one's "people" and one's "place." Heritage tourism in Scotland is about experiencing "Scottishness," about being for a couple of weeks where all seems homogeneously Scottish. Americans who at home have to seek out others interested in Scotland describe being surrounded by "everything Scottish" as a "transporting experience" through which their "heritage comes to life." Heritage tourism is also explicitly about seeking connections with ancestors. The heritage tourist as pilgrim seeks an association both with those who went before and those with whom he or she may feel a living kinship and shared sense of community—associations which, without a purposeful search, would not be otherwise obtained through daily life.

The sense of *communitas* often achieved in community events is perhaps most intense on group trips to the auld sod. Rather than breaking new ground in their own experience of the heritage by traveling without a group or visiting sites of interest not included in the tour, those who say they have "always known" about their "inheritance," or who have been to Scotland before, may serve as "heritage guides" on group tours. These community members interpret sites and recite clan lore for those whose inheritance must be worked for, sought, and discovered. Informants who have toured Scotland more than once speak of the "thrill" they feel from watching others experience scenes of clan history for the first time.

In the search for identity and community as a complement to one's present world and perspectives, the religious connotations of pilgrim also finds application here. When heritage tourists visit clan lands or Culloden Moor, they visit sites sacralized by their connection to ancestral action. The commemorative activities pursued in reverent visitation of these sacred landscapes have ritualistic and religious qualities (in the order in which sites are visited; in the giving of histories and personal reflections that evoke the memory and spirit of the ancestors; in the moments allowed for silent reverence; and even in the taking of group photographs at a site following its "experience"). Travel to Scotland may also involve a sense of religious pilgrimage for Presbyterian community members. Many heritage tourists attend religious services while in Scotland, the homeland of their faith; and many church groups from North Carolina travel to the land of Knox and the Covenanters with the expressed purpose of learning about their Presbyterian heritage.

Beyond the many religious analogies that apply here, I interchange the term pilgrim with heritage tourist, because community members describe their own travels as pilgrimage, and also because their travels are structured by, and have meaning as pilgrimage because of, a set of beliefs specific to the community.[10] As Bonnie Prince Charlie's defeat, the Highlanders' persecution, and the clan diaspora have become root paradigms within the Scottish-American community, travel in clan lands revolves around these themes and becomes a "return" or "quest" rather than tourism.

Sir Walter Scott's writing spurred a Scottish tourist industry that still thrives on the romantic themes of his work, but he never could have expected that his vision of Highland life would draw descendants of Scottish emigrants to the lands from which so many were evicted and exiled. In fact, he concluded his essay on the "manners and customs" of Highlanders by noting that should the pipes summon the clans, "the summons will remain unanswered. The children who have left her will reecho from a distant shore the sounds with which they took leave of their own. 'We return—We return—We return no more'" (1826). The endurance of Sir Walter's reinterpretations of the Scottish past have disproved his prophecies for the future.

Return of the Diaspora

"MacLeods come Home!" was the famous call of the Dame Flora MacLeod during her 1953 visit to America as clan chief. In community literature and as honored guests at Scottish-American heritage events and Highland Games, other clan chiefs repeat this plea and many clansfolk have answered the summons in their new-found, "ancient" loyalties. Dozens of annual clan-based tours to Scotland feature visits to those places seminal to heritage lore and confirm their importance as the linchpins in the development of both clan and Scottish-American identities.[11] So well-developed is this tourism specialty that many clan societies caution members to investigate the details of any Scottish tour that claims to cover the clan properties and to call designated society authorities before planning a trip. Clan newsletters and other community literature encourage travel to clan lands and educate the would-be pilgrim about what to see in Scotland that relates to their "family."[12]

Beliefs of shared kinship and a united identity among Scottish Americans are dramatically enhanced through clan society pilgrimages to Scotland. Tourism promotions promise "a journey of exploration into the past—your family's past, and Scotland's past—during which you will continually encounter buildings and objects which were in existence when your ancestors were around" (MacDonald 1993:48). Most clan societies arrange tours to Scotland, some on an annual basis, and display photo albums from clan travels and gatherings at Highland Games tents. Some clans whose names combine Scottish and Viking or Scottish and Norman origins arrange tours of much broader "homelands." (The Norman-descended Montgomeries, for example, arranged 1995 clan trips to Scotland, England, and France, whence the Normans came.) Some clans organize trips to celebrate anniversaries in clan history or to attend a Highland Games, especially when an American member of the clan is competing abroad.

When a clan chief exists, a visit to the chief's residence is essential. Many chiefs actively organize tours for their clansfolk themselves; on "Clan Maclaine of Lochbuie's 1994 Grand Tour of Scotland," for example, the Chief and Lady Lochbuie even toured with clan members, as did Clan Anderson's chieftain for his clansfolks' 1996 "Homeward Bound" tour. One of the main aims of many clan societies is the preservation of the chief's residence and/or clan lands. A few of my informants expressed a desire to see their clan society become more of an actual *Gemeinschaft* in the home territories. In a book often cited by clan society members, Sir Thomas Innes of Learney's *Tartans of the Clans and Families of Scotland*, the author notes his disappointment that descendants of the clans have not returned to Scotland. "It is unfortunate that few have gone beyond dinners, bursaries, etc. in place of the wider, more permanent scope, of acquiring heritage in the clan country and starting, even in a small way with a few crofts, to re-settle the clan races upon the soil of their native districts" (1971 [1938]:55–56).

While only a few would actually support the reestablishment of the community in a physical and geographical sense, a great drive does exist among clan societies not only to visit clan territories, but to enshrine the original site of clan residence as a focus of affections.[13] It is one of Clan MacIntyre's stated objectives, for example, "to secure and preserve all or part of Glen Noe as a symbolic homeland for members of Clan MacIntyre the world over." Clan Colquohoun takes pride in having "occupied and controlled an estate of thousands of acres on the west banks of Loch Lomond for over 800 years."[14] Clan Carmichael emphasizes its fortune that "though many Scottish clans have no lands or buildings left," the thirtieth Carmichael chief donated 500 acres of clan lands to the Carmichael Family Trust that "will live on forever for the benefit of all Carmichaels, never again to be diminished by taxes."

Despite the presence of Clan MacLeod's seat at Dunvegan Castle, much of the Island of Skye is considered "homeland" to MacDonalds. Clan Donald has a clan heritage center with a research library and resort cottages at Sleat on the southeastern portion of the island beside the ruins of the High Chief's former home, Armadale Castle. Those without a surviving ancestral estate, or chiefship, are increasingly re-"placing" their clans by establishing heritage centers. Clan MacLaine of Lochbuie plans to establish a center at Lochbuie. Clans MacPherson and Clan Donnachaidh have heritage centers and the Lyon Court–appointed commander of Clan Gunn has helped acquire a clan center that "provides a focal point for clansfolk to consider their ancestral home."[15]

The presence of the centers in the clanscape mark, much like neolithic cairns, the clan's ownership (though now a spiritual ownership) of all that surrounds them. They are monuments to the ancestors, but instead of holding ancestral bones, they enshrine walls of text proclaiming the heritage; the walls wind, much like an elaborate passage tomb, but past exhibit cases of tartan and pipes instead of stone carvings, and lead to the light of the audio-visual display instead of the winter solstice. The clan museums offer an abstract of Highland life, a selection of artifacts presented to convey a sense of unique identity. Quite beyond the cultural tourism of nineteenth-century Highlandism, the more specific clan centers offer not the exotic Highland other, but a glimpse of one's own exotic past, paralleling familial relations of Highland society with those of the present. A strong sense of connection to a clan nucleus may particularly appeal to those whose American ancestors and recent generations of family members may have dispersed geographically. In lieu of a shared sense of place with kin in America, a Scottish site tied to the origins of one's surname (and therefore family) becomes the point of reference for heritage and for "beginnings." Its landscape becomes a clanscape and the history of the area becomes family heritage.

In an article praising the accomplishments of the Lowland "Clan" Carmichael chief, Roddy Martine notes that now reunited as a clan and reunited with its land, "the Carmichael family are once again making a positive contribution to the Lanarkshire community from whence they came" (1988:36). International clan societies do indeed contribute to local communities through jobs and sales provided by the restoration and upkeep of clan properties (works enabled by society dues and the organization of special funds and trusts). The reunions and gatherings represent a physical, if temporary, return to the homeland, while the society-funded developments of heritage centers and the repurchase or consolidation of clan lands into a kind of clanscape/heritage park represents a spiritual return to the land by those whose homes are now elsewhere. Descendants of the absentee landlords (often former clan chiefs) who drove their tenants to emigrate now reside in clan lands once more, supported by absentee tenants.

Clan members express pride in contributing to the foundation of a clan center or paying for the upkeep of a chief's castle (though the burden of doing the same may have led their ancestors to emigrate) because they say they are "investing in their heritage." Clan members say that having a "clan homeland" affirms that they are not alone in a rootless world. By contributing to the upkeep, preservation, or construction of a tangible, visitable location, their feelings for their heritage are given focus and substance, and they memorialize the clan of their own period for the future.

Visits to the chief's home always feature in community discussions of travels in Scotland. Describing their trip as one "truly to remember, leaving you to feel a part of the great Clan Legacy, not just a dream," members of the MacDougall clan relate how their society president "pointed out sites where the Clan had been engaged in great battles" on the way to lunch with the chief "in the ancestral dining room." As with many clan tours, the MacDougalls visited Pringle Woolen Mills and Culloden Battlefield, and had dinner at the Culloden House Hotel where the proprietor "regaled" clan members "with tales of the Battle" (Wolf 1994:2). Significantly, the trip commenced, as many clan trips do, with the chief welcoming home her or his "children." Clan tours have developed a somewhat standardized order that participants find a compelling progression. After an introduction to the chief at the clan stronghold and a tour of clan territories and museums, the clan trip culminates in the visit to Culloden (which marks "the end" of the clan system) and concludes with descendants of the exiled clans shopping and dispersing to their other homelands.

Clan/"family" reunion tours represent not only a return to the home-land, but a pride in the maintenance of "a presence" in the clan area.[16] This presence is maintained by the permanent enshrinement of a par-ticular site or it is maintained in spirit by gathering at a place sacred to the clan. In the public eye (that of other nonclan residents of clan areas), clan members demonstrate clan presence by appearing en masse at public festivals such as Highland Games in the clan tartan, or even by parading through town, as two hundred Moffats did in the town of Moffat during their first international gathering in 1993 and as the Macphersons do annually in Newtonmore. Announcing the emigrants' return, clan reunions and tours also reestablish the importance of a name and of a group in local history and affairs. However, the "home-lands" to which clans symbolically return are framed by castles and battle sites today. The castles, rather than the actual relict landscapes of black houses and clachans abandoned in the Highland Clearances, fig-ure in images of clan heritage.[17] Cognitive mapping of the clanscape is oriented toward the homes of the elite rather than those of the actual emigrants in alignment with a reference system that ends in 1746 "with the clans."

The creation of clan trusts and clan lands foundations is an active effort to preserve the memory of a certain period and a certain historical perspective in perpetuity. What exists and remains in the landscape is as much a mirror of present power relations as of the past powers that created it. Archaeologists Carole Crumley and Bill Marquardt write that landscapes are manifestations of "a dynamic tension between in-frastructure (the realm of material production and social relations) and the superstructure (the realm of ideas)" that characterizes human life (1987:6). What constitutes a desirable, symbolic, or evocative landscape may change over time: the wild Highland landscape became sublime at the same time that wild Highlanders became quaint and the English elite became tourists in Scotland. The establishment of clan centers is a direct result of the affluence of descendants of Scottish emigrants, the development of a tourism market for the same, and the phenomenal post–World War II interest in kin and place origins. The clanscaping of Scottish landscapes is a further evolution of the way Scottish land-scapes, peopled and unpeopled, have been invested with varying mean-ings by and for various "others": elite others, tourist others, even re-turned others.

Generational Perspectives on
Traveling to the Homeland

The generational differences, mentioned in Chapter 3, emerge in community approaches to travel in Scotland. Whether community members plan their own journeys or take a tour, what they visit and what they emphasize in describing their trips generally relates to generational interests. With the exception of the Celtic Fringe, the mainstream community members use basically the same framework and reference system in "experiencing Scotland," but the vocabulary used in discussing their travels reveals distinct perspectives on the experience.

The first generation speaks of going to a location, while the second generation describes their tours as "driving through." Older members speak of points and places where their own research or that of their tour guide indicates events happened; they then focus on the import of those events for their clan or for their ancestors' immigration to America. First-generation heritage members work from a cognitive map gained through reading tourist literature, clan lore, and popular histories. They speak reverently about the places they visit and describe them in relation to their (sometimes recently discovered) heritage.

The first-generation heritage revivalists have actively cultivated the significance and meaning that certain sites now hold for them. That such knowledge is hard-earned perhaps leads them to describe their travels as pilgrimage. They have made the journey to have place and past impressed on their memory and incorporated into their own experience. Their mental maps of the homeland are dotted with battlefields, castles, and sites of clan history. The second generation may visit the same sites, but more often travel in smaller groups with rented cars and stop at other historic sites and pubs along the way to the major sites of heritage lore. When they take clan tours, they may remain in Scotland after the tour's conclusion to pursue specific interests in weaving, re-enacting, or music, either through personal contacts or specialized museums/shopping.

In contrast, the Celtic Fringe travelers visit Scotland without group tours and report visiting more archaeological sites and pubs (in search of music sessions).[18] Their descriptions of landscapes reference their more distant Celtic, or more contemporary, interests rather than clan or military history. They will travel further and go to more trouble to see the "Stones of Callanish" on the Isle of Lewis, or at Stenness on the Orkney Islands. They speak of how landscapes evoke the "unknown" rather than the known that the first generation seeks. Fringers are more

Donald MacDonald regularly conducts American Scots to "Carolina Hill," near Skeabost on the Isle of Skye. MacDonald convinced the Ordinance Survey of Great Britain to mark the site on the Map of Scotland. The hill was home to Captain Kenneth MacDonald, who had settled in Cameron Hill, North Carolina, but returned to Scotland after fighting for the Crown in the American Revolution.

interested in the legacy of nameless people, while the first generation documents its heritage to the last Mac. While others of their generation visit sites connected to Bonnie Prince Charlie, many fringers seek a heritage they can explore without the reference system of clan societies and about which they can develop individualistic interpretations. They seek communion with more distant ancestors and/or with living Scots. They pursue another Scottish heritage in which many have become interested through the New Age Movement. They speak of visiting pre-Viking sites in terms not unsimilar to other community members' descriptions of attending Edinburgh's Presbyterian St. Giles' Cathedral.

However different their approaches, all of these perspectives on travel in Scotland relate to pilgrimage, whether the pilgrimage center be a historic site, a landscape, or the whole of Scotland. Anthropologist Gwen Neville writes that the pilgrimage center "from the standpoint of the believing actor, represents a threshold, a place and moment 'in and out of time' " (1979:104). Visits to both those pilgrimage points related to community lore, and those connected to more personal visions of heritage, remove the heritage pilgrim from everyday life to a liminal space where one may experience the spirit of identity and heritage. Many community members describe a mental reliving of history at such sites. An obituary in the *Armstrong Chronicles* for Colonel John Armstrong described his long military career and his visit to Armstrong lands:

> Clan Armstrong Trust historians told of events in the ancient Armstrong past at the sites where they happened. Jack found it gripping. Standing on a razed foundation at the east end of Gilnockie Bridge, he judged terrain in light of weapons of the early 1500s. . . . Two battle tested John Armstrongs, about 20 generations apart, had considered how best to defend Scotland there. Across the gap of centuries they had agreed, identically. There was silent communion. (Armstrong 1994:7)

Visitors' knowledge of ancestral activities allows them to achieve a certain intersubjectivity with their real or presumed ancestors at the scene of events. By traveling to ancestral sites, a feeling of union intensifies through which temporal distance dissolves in the experience of place. Belief in the power of landscape and locality can convey one from present existence into a communion with whatever one feels is one's heritage—a communion that may be unachievable "in time" with ordinary life and in a more familiar place. The communion experienced in travel to Scotland or to the Scotland-like landscape of the Grandfather Games comes, in part, from being "removed" from the familiar and ordinary. The act of pilgrimage itself instills greater significance and meaning to a place because of the very effort exerted for its visitation.

"Family" Reunions

International clan gatherings and family reunions with Scottish themes have become especially popular within the last two decades. The family reunion is an American tradition particularly strong in the South. Gwen Neville notes that "gatherings of this type are not celebrated in Scotland, nor is there a record of such gatherings in the history of Scottish Presbyterians" (1987:8). However, today's international clan gatherings, though perhaps initially and inextricably linked with the promotion of tourism, have come to celebrate a sense of kinship and of place in combination with religious heritage. In the American South, Presbyterian church homecomings of the Cape Fear area celebrate both Scottish Presbyterian and family heritage with a regional interpretation of Scottish-American identity. Unlike the Catholic pilgrimage system of traveling "outward from home to seek one's spiritual 'fortune' in the

form of salvation or expiation," Neville writes that the Protestant pilgrimage is based on "returning home from wandering out" (1987:4).[19]
The Protestant pilgrimage, especially as undertaken by heritage pilgrims, is to find roots and familial links and thus to find "salvation" from
the anonymity and rootless existence of contemporary life in the perceived stability of the past.

Unlike family reunions, clan gatherings require advertising and other
promotion, since the "family" is not so familiar. Also unlike family reunions in the American South, clan gatherings in Scotland are not
usually annual events and among those eligible to attend, many may
do so only once in their lives. However, my informants describe clan
gatherings as "family reunions." As I have emphasized elsewhere, "clan"
and "family" have become interchangeable in the Scottish-American
community, and fictive kin relationships have taken on connotations of
blood kin. The idea of family used here is not nuclear or extended, but
what Neville calls a cognatic descent group, a "group consisting of all
the descendants of one common ancestor, figured through both male
and female descendants" (1987:57). While a preference for agnatic over
cognatic descent exists in Scotland, the Scottish-American community
follows a cognatic kinship system in the assignment of clan tartans and
in the joining of clan societies. National clan societies that gather at
Highland Games and draw together those with the clan name or a
surname of a clan sept are therefore more free with billing events as
family reunions.

The generalized vision of kinship favors the use of the all-embracing
"cousin." Promotions for trips to Scotland, Highland Games, and other
heritage events beckon participants to "come and meet your cousins" or
"share in the cousinship." Event programs set aside time for "talking
with your cousins." Not only is surname associated with clan and kinship, but any Scottish ancestry draws one into a more general cousinhood extending between clan societies and to "cousins" in Scotland,
Australia, New Zealand, Canada, and other places around the globe to
which the clans dispersed.

Family reunions draw together relatives, and sometimes family
friends, who have scattered because of work demands and urbanization,
while clan gatherings draw those who may only share a surname but
who conceive of themselves as sharing a heritage and a kinship that has
been denied them through the diaspora of the clans. Reunions frequently
honor common great-grandparents or even a family's further-removed
founding immigrant ancestors. While international clan literature does
advertise family reunions of those related to a specific Scottish immigrant ancestor, the basis for clan gatherings in Scotland and the United

States is often hypothetical descent from an apical ancestor, sometimes one thousand years removed. Though acknowledging such an ancestor, these reunions generally do not focus on such distant and often mythical figures. Instead, the emphasis is on the founder(s) of the clan society or upon the clan chief and famous "members" of the clan (i.e., those who share the surname). The experience of *communitas* at American family reunions and at clan gatherings and society events is with both living cousins and the dead clan ancestors, known and (mostly) unknown.

The Southern Sense for Scottish Places in Carolina

North Carolina's uniqueness in the Scottish-American community may be again felt in gatherings of Carolina Scots where those returning from hundreds or even thousands of miles away may still be recognized by family resemblance. In the introduction, I quoted Cape Fear–native Ed Cameron's description of Cameron Hill in the Highlander settlement area as "a wee bit of Scotland removed."[20] Cameron's sentiments convey the feelings of many for both the homeland centuries removed and the often-expressed empathy for the homesick pioneer Scots. As clan heritage centers or clan castles are the chief shrines visited by the Scottish-American community in Scotland, the centers of pilgrimage for ritual commemoration of the Cape Fear settlement are the early Presbyterian churches and cemeteries, or the surviving homesteads of second- or third-generation Scottish immigrants.

Attachment to place is not peculiarly southern, but Scottish celebrations in North Carolina and other southern states incorporate a peculiarly southern sense of place. Describing how southern ties to the land are often implicit in daily conversation, folklorist Barbara Allen notes that landscapes become symbolic genealogical records "with historical and social as well as physical dimensions, a complex structure of both kinship networks and land ownership patterns" (1990:52). Those who assemble for Cape Fear Valley church homecomings and family reunions introduce themselves as the child of so-and-so, who was the great-great-great-grandchild of Scottish settler X. The focus of many dinner-on-the-grounds conversations involves locating each other in the landscape and in the Scottish community genealogy. Once one is known to be the second cousin once-removed of Alexander, son of Lachlan, who had that place at Gum Swamp, then further associations between the conversationalists' families come to mind.

Of communities across the rural South, Allen notes that a sense of place "is inseparable from a sense of the network of relations, past and present, that bind people in a neighborhood together" (1990:161).

While many of those who come to the Cape Fear congregational and
family reunions have moved elsewhere and are no longer part of "the
neighborhood" (now home to Fort Bragg), they still recall local associations and geography. After a long discourse on one's origins, one may be
identified as someone's grandchild, with a story of the grandparent's
youthful antics to follow. Though the conversants may have never before met, stories about a particularly eventful fishing trip shared between the teller and the listener's father/grandfather establish an in-
stant bond and feeling of mutual trust. The teller may relate the same
story on every subsequent meeting, but it only serves to reinforce the
relationship and a right to congeniality through transgenerational
association.

Location is an essential key to appreciating such stories; if you do not
know the pertinent place, the teller will verbally take you several different routes past landmarks you would be expected to know until he or
she can situate you there. Only then may the story begin. (After particularly long attempts to blend your cognitive maps, the story itself
may be anti-climactic.) It is important to first know *where*, then *who*, and
vaguely *when*. A fix on the scene of events makes the story more potent
and memorable and tags another spot in the landscape that the receivers
may then call their own. The teller is giving a gift, not just of a story, but
of a personal bond to be remembered by association with place. Such
gifts are especially significant for those whose ancestors or who themselves have left the area and are seen by locals to be making an effort to
reacquaint themselves with the place and community of their forebears.
I have seen many older community members, shocked at their conversa-
tional partners' ignorance of a place, either promise to take them there
and "show" it to them or drive them there on the spot.

Community members mentally map the Cape Fear Valley with stories
and visitable reference points such as the Shaw House and the Malcolm
Blue Farm, both in Aberdeen. The Malcolm Blue Farm, settled by a
Scot in 1825, has an annual festival featuring Scottish and Bluegrass
music, crafts, and a Confederate encampment. The yellow and red Royal
Standard of Scotland flies above the entrance of the site's museum that
displays permanent exhibitions on the story of Culloden and clan exile
as well as on agricultural artifacts and naval stores. One of the major
sites visited by those participating in nearby heritage conferences and
events is Mill Prong House built in 1795.[21] Its application for National
Register status notes its significance as "a focus of sentiment and interpretation of the important Highland Scots community in North Carolina." Other heritage sites include the home of John Charles McNeil,
the early twentieth century "poet laureate of North Carolina," who

wrote about growing up in the Scots area. Community members also take visiting speakers and games guests to view historical markers related to famous settlers such as John Bethune (an early Presbyterian pastor) and to reputed house sites and springs associated with Flora MacDonald.

Gaelic-speaking societies passed on lore about places and the origins of place names, a *dinnsenchas*, as a kind of oral gazetteer that maintained interpretations of ancient ruins, and historical events considered significant, in communal memory. When the Highland Scots immigrated to the Cape Fear Valley, they named many areas with place names from home and after the people who settled on them. Knowledge of place name origins is still important lore in the Cape Fear Scottish community. One of the most familiar, and perhaps bizarre, name-origin stories is that of Barbecue Presbyterian Church, which Flora MacDonald attended. A sign in front of the church still wishes guests "Ceud Mile Failte" (100,000 welcomes, in Gaelic). By tradition, a former sailor and early settler, "Red" Neill MacNeill, so named Barbecue Creek because a mist rising from it reminded him of barbecue smoke he had seen in the West Indies; the church built nearby in 1758 took the name of the creek. Buies Creek and McLendon Creek took the names of those who settled beside them. Some famous settlers even took their nicknames from the landscape: "Bluff Hector," famous in settlement lore, was so called because he settled on a bluff by the Cape Fear River. A few families are still referred to by their place association; hence "the Anderson Creek Shaws" or "the River Blues."

Members of the Cape Fear Scottish community still refer to a few local areas by the place from which settlers in that area had come: the "Knapdale" community refers to an area at today's Parkton, south of Fayetteville. Names of Revolutionary battle sites where Highlanders participated also form a part of the North Carolina *dinnsenchas* (McPhail's Mill, Kings' Mountain, the Widow Moore's Bridge, Piney Bottom, Raft Swamp). These sites draw visitors as known locations of ancestral activity and as significant sites in the history of the Cape Fear community. (Many Highlanders were captured and/or emigrated from North Carolina following these battles.) Today's community members value place names for what they reveal about their Scottish ancestors and because they serve as markers that, in the words of local historian Malcolm Fowler, "they passed this way" (1976).

Following the Civil War, place-naming continued to evoke Scotland (as it still does today), but names were selected simply because they were Scottish, not because they related to home areas of the original Cape Fear settlers. "Blues Crossing" was renamed "Aberdeen" in 1887.

Traditional Highland cairn in the Creag Meagaidh
Nature Reserve in the Grampian Mountains, Scotland.

Grandfather Mountain memorial clan cairn.

Scotland County was formed in 1899. "Dundarrach" in Hoke County was incorporated only in 1911. New streets, housing developments, and shopping centers continue to employ Scottish place names. For example, on the outskirts of Fayetteville, one may find the Loch Lomond and Arran Lake subdivisions, the Highlander Apartments, and street names such as Glencoe. Near Southern Pines are the Dundee and Scotsdale housing estates, to mention but a few.

By using such place names, and occasionally by "Scottish" additions to the built environment, many try to evoke local heritage and restore a Scottish sense of place in North Carolina. John McKenzie Panagos, a member of Clan MacKenzie, has constructed a clan-themed bed and breakfast in Murphy, North Carolina. Each of the guest suites and cabins is dedicated to a specific clan and decorated with the appropriate tartan. Expansion plans include the construction of a replica Scottish castle complete with moat, great hall, and a genealogy library for clan research on each of the featured clans.

Invoking the Burnsian line "from scenes like these old Scotia's grandeur springs," the owners of MacRae Meadows planned to model a Scottish village in Linville after vernacular architecture from Fife, Scotland. Though the "Invershiel" project had to be abandoned for financial reasons, the completed Scottish tollbooth and the former home of the Linville "Everything Scottish" shop (now occupied by a chain convenience store called "Scotchman") still provide a sense of the homeland. Less expensive ways of integrating reminders of Scottish heritage into North Carolina landscapes include the erection of memorial cairns for ancestral immigrants and the community's dead at each of the Scottish Highland Games fields.[22] The cairn at Grandfather Mountain has inset panels with seventy-four polished stones contributed by as many clan societies, most brought from the clan's homelands in Scotland.[23]

Dedicating the memorial cairn on Grandfather Mountain, Presbyterian minister James Hanna proclaimed:

> When our forebears left their native moors to settle in new lands, no cairns were built. Instead they built homes, schools and churches. There are thousands of Houses of God that stand as living cairns, reminders to all who pass that once they lived, loved and worshipped here. . . . May our Cairn on MacRae Meadows . . . always stand as a . . . covenant that we shall be as faithful as they in passing our Christian Heritage onto the generations yet to come! (Stewart 1994:22)

Descendants of the eighteenth-century Highland immigrants have also constructed new pilgrimage points in the form of Highland cairns at the

early Presbyterian churches. These memorials connect pledges to perpetuate the "faith of the fathers" and pride in Scottish heritage to places
where ancestral Scots first honored the same.

Much of what we know about the Cape Fear settlement relates to its
early churches, and their specific celebration combines with general
celebration of the eighteenth-century immigrant ancestors. The culturally constructed dichotomy between sacred and secular life collapses
when both become heritage. When Barbecue Presbyterian Church
erected a memorial cairn in 1969, local historians Malcolm Fowler and
Rassie Wicker gave fellow local historian and minister James Mackenzie
a stone from what they believed to be Flora MacDonald's chimney for
placement in the cairn. Positioned in church cemeteries and designed
specifically to serve as pilgrimage points, cairns are the scene of reverent commemorative ceremonies or group photographs, and serve as a
stopping point for community members touring local heritage sites.
Evoking the symbolism of such monuments, homecoming sermons
make frequent reference to "those people out there" (in the cemetery)—
ruminating on their struggles and their perseverance as examples that
their descendants should look to today for inspiration. Most of the pre-
and post-service socializing occurs while walking about the graveyard,
and dinner often takes place immediately adjacent to the headstones.

North Carolina's heritage pilgrims have many predecessors in celebrating that comforting sense of continuity provided by ties to particular locales and the possession of a heritage. A centennial address by
James Banks on October 18, 1858, at Bluff Presbyterian near Fayetteville appears in recent event programs and still reflects the themes in
celebration today:

> When a thousand years shall have passed away and cast their
> shadowy wings over this republic, our descendants will sit here
> beneath those towering trees, listening to the truth as it is dis-
> pensed, to the faith once delivered to saints . . . beneath a south-
> ern sun. And they will thank God that the Presbyterian religion,
> with all its blessing, is theirs by inheritance, and that their heritage
> is within the bosom of North Carolina. . . . A State of which it
> may be said, as it has been of Caledonia: "A nation fam'd for song
> and beauty's charms, Zealous yet modest, innocent though free,
> Patient of toil, serene amidst alarms, inflexible in faith, invincible in
> arms." (1858)

These thoughts echo in a poem written over a century later by Melvin
Hartley. A framed copy of the poem, which was inspired by the nation's
bicentennial year, now hangs at Old Bluff Presbyterian Church:

Walk quietly among these generations sleeping on this Holy Bluff;
Touch these ancient trees; read reverently these faded stones.
Then be still and listen to the faint sounds of the distant past:
The carpenter's mallet raising this, God's House, while we were
    still under England's yoke; eighteen full years before we were
    free;
Steeds stepping spiritedly across open fields, carrying fore-fathers
    in their full hats, their bonneted ladies riding side-saddle to
    worship in this Holy Place. Listen to the hushed discussions in
    the churchyard on the matter of Independence, the Continental
    Congress, and think of freedom.
Your fathers, and their fathers, and their fathers before them sleep
    here. Your heritage sleeps here. Walk quietly among these gen-
    erations sleeping on this Holy Bluff; Then be still and know that
    God walks here—and has—and will.

These works sacralize sites connected with the early Scottish settlers, emphasize the moral value of place and ancestral precedent, express patriotism and affirm Scottish associations. An active member of
the Cape Fear community, the Reverend James Mackenzie spoke of the
valley's historic sites as sacred simply because they are ancestral. In his
Historical Sketch of Bluff Presbyterian Church, he wrote:

> This is not only a historic place, it is a holy place . . . ground forever
> sanctified by those who met here to worship their God. . . . Here as
> infants they were carried to be baptized and here in later years they
> carried their own, generation after generation. Here, before this
> pulpit, they knew their joy and their sorrow. Here they were mar-
> ried, and here they were buried. (1966:23)

I reprint these poems at length to demonstrate a continuity of tradition within the North Carolina community and to illustrate the obvious
connections that they draw between place, heritage, and faith. Landscapes become more than storied places; they remind and instruct the
pilgrim in the values for which ancestral lives are venerated. These sites
have indeed become holy sites, not only for direct descendants of their
members, but for all members of the Scottish community. It is perhaps
curious that just one to two hundred years on, Americans are so nostalgic about these places. I have not found like poetry about churches built
nearly two hundred years ago in the Scottish Highlands. I connect the
sacralization of these relatively recent North Carolina sites with the fact
that the faith and heritage celebrated there were reft from their own
place in Scotland. Instilling places with a sense of ancient tradition is

especially important in a new land. Expressed through a southern sense of place, the creation of Scottish sacred sites combines two traditions and enshrines them to the memory of their creators and to the edification of their perpetuators.

"Re-placing" the Highlands in Carolina

While the Cape Fear Valley settlement is an important point of reference and place of pilgrimage for the North Carolina and wider Scottish-American community, the state events that draw the most participants nationally and internationally tend to occur "where there are mountains." As Highland landscapes became representative of Scotland, the major sites of ritual gatherings in America are often selected for their similarity to the Highland image of the homeland. Hence, the Grandfather Highland Games and the Scottish Tartans Museum and Heritage Center are not in the original Highlander settlement area, but in the uplands more similar to the Scottish Highlands.

Memories of the Cape Fear settlement, of which North Carolina community members are so proud, are transplanted and celebrated in "more Scottish" places. Active community member John Flowers writes, "Each summer when the clans gather on MacRae Meadows . . . and the massed pipers sound 'Scotland the Brave,' and clan standards float above thousands of kilted clansmen, Flora MacDonald is again among her people" (1980:28). Though in a Scots-Irish–settled area, the Scottish-looking setting seems to validate the integration of disparate traditions into a unified vision of Scottish heritage. Lowland religious and country dancing traditions merge with Highland music and dress in a setting that evokes a collectively ancestral sense of place. The united celebration of various Scottish traditions perhaps seems more "natural," rather than cultural, because of the presumed resemblance of Grandfather Mountain to a Scotland romanticized in the nineteenth century as the "land of mountain and stream."

Donald MacDonald attributes much of the success of the Grandfather Mountain Games to its Scotland-like setting. MacDonald notes that "the rugged terrain, the wildflowers and even the weather are similar to Kintail in Scotland's Wester Ross. The Alleghany sand myrtle which grows on the mountain is a member of the Heather family. Thistles bloom in late summer and scotch mists blow through MacRae Meadows" (1998). (Kintail is Clan MacRae territory and the most obvious parallel for a place named "MacRae Meadows.") The Grandfather Games tartan employs a sett symbolic of the landscape, with green for MacRae Meadows and gray for the granite of the mountain that overlooks the gathering. Clan society members note that "one might think a large slice of Scotland has been transferred to Linville" (Clan Forrester 1994:1). In lieu of the ultimate pilgrimage to physically experience the ancestral clanscapes, participants say that MacRae Meadows is as close as they can get to clan lands in America.

Landscape becomes an aid to celebrating and experiencing heritage. Participants claim the Scotland-like scene created on Grandfather allows them to feel "transported" to their spiritual home, to shut out the "ordinary world" and more easily remember and emplace their ancestors. As the clans annually converge on MacRae Meadows for the pregames torchlight ceremony, an emcee sets the scene by asking participants to quietly "consider the mountain. Its strength and size shield us from the world beyond. . . . Time starts to slow, we move to a different pulse, a different age. . . . It is time to wonder, to remember. . . . The blood calls. . . . Be silent and listen to the old long since" (Taylor 1995).

As sites of ritual reunion, the games fields themselves accumulate their own histories and place lore. Topographical associations with events map the field; "Pulpit Rock" designates a large outcrop where the annual Sunday Kirkin' takes place, and musicians play in the "Celtic Groves" (wooded areas to one side of the field). Gary Morrison says that as the "spectacular forest of Grandfather Mountain surrounds you, and, with the sound of bagpipes or harps or guitars, it isn't hard to imagine yourself in the Scottish forests of long ago" (Morrison 1999:43). Several people told me that they met, married, or remarried their spouses by such-and-such a tree or by a certain rock outcropping during the Grandfather Games. MacRae Meadows not only features memorial cairns to "The Flowers of the Forest," but has also become a burial ground. After carrying the kilts, shoes, or ashes of deceased friends in the annual tartan parade, community members have placed their loved ones' ashes around the games field. The Cape Fear Valley was home to America's only direct Highland settlement—"a wee bit of Scotland removed" in terms of culture and community, but for many community members, the landscape of Grandfather represents a wee bit of Scotland in the physical sense. Almost every year, one of the Psalm readings for the Sunday morning service is Psalm 121—"I to the hills will lift mine eyes"—but despite the connection to the original settlement, the sandhills of the Cape Fear Valley do not look the part.

Failing sufficiently Scottish settings at other gatherings, celebrants employ verbal allusions to places known mostly through literature or oral lore. Verbal evocation of the homeland landscapes occurs at most heritage/clan society events in speeches, toasts, and songs. Honoring the Highlanders' effort at Moores Creek, participants leave bunches of

Jimmy Patton salutes after laying the wreath at the Highlanders'
monument at Moores Creek Bridge Battleground, as the president of
the Wilmington Scottish Heritage Society, Grover Gore, looks on.

heather on the marshy ground around the Loyalist monument as they
describe places in the "beloved homeland" from which those who died
were exiled. During tartan parades, or while tossing a torch onto their
opening bonfires, participants yell their clan's war cry, which is often a
place name. The MacLaren's "Creag an Tuirc" means "The Boar's
Rock." Clan Fraser's "A 'Mhor-fhaiche" translates to "The Great Field."
Clan Campbell's "Curachan" refers to a mountain near Loch Awe, and
the MacLennan's "Druim nan deur" reminds clan members of "The
Ridge of Tears."

The yelling of the war cry both reinforces the image of Scots as "born
warriors," the subject of the next chapter, and communicates a knowledge and pride of place. It strengthens group feeling by reminding clan
members of a significant incident and place association in clan history.
In conjunction with parading the clan tartan, the repetition of the war
cry asserts a unique (clan) identity within the community by proclaiming a place of origin in the homeland. As clans representatives gather
and one by one declare the names of the hills, glens, and shores from
which they hail, they name places in Scotland. The dispersed clans,
when they gather "in exile," still gather, spiritually, from the homelands
and in a setting that evokes the ties of kinship, faith, identity, and community symbolized for the heritage pilgrim by the Scottish clanscapes.

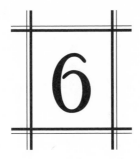

Warrior Scots

Beside wood-framed canvas tents, fires flicker in opposing camps of Revolutionary Loyalists and Patriots as soldiers fortify themselves for a cold February night on swampy terrain. Throughout supper and the low uilleann pipe music that follows, kilt-sporting members of the Eighty-Fourth and North Carolina Highland Regiments exchange playful accusations of treason with the Patriot Guilford Militia. Both sides prepare for the morning's "battle," the beginning of a weekend of living history demonstrations featuring weaponry drills and colonial medicine.

Twenty miles from Wilmington, North Carolina, the scene is the battlefield at Widow Moore's Creek that, on February 27, 1776, became America's Culloden. Like Culloden, the event at Moores Creek Bridge was more a massacre than a battle. As the Highlanders' famous downhill charge proved futile against Hanoverian artillery and cavalry on the boggy Drummossie Moor, an attempted charge across the greased girders of a partially dismantled bridge and the waterlogged ground at Moores Creek ended in minutes, leading to the deaths of approximately 50 untrained, largely unarmed Highlanders in a salvo of Patriot artillery and musketry. Over 850 of their fleeing comrades were captured, imprisoned, and/or banished. (Only one Patriot died.)[1]

Since the bicentennial anniversary of the event in 1976, annual gatherings of Loyalists and Patriots have encamped on the historic landscape of Moores Creek. Local boy scouts place candles for late evening tours of the battlefield and its monuments in which "Patriot" and "Loyalist" guides ask participants to consider which side they would have joined as Scottish immigrants familiar with Culloden. An ultra-patriotic celebration, the weekend of living history events nevertheless focuses on those Scots who fought against pro-independence "Patriots." In com-

A young Patriot watches Loyalist Highlander Ken Bloom at the
1995 Moores Creek Bridge encampment. An instrument maker,
Bloom measures a replica of eighteenth-century bagpipes to copy.

memorative rituals, the American national anthem and pledge of allegiance *follow* a bagpipe band's performance of "Scotland the Brave."
Typifying the blended patriotisms entailed in a hyphenated heritage,
the Moores Creek events also exemplify other aspects of Scottish heritage central to celebration in the South.

Southern Scottish heritage lore and celebration employ ubiquitous
male and military themes and rituals distilled by Highlandism suggesting that Scots are "natural soldiers." Such a focus attracts a remarkable
number of participants with military backgrounds. These members of
the southern Scottish-American community tend to be not just the rank
and file, but members of the Army's Special Forces, the Navy Seals, and
officers from various branches who attribute their successful careers to
their Scottish and southern heritage. While praising the "warlike character" of the Scots, heritage lore and events simultaneously tie the loss
of Scottish traditions and the Highland way of life directly to military
defeat—a paradigm with which southerners are well acquainted.

Highlandism has left a strong military imprint on the Scottish national identity and contemporary perceptions of Scottish heritage. Focused initially on the romance of Jacobitism, Highlandism evolved with
the needs of the British Empire. The seemingly antithetical defeat of

A 1740s encampment of the Oglethorpe Highlanders
at the 1997 Stone Mountain Highland Games.

Prince Charlie and loyal service in the Hanoverian imperial cause both
came to identify not only Highlanders, but Scots in general during the
Balmoralism of Victoria's time. By the late nineteenth century, the
British military required all Scottish regiments, Highland and Lowland alike, to wear tartan. Once emblematic of treason, the "Highland
habit"—as revived in the military context—became not only "the national dress of Scotland," but symbolic of Scottish military prowess.
Military recruitment strategies, period literature, and popular media
drew upon visions of a Gaelic Highland warrior heritage and helped to
Highlandize Scotland as a warrior nation. The glorification of war and
empire in nineteenth-century Highlandism remains prevalent in the
Scottish national imagery perpetuated through the tourism industry
and in that adopted by twentieth-century heritage movements.

In the South, male images of the soldierly Scot find ready parallels
with southern stereotypes of chivalrous and military-minded "gentlemen" and "colonels," and southern Scottish heritage celebration perhaps most strongly exhibits a military emphasis. Military encampments
are standard at most southern Highland Games and relate not only to
the Jacobites or to Highlanders in the American Revolution, but to their
descendants' role in the American Civil War. Confederate living history
encampments, and even battle reenactments, are common to southern

Scottish heritage events. Their presence exemplifies the heritage belief that a perceived southern character and its bellicose proclivities directly stem from a perceived Scottish, battle-prone temperament.

Expressions of a Warrior Culture

Community members describe the most basic aspects of clan, religious, and artifactual Scottish heritage with consistent reference to a "warrior culture" and its ethics. For many informants, admiration for the ideal soldier's strength of resolve, loyalty to kin, and sense of honor adds a powerful, emotional dimension to their vision of ancestral warriors. For others, the appeal of Scottish military history lies in a different type of romanticization more similar to the drama of today's professional wrestling. From either perspective, military interests predominate in both heritage literature and event conversation, in which any military endeavor engaging Scots becomes evidence of the innate military talents of "Scotia's sons." In clan tent or campfire discussions of the American Civil War or any subsequent war, heritage group members are quick to point out how someone was motivated by "his Scottish courage," though his ancestors may have been Americans for well over a century.

Identifying the founding apical ancestor of a clan as a great warrior, many clan societies use the clan war cry for banners, in clan tent display, and as a title for their newsletters.[2] Recognition of clan military prowess is a recurrent theme of society literature, events, and organizational purposes. Among the Clan Fraser Society's listed goals is "to mark with plaques and statuary, historic battle sites in Scotland and North America where members of the clan have gained undying fame" (1994:2).[3] Because of their exposure to military heritage within the community, even Scottish Americans who claim not to be particularly interested in military history can detail their clans' military exploits and stress the importance of "the Scottish impulse to battle" in the clan system's demise.

Clan histories focus overwhelmingly on military episodes, in descriptions of both early and recent history. Community members' self-published booklets on Scottish traditions record beliefs in a biological propensity for soldiering, which also surfaces in toasts, commemorative speeches, and clan tent discussions. In his *Scottish Character and Lifestyle*, Christian McKee writes, "The Scots have always been known as great warriors. The value they placed on deeds of valor, heroism and prowess in war certainly played a part in forming their distinguishing characteristics. The early Highlanders were always dressed and ready for war, even when going to church. Their primary weapons were knives, which were almost an integral part of their bodies" (1989:28). Clan Henderson's promotional literature notes that though "a small clan, we have been involved in the mainstream of history, from clan battles in the Highlands to the Jacobite uprisings, and the Massacre at Glencoe" (1994:1).

Military endeavors then represent the "mainstream" of Scottish history, and when a Lowland "clan" cannot claim a continuous military (or even clan) history, a military reason often explains the lack. Accounting for the scarcity of information on group origins and its role in the "principal" events of Scottish history, Clan Davidson asserts that its forebears were so eager to fight that they nearly died out before being fully established as a clan. Clan literature notes that while little is known of the Davidsons' remote history, "they distinguished themselves throughout the fourteenth century by the protracted and sanguinary feuds which they maintained with such bravery and determination that they were almost exterminated before they could be effectively suppressed" (1993:1). A reputation for feuding only proves a clan's "true Scottishness" and becomes a source of clan pride.

The much-quoted assertion of the Cape Fear historian Reverend James Mackenzie that "each clan was both a family and an army" has become a pivotal tenet of community lore, as it was a central theme of Highlandism (1969:5). While all history is the product of selective recording of events, the southern Scottish-American community largely interprets the marked focus on warfare in Scottish history not as the survival of the most dramatic events in oral tradition, or in terms of the interests of the literate, but as the very driving force that made Scots Scots—their "love of the fray."

The "Scottish Warlike Temperament"

Celebration of a "genetic" martial strain and its presumed impact on a southern temperament relates to differential recording and valuation of historical happenings and clearly echoes Highlandism and the literature of its period. Reprinted Victorian texts are still prominent reference material for clan societies and heritage groups.[4]

Published in 1851, James Logan's *The Scottish Gael or Celtic Manners as Preserved Among the Highlanders* devotes three of seven chapters to military characteristics of the Highlanders and sets out the now-accepted codification of clan badges, plants, and war cries.[5] Logan had previously published a collaborative work, *The Clans of the Scottish Highlands: The Costumes of the Clans*, with illustrator Robert Ronald McIan. Purposely issuing their work in 1845, the centenary year of the last Jacobite Rising, Logan and McIan began what has now become a genre,

A reproduction of MacIan's famous 1845 print of a MacLachlan.

coupling clan histories with clan tartan illustrations. The Walter Scott–
influenced text paired with McIan's visual representations compose one
of the more popular and enduring products of Highlandism from Queen
Victoria's early reign. One hundred years after propaganda and proscriptions against "wild Highland savages," McIan captured public
imagination with his images of Highland clansfolk as fresh-faced, athletic, young warriors and demure young women of the Victorian ideal in
neat, modest tartan attire. Barbarous Highland warriors of the public
imagination were transformed into virtuous and model Scottish soldiers. A perennial presence in clan tent displays and in community
members' libraries, *The Costumes of the Clans* continues to shape gentled,
yet militaristic, conceptions of Highland heritage.

Such beliefs about "the nature" of personality and aptitudes are themselves traditional stereotypes created through millennia of biases in re-

David Dysart displays a spiked targe and a MacIanesque attention to detail.

corded history, rather than millennia of cultural continuities as claimed by Highlandism and several current historians popular with community members. Grady McWhinney's *Cracker Culture: Celtic Ways in the Old South* (1988) asserts not only that Scottish and Irish "temperaments" are direct and undiluted products of ancient Celtic society, but that a southern temperament is also a survival of Celtic traits via the Scottish and Irish immigrants who settled in the South.[6] As Logan linked the ancient Celts with early modern Highland clans through military lore, claiming that "the Celtic muster rolls are exactly similar to those of the clans of Scotland," McWhinney suggests that southern military traditions evidence the Celtic "nature" of American southerners (Logan 1851:76).[7] Essentializing the disaccord between the American North and South to differences between "sober" Anglo-Saxons and "hot-headed" Celts awakens the nature-versus-nurture debate, an argument that itself has ancient roots.[8] From the anthropological perspective, I consider perceived behavioral similarities in terms of similar cultural and historical experiences rather than continuous traditions or natural predispositions, and certainly parallels between the Scottish and southern experiences do present themselves.

Both Scottish and southern identities have militaristic stereotypes related to (or despite) cataclysmic military defeats at the core of their traditions. As historian Nina Silber writes, "Having been enshrined in their lost cause, southern men seemed to be permanently cast in a military mold" (1993:173). Likewise, the Highlander, once defeated, is perpetually dressed for battle with claymore in hand. Viewing these similarities as the effect of historical experience, rather than cause, we may explore the military themes of Scottish heritage from a different angle.

Stereotypes generally burgeon around a kernel of truth, and what we know most about the Highland Scots, and about the ancient Celts, relates to their warfaring activities. As noted in Chapter 4, the Scots were actually Irish who raided the western coasts of Britain following the Romans' fourth-century withdrawal. Ulsterian raiders settled in the Argyll area of what is now southwestern Scotland and named their kingdom Dalriada after a northern Irish tribe. Eventually giving their name to Scotland, these invaders are known to history as the "Scotti," which T. G. E. Powell tells us is a descriptive appellation for bands of Irish adventurers (1986:203). Considering the historical origins of the term Scots, "Scotland" indeed translates to the land of raiders and soldiers. The particular clan system that developed in the Highlands did have an overtly military basis: clans allied against clans and against non-Highlanders. Clansfolk owed military service to their chief rather than taxes. However, are these truths actually evidence of a warlike temperament inherited from Celtic ancestors? Why do we know more about the Celts and the Scots in war than in daily life?

The domain of the Celts extended from Ireland and Spain to modern-day Turkey during the European Iron Age.[9] Greek and Roman writers such as Polybius, Posidonius, Diodorus Siculus, and Caesar left many descriptions of Celtic social and military organization, the latter being the classical authors' chief concern. While the ancient Celts and historic Highlanders are both described in historical texts as warlike, we must consider the biases of those telling their tales. Romans commenting on Celtic practices were not documenting cultural traditions for posterity; they had a propagandistic agenda. The Romans related, in exaggerated form, what they found most exotic about Celtic society to justify their expansionist policies and military campaigns against the Celts to their

readers back home. Likewise, the unsympathetic, and frequently antagonistic, English and Lowland Scots recorded most of what we know
about aliterate Highland culture. At the time of Culloden, a Highland
chief's status was, to an extent, still reckoned in the number of men who
would follow him into battle, though professional troops had replaced
such feudal levies across the rest of Britain. What seems characteristic
of Highland life in subsequent lore perhaps results from disproportionate emphasis on what those recording events regarded as an interesting
anachronism rather than a unique practice.

Arguments for enduring, truculent tendencies also draw on archaeological finds. Archaeological evidence (largely from grave or votive
deposits) tells us mainly about the elite, perhaps warrior, class of the
Celts, but not much about the common folk. Artifacts from Celtic times
are differentially preserved according to the environmental conditions
in which they were deposited and their own material constitution.
Metal artifacts, such as swords and other weaponry, survive where
organic materials do not. Large forts and defensive earthworks remain
in the landscape when smaller settlements and homesteads have been
plowed away by millennia of farming. Likewise, cultural identities result
from differential preservation in both historical record and folk memory. Highland targes and basket-hilted broadswords remain emblematic
of a regional culture both because of the romance surrounding the
eighteenth-century events with which they are connected and because
of how we prioritize history.

Battle-driven histories yield battle-mad characters, yet it was because
warfare was not a daily reality that it was recorded. Surely Scottish men
and women were more commonly engaged in other, peaceful activities
between clan battles and regional risings against the central government, yet folk tales and legends grow around what is most unusual and
dramatic in impact. By crystallizing one significant aspect of Highland
experience, the legends that grew around clan feuds and Jacobitism
have attributed martial inclinations to the whole of Highland society.
Heritage lore of Scots abroad gives even more prominence to perceptions of "character" in the search for roots and identity, and to legendary
Jacobite events as the point from which later Scottish history must be
seen through the eyes of exiles. Heritage lore fixes Highland, and by extension Scottish, culture at Culloden. Perceived as the reason for ancestral migration, the dramatic and military nature of this event continues
to color conceptions about the way of life it is deemed to have ended. A
combination of forces, intentional and unintentional, have combined
through the centuries to fix Highland culture as a warrior culture. For
those who now claim that culture as ancestral, perceptions of a warrior-

dominated society shape visions of identity and values in the present, in public rituals, and in gender roles within the heritage community.

Scottish-American Military Professionals
and the Warrior Inheritance

In his book *Soldiers of Scotland*, John Baynes defines a Scottish soldier as "having been born in Scotland or born of Scottish parents, or else by descent, having a Scots name and belonging to a family retaining its original, national traditions even if living in another country" (1988:xv). Such a liberal definition is popular among Scottish Americans with military careers who are, accordingly, also "Scottish" soldiers. In my initial encounters with North Carolina's Scottish community, I was continually impressed by the large numbers of career military people whom I met at each event. Their military identities and branches are immediately recognizable in their attire. They combine military shirts, badges, and medals with kilts of clan tartans to express a blended pride in career, American patriotism, and what they perceive as Scottish family heritage.[10]

Community members within and outside the armed forces similarly explain the appeal of Scottish heritage for career military people with regard to the martial traditions, music, and history of Scotland. Those with military backgrounds discuss presumed parallels between ancestral Highland life and their own military culture as a primary reason for their affinity with things Scottish. The military has some analogues with the clan system. The hierarchy of Gaelic Highland Society dictated one's rank in any clan military endeavor, as distinctions between officers and enlisted personnel flow over into the social lives of career military people. Providing distinct indentities, today's various military branches and regiments or units also construct a further set of loyalties and a sense of "family" within the military. While united against common enemies, military groupings hold traditional animosities and competitive relationships as did the clans.

A particular attraction of the community is the clan chief's celebration as military leader and the hierarchy present in Clan societies, reminiscent of military rank. Informants Dan Matheson and Mitchell Mclean (retired and active military, respectively) specifically compared clan society rankings with those of an eighteenth-century chief's bodyguard. Older military members also comment on the predominance of pre–baby-boomers in the community with whom they share worldviews shaped by the experience of World War II and the Cold War. In practical terms, military men also suggest that Scottish interest groups

Retired and active military men "pulling a coin check" at the Grandfather Games. Coins received on achieving a certain status are to be carried at all times; if someone does not have his coin, he owes all present a drink.

are easier and more affordable to join than golf or country clubs. Though perhaps an after-the-fact rationalization, retired military men explained that despite the initial costs of outfitting oneself in "Scottish" attire, heritage activities are an affordable hobby.

Scottish activities engage career military people, battle reenactors, and military bands across the country, but a military emphasis and presence is especially strong in North Carolina. Fort Bragg, one of the world's largest military complexes and home to the Army's Airborne Corps and the Special Forces, is located in Fayetteville and occupies 160,000 acres at the heart of the original Highland settlement. Most of the military professionals whom I met did not have a direct connection to the Scots of the Cape Fear, but became involved in the area's Scottish activities through other military friends, often knowing very little about their own Scottish ancestry at the time of their initial involvement. Many of those posted at Fort Bragg remain in the Fayetteville area on retirement and become involved in local Scottish activities through membership in military bands and honor guards, or through interest in Scottish military or local history. Active military join for many of the same reasons. Informants Steve Johnstone and Dale Mc-Cain also note that Scottish events provide an extended-family environment that they feel is positive for their children—especially since they

A Scottish-American Military Society color guard in
the 1995 Culloden Games Tartan Parade, Georgia.

are stationed far away from relatives. For both active and retired military coming to the area through Fort Bragg, genealogical interests
were not a prime motive for joining the Scottish community. Participants may have known their name was Scottish, but generally an interest in researching their Scottish ancestry developed after becoming
involved with Scottish heritage activities. To quote one North Carolina
participant, Thomas Grant, "Scots come from a warrior culture.... We
[military men] are naturally drawn to military careers and Scottish
events to begin with and find out why (because we're Scots) later on."

One community organization focusing exclusively on military heritage is the Scottish-American Military Society (sams), organized at
Grandfather Mountain in 1981 to celebrate the patriotic activities of the
Scots/Scots-Irish during the Revolutionary War and beyond. Though
Highlanders were of course known for their initial lack of pro-American
sentiment during that war, the merging of Highlander and Scots-Irish
identities as born soldiers easily plays on the frontiersmen/warrior
stereotyping of the Scots-Irish. At many Highland Games, especially in
the South, sams operates tents and provides honor guards. Its members
also explain that these honor guards "provide color" and pipers for
weddings, parades, festivals, kirkin's, and Scottish-American funerals.

The society's motto, "With fire and sword," refers to the British threat to destroy settlements of Kings Mountain, North Carolina, a threat that Patriots met "with fire and sword."[11] The group's crest shows a backcountry rifleman, looking much like the images of Scots-Irish Davy Crockett, in a hunting shirt with a rifle and belt-ax, against an image of Kings Mountain. Representing allegiance to a chief when placed about a clan crest, the belt and buckle also encircles the SAMS's emblem as a symbol of fidelity "to the principle that liberty was won and has been preserved with armed force" (Nichols 1994:1).[12]

Stated aims of the society include the "preservation and promotion of Scottish and American Armed Forces customs, traditions and heritage," and the provision of "a forum for the exchange of military history and genealogical information" (Nichols 1994:1). Membership numbers nearly two thousand and is open to war veterans of Scottish ancestry and those who either have served, or are serving, in the American armed forces. In addition, SAMS grants honorary life memberships to recipients of the Medal of Honor or the Victoria Cross. Members from local and regional "posts" set up information (often called "recruitment") tents next to clan tents at Highland Games. Society members generally maintain an active interest in current military affairs and politics. They emphasize their belief that "Scottish-American history is still being made today": "SAMS and its membership serve to continually remind us of the contributions of the military in our own context; that peace has been won on the battlefield and maintained by a strong military presence and that, well prepared, we need to continually keep our guard in the ready position . . . lest we forget" (Stewart 1994:28).

As SAMS headquarters in Charlotte, I asked members why North Carolina Scottish events have such a strong military emphasis. Several collectively answered that North Carolina has always had one of the highest rates of voluntarism for joining the U.S. Armed Forces. Voluntarism is also an important aspect of the southern cult of chivalry and a southern theme that easily merges with an emphasis on the Scottish clan system's military basis. Just as Highlanders provided the bulk of Prince Charlie's all-unconscripted army, community members are quick to note that, although North Carolina was one of the last states to withdraw from the Union, it provided more troops to the Confederacy than any other state; furthermore, North Carolinian soldiers accounted for approximately one-fourth of all those lost across the South. Because the Highland Scots' heritage in the state is also one of voluntarism (in the Revolutionary War and in subsequent wars), SAMS members told me that the celebration of Scottish and southern military traditions "naturally come together."

The Scottish-American Military Society is the largest of several military-Gaelic/Scottish societies. Its prominence within the Scottish community demonstrates the strength of military themes in Scottish heritage, and the beliefs of military community members that their American patriotism is a natural continuation of the patriotic tradition of military service "from which they came."

A Hyphenated Heritage and Multifaceted Patriotism

In heritage discourse, the rise of America from colony to world power in two centuries is often attributed to the "warlike" yet "noble and righteous" character of its many Scottish settlers and leaders. Jacobite interests dominate dress codes, music, dancing, and community literature, but military exploits by any Scot or American of Scottish descent may become "Scottish heritage." During the fiftieth anniversaries of World War II events, almost every heritage event I attended throughout the South paid tribute to war veterans, sometimes recognizing the names, units, and battles seen by those present. Reenactment groups displayed World War II artifacts and researched particular Scottish regiments. Having studied the uniforms and movements of the 15th Scottish Division of the 2nd Gordon Highlanders (disbanded after the war), one group of junior high school and high school boys collected uniform pieces and set up a display of mess kits and period equipment at Highland Games. Community literature devoted many articles and tributes to Scottish-American heroes of World War II that coupled histories of their campaign successes with genealogies tracing their immigrant Scottish ancestors.

A mutual respect for military accomplishments exists between clan societies. Once-feuding clans join together in veneration of "Great Warrior Scots." The introductions of speakers and guests at heritage events and Highland Games always include their military credentials, mention any military service or military schooling, and often note ancestral military heroes. Honored event guests who are descendants of famous fighting Scots important in heritage lore are welcomed as if they were that historical figure incarnate.

Having discussed Scottish-American events as ethnic celebrations, I wish to emphasize that the Scottish-American community is the Scottish-*American* community. Instilled in commemorations of Scottish diaspora and struggle is an appreciation and celebration of the opportunities ancestral hardships have yielded for Scottish Americans. Scottish Americans, especially older members of military and clan societies, are careful to underscore pride in their American identity, as if embracing their Scottish identity exclusively at events would seem unpatriotic. They suggest that by honoring one's Scottish heritage, one honors the roots of one's American heritage. Community members credit the military achievements of Americans with Scottish ancestry to that descent, but stress that such accomplishments were in service of "the greatest country on earth." The late Grandfather Games chaplain Reverend Dougald Lachlan Maclean emphasized that while the Scottish origins of "our beliefs" should be recognized, "we are also proud Americans. It is no accident that the Games weekend always follows July 4th weekend. We have our priorities straight."[13]

Events often begin with the singing of Scotland's unofficial national anthem, "Flower of Scotland," occasionally "God Save the Queen," and invariably "The Star-Spangled Banner."[14] In the contemporary South, Scottish-American heritage concomitantly entails several historically opposed sets of loyalties. Southern community members have what might be called a multifaceted patriotism to the eighteenth-century, undemocratic Highland clan system, to the British Crown, to the Confederacy, and to the egalitarian ideals symbolized by the American flag. They are patriotic and proud about several countries and regional cultures in several time periods all at once.

Though community members view Culloden as the deathblow to the clan system (and the likewise romanticized inter-clan rivalry), Highlanders' loyalty and service to the Crown almost immediately following Culloden engenders pride thanks to Highlandism's simultaneous glorification of empire-building and the Scottish soldier.[15] That Highlanders fought, despite a convoluted (and often contradictory) sense of loyalties, merely indicates to heritage celebrants a consistency of "the warrior ethic," which in today's interpretations has evolved into patriotism. The immigrant ancestors of southern "Scots" may have had family on the losing side at Culloden; their descendants may have fought on the Loyalist and losing side in the Revolutionary War; they may have fought on the losing side in the American Civil War; and they may have finally won in the World Wars. Whatever their legacy, Scottish Americans express pride because these ancestors fought, as Scots "are bred to do," for "what they felt was honorable and right." Granted, all patriotism is based on this idea, but in heritage lore, "patriotic duty" flexes to fit the many past and present identities of participants and their ancestors. Serving in the U.S. Armed Forces and proudly commemorating ancestors who fought for the Crown during the American Revolution are not contradictory when both expressions of patriotism are linked by a shared Scottish military tradition.

Weaponry and Wappenschaws

Weaponry displays and military-styled encampments of reenactors accompany the celebration of a warrior heritage. Those aspects of Highland material culture forbidden by the 1746 Disarming Act and the 1747 Act of Proscription (targes, dirks, claymores, tartan, and bagpipes) have become central artifacts of Scottish heritage today. In tartan parades at Highland Games, men often carry reproduction Lochaber axes, halberds, and broad swords that they lower as they pass a review stand of honored guests. Clan MacFie, and other clan societies, attach pendants to their tartan parade banners that note the battles in which the clan participated (e.g., Harlaw, Flodden, Sherriffmuir). Where other ethnic groups might decorate an assembly area with murals, saints' statues, flags, or crafts, it is the weaponry—now symbolic of a warrior culture, Jacobitism, and exile—that forms an integral part of event decorations, providing a Scottish feel to rented assembly rooms and dining halls. Heather and leather targe centerpieces ornament dining tables and clan tent information booths. (A targe is a spiked shield, though as a recent article in *The Highlander* explains, "A dyed-in-the-wool Scot takes offense if a targe is referred to as a shield. With a ten-inch spike jutting from the center . . . it is an offensive weapon. A shield is something you hide behind" [Huddleston 1998:60].)[16] Claymores and basket-hilted broadswords cross above entranceways to dances and ceilidhs, and individuals regularly display personal weaponry collections in clan tent exhibits.

Weaponry also functions as trophies for home display. Athletes at the first annual Culloden Games in 1995 received basket-hilted broadswords as prizes. Clan Shaw awards "The Order of the Dagger" to those who have contributed to clan society activities and organization. At the Loch Norman Games, designers of the "best clan tent" receive a battle ax, and the outstanding amateur athlete in "the heavies" receives a dirk inscribed "Expect No Mercy." And SAMS awards dirks to outstanding graduates of selected southern military schools.

In recognition of the late medieval muster practice called a "weaponshowe," the Napiers call their annual meeting at the Grandfather Mountain Highland Games the "Annual Wapenschaw." As small arms did not even begin to replace the bow and arrow in the Highlands until the late seventeenth century, these musters were often archery drills. In recognition of this, the Grandfather Games held an archery competition (until it was deemed too dangerous around the annually growing crowds). The Loch Norman Games have started a longbow competition, but rather than relate the event to the Wapenschaws, games organizers link it to the more distant Viking-Scottish military tradition: "The Long Bow has held a prominent place in the history of Scottish warfare. Norse raiders, who counted it as standard equipment for their troops, apparently introduced it to the British Isles" (Taylor 1995:41).[17] The longbow is not the only weapon in which interest has grown beyond display and demonstration to competition at North Carolina's newest games.

Other nontraditional competitions with Scottish weaponry involve the battle ax, also drawing on Scottish Americans' "Viking heritage." A third new event, organized privately, is the Highlander Sword Competition. Inspired by the television series, competitors report the results of secretive challenges throughout the year to select final contestants for a championship fight the evening before the games. During the games swordsmen show curious visitors how to wield the "twa handed claymore" and its lighter version.

Scottish weaponry also forms important accessories for varying styles of male attire. Some clan societies, such as Clan MacNeil, have now appointed "clan armorers." Nineteenth-century Highlandism restricted the use of the Claymore to full dress formal occasions, but today a variety of weapons may accompany both casual and formal, day and evening apparel. Twentieth-century descendants of "Jacobite warriors" might strap on a targe or broadsword when attending events in eighteenth-century garb, while those in "modern" dress will settle for an ornamental dirk or sgian dubh ("black knife," worn in the sock). Reenactors are quick to point out that "the Highlander" would have far more weapons about his person than the sgian dubh that survives today in decorative form, much like the tie survives from the cravat. At several events in which the 84th Highland Regiment participated, members surprised audiences in the disarming of what they called an average Highlander by removing ten swords, daggers, and dirks hidden within his apparel.

Reenacting the Experiences of Soldier Ancestors

Heritage drawn from a history framed by military events transforms all such events into ancestral experiences. Reenactments and living history displays interpret ancestral Scots primarily through scenes of war. Basing their activities most commonly on the Jacobite period or on a particular Colonial war effort in which post-Jacobite Scots were involved, reenactors and living historians provide a military presence at heritage events and are never absent from southern Highland games. Along with the growing number of weapons vendors, they set up full displays of pikes and firearms, bows and swords. Demonstrations in the correct use of traditional weapons as well as muskets and cannons have become standard at most games in North Carolina.

Reenactment groups associated with Scottish events are ceremonial military units participating in parades and presenting battle vignettes or short reenactments of a famous charge. Living history activities also revolve around military encampments. The 84th Highland Regiment, the North Carolina Highland Regiment, and members of the Fayetteville Independent Light Infantry (a military history society/reenactment group based in the heart of the original Cape Fear settlement) attend the annual commemoration of the "battle" at Moores Creek. These regiments, along with nationwide units of the 78th Regiment of Fraser Highlanders, the 42nd Royal Highland Regiment (Light Infantry Company), and other groups based on the French-Indian and Revolutionary War periods in which Scots-Highlanders were active, appear at Scottish events across the South.[18] Their members lecture about eighteenth-century Scotland and about Scots in America at museums, schools, and elder-hostels. They also appear at heritage society Burns's Nights, Scottish-interest conferences, weddings, and local charity and ceremonial functions.

Proposed as a way to explore "ancestral Highland life" before the impact of "the Forty-Five," new reenactment groups that are focused on the Highlanders in the Highlands continue to form, such as "The Stewarts of Appin" and "The United Regiment of MacLachlans and MacLeans, Circa 1745." Explaining the rationale behind "The United Regiment," organizer Jim Finegan comments,

> "Why would we want to do this?" The only answer we can give you is that it will be fun! It's an opportunity for us to get dressed up in silly costumes, listen to a musical instrument that has been declared a weapon of war . . . and serve our community as teachers in one of the lost cultures of the past . . . to present a living memorial to those Highlanders who fought for a cause that ultimately led to a devastating defeat that irrevocably changed the Highlands forever. (Finegan 1996:1–3)[19]

In the context of Scottish Highland games and other heritage events, military-themed reenactment and living history has become a popular form of acting out perceptions of ancestral lifestyles and communicating to new comers and children the core tenets of heritage lore.

Reenactors also supply a military presence at religious services such as church "Scottish heritage" days and Kirkin's o' the Tartan, symbolically uniting the military and Presbyterian heritage of Scots. The kirkin's themselves have a quite militaristic format as formal parades led by a piper alternating hymns with martial airs. Participants carry large banners of their tartans (now seen as symbols of clan loyalty), which are held up much like flags evoking clan patriotism and rivalries. The kirkin' is said to be a rededication of tartan to God's service. It has been reasoned in the Scottish community that tartan was worn by men marching off to battle; thus the kirkin' suggestively links "God's service" with battle. Certainly such a link ran through the experience of the Lowland Covenanters and the sermons of John Knox.[20]

John Knox would also have approved of the long sex segregation of Grandfather Mountain's Tartan Parade. Though young boys could lead the parade holding swords, women were barred from participation for the parade's first three decades. In 1980, the parade's inventor, Murvan Maxwell, defended the exclusion of women "due to space limitations," though marchers walk in variously shaped groups, not abreast, on the large games track (Maxwell 1980:55). Through the 1980s, the stated reason for an all-male parade was that only men marched off to battle wearing the "clan tartan." By 1989, Maxwell argued more creatively for women's passive spectatorship in the Grandfather Games Program:

In the old country, Scots liked to march to the sound of pipes and drums—in true military fashion. Scots are born soldiers and off to the wars they would go, ever parading, with wives and loved ones watching and cheering. So why not a GMHG event to arouse their male martial spirit, to knit together their clanship and to provide a format for their ladies to cheer them on, arouse their clan pride and excite their old-country interest? A semi-military type of parade, the males stepping along to the cadence of pipes and drums, marching in individual clan groups with their own tartan fluttering in the breeze while the lassies cheered and applauded from the sidelines, seemed to be made to order for the natural outleting of the Scottish spirit. (Maxwell 1989:31)

Women have always marched in the Parade of Tartans at other Highland Games in North Carolina, but they first marched at Grandfather only in 1994. Many women claimed they were not bothered by the exclusion, while others expressed indignation. However, discussing the issue at the Waxhaw Gathering, Jean Ross and Annie Montgomery concluded that although the men did not know it, they had a point about only males wearing tartan to battle. As classical sources tell us, when Celtic women joined a battle in Roman times, they did so naked to terrify the opponent.

While drawing on the idea of a Celtic warrior inheritance, Scottish heritage exhibits a selective historical memory by ignoring the role of

Celtic women in warfare. The celebrated warrior culture remains essentially a male culture, although both history and legend provide us with female Celtic warriors. Historically, Tacitus and Cassius Dio document the Celtic examples of Boudicca, who led the Iceni tribe against the Romans in A.D. 61, and of Cartimandua, who led the neighboring Brigantes. Diodorus and Ammiamus Marcellinus, among others, describe women in warfare on the continent. Quite short of keeping women safe and secure, cheering on the sidelines, women of slave status in Celtic Britain and Ireland were forced to fight in battle either as front line soldiers or as servants of other male or female warriors (Rankin 1987:254).

In the early Welsh tales from the *Mabinogion*, we see heroes seeking martial education from groups of women. In the Ulster Cycle of Irish sagas, we learn of women warriors such as the Scottish Dordmair, Scatach, and Scatach's daughter Ualtach "the very terrible," who taught the formidable Ulsterian hero Cu Chulainn the martial arts. We also learn of women like Nes, the mother of King Conchobar, who led bands of warriors, and Queen Medb's undisputed authority over her warriors and her famous creach, the Tain Bo Cuailnge. Yet Celtic heroines are lost in Highlandisms' emphasis on the Highland soldier of the British imperial period.

Rooted in Highlandism, contemporary celebrations neglect even the heroines of the better-known Jacobite period. On horseback, Jenny Cameron led her clansfolk from Glen Dessary to join Prince Charles at Glenfinnan, and for her active patriotism was vilified as Charlie's harlot by the Hanoverians (Craig 1997:44). While her Mackintosh husband served as a Hanoverian officer, "Colonel Anne" (a Farquharson) raised her husband's clansfolk for the Jacobite cause. Staunch Jacobite Lady Nithsdale secured her place in history after the Jacobite rising of 1715 by rescuing her condemned husband (a Maxwell) from the Tower of London on the eve of his execution. Yet when women appear in living history scenarios, they appear as camp followers. While women now march in tartan parades across the country, the most stereotyped aspect of the Gaelic clan system retains Highlandism's masculine focus in reenactments of ancestral moments.

Military Origins of "The Scottish Arts"

Many aspects of heritage celebration that may seem quite unmilitaristic to non-Scots in fact have military origins. The dancing and piping traditions featured at nearly every heritage event continue to play a part in the Scottish military traditions from which they derived. Several

Highland dances draw on eighteenth-century military themes, such as "Barracks Johnnie" danced to the late-eighteenth-century recruiting song, "Wilt Thou go to the Barracks, Johnnie?" In the twentieth-century evolution of games traditions, Highland dancing has become the only event in which women are now the predominant participants.[21] Historically, men performed the Highland dances in honor of a chief or a new marriage, or to celebrate victory in battle. Current dancing competitions often include jigs and hornpipes known as "national dances," as well as the more balletic "Village Maid," "Earl of Errol," or "Blue Bonnets over the Border" introduced in this century; but the standard competitive dances are those whose distant origins retain an association with military lore.

Men still perform the oldest dances, the "Highland Fling" and the "Sword Dance," at games in Scotland and in Scottish regimental pipe bands' international performances. Originally performed around a spiked-targe, the Highland Fling celebrated performance in combat. By tradition a divining ritual to predict the outcome of a battle, the Sword Dance was performed over two crossed swords or a sword crossed with its scabbard. If the dancer did not touch the swords while executing the steps, victory was assured; if he did, death was expected and he braced himself to glory in a warrior's death. Several informants relayed varied but consistently gory tales of the dance's eleventh-century origin. The most popular version suggested that MacBeth first performed the dance over his bloodied claymore and the head of a man loyal to his archrival for the throne, Malcolm Canmore (of Highland Games fame). More moderate accounts replace the severed head with the vanquished's sword, and still others suggest links to the ancient Celts.[22]

The remaining favorites among competition dances evoke Jacobite motifs. "Seann Truibhas" (old trousers) refers variously to the Highlander's discomfort in wearing the trousers when the kilt was proscribed, or the shedding of the trousers in favor of the kilt with Proscription's end in 1782. Performed in a modified version of the eighteenth-century earasaid, "Flora MacDonald's Fancy" recalls her assistance to Prince Charlie.

Of Lowland origins, Scottish country dancing also carries military themes. Country dancing is somewhat akin to square dancing, but is gentrified as "Scottish ballroom dancing" in Scotland and abroad with standardized Highland apparel.[23] Dances such as "Dashing White Sergeant," "White Cockade" (the emblem of a Jacobite), and "O'er the Border to Charlie" draw upon Jacobite themes. According to Scottish country dance instructor Sandy Gallamore, new country dances with more recent military origins have also become popular with transnational Scots. Choreographed in 1984 for the 350th year of Britain's oldest infantry regiment, the "Reel of the Royal Scots" is now a familiar exhibition dance for country dance groups. During the recent anniversaries of World War II events, all-male dance ensembles performed the "Reel of the 51st," conceived during World War II by Scottish soldiers in a German prisoner-of-war camp. Less militaristic fiddles and, much to the purists' chagrin, accordions, provide the steady tempos of today's country dance music, while bagpipes always accompany Highland dancing.

Though bagpipes are traditional instruments in many cultures, their strongest associations are with the Scots. Outlawed as weapons of war after Culloden, bagpipes have a special association with the persecution of Jacobite Highlanders. At least one piper, James Reid, was executed during proscription for playing the pipes. Bagpipe music has many expressions in Highland culture, but with Highlandism it came to symbolize loyal and dependable (not to mention expendable) Scottish soldiers. Even Lowland Regiments such as The Royal Scots, Scotland's national senior regiment, acquired bagpipe bands in the nineteenth century. Pipe bands now evoke the days of the Empire, especially in former colonies. Today, local pipe bands based on the Scottish model play in full Highland dress from Vancouver to Hong Kong. As military bands from the United Arab Emirates go to Scotland for training, members wear a tartan sash over their uniforms. Scottish military bands travel worldwide to perform, and several of my informants linked their early interests in Scottish heritage to attending a concert by one of the many regimental bands.

Deftly integrating Highland and military themes (now a traditional association) through costume, narration, and music, the performances of touring bands play on clan rivalries, historical incidents, and patriotism tied to current events. Displaying full Highland dress with military badges and medals, and a specific tartan linked to the regiment, band members wear decorative Highland weaponry and some Drum Majors carry claymores. The Scottish regimental bands are the original model for heritage and military pipe and drum bands around the globe.[24] Pipe-band competitions and "massed" pipe-bands performances are an arresting part of larger Highland Games. Many games give their name, and increasingly their own tartans, to their host bands that carry local and regional pride into national and international competitions. Just as Scottish bands tour the globe, many civilian and military pipe bands begun in the former colonies now come to Britain to perform and compete in Highland Games, but all emulate bands like that of the senior Highland regiment, the Argyll and Sutherland Highlanders.

Much of the pipe music heard at games events focuses on clan feuds, battles, massacres, or other like incidents in the history of "Scotland the Brave."[25] Pride in the military prowess of ancestors is one of the most common subjects in clan songs and community literature. Some of the best-known Scottish tunes originated as military marches or have developed around military themes. Scottish Regiments have their own martial airs (or marches) and many clan societies, perceiving clans as small armies, have adopted their own military tunes. "The Battle Hymn of the Hendersons," for example, blends the names of clan "fathers" with military virtues in a brief review of clan history. Women rarely figure in these songs, and when they do, as in the penultimate line of the Hendersons' Hymn—"Our daughters all are lovely with their beauty, charm and grace"—they appear as passive ornaments of the actively "virile" clan.

An enduring musical allusion to Scottish military prowess comes from the early years of the Highland regiments, when Highlanders were realigning their loyalties from the defeated Stuarts to the job-providing Hanoverians. Written by a major of the 42nd Regiment (The Black Watch) in the second half of the eighteenth century, "The Garb of Old Gaul" refers to the tartan kilt (Gaul being the continental Celtic stronghold against the ancient Romans).[26] More often reprinted as a poem or quoted in speeches and toasts, the song's title is a recurring phrase in community explanations of clan tartans and of the Scots' military heritage and patriotism. "In the garb of old Gaul . . . We'll bravely fight like heroes bold. . . . No effeminate customs our sinews embrace; No luxurious tables enervate our race; Our loud-sounding pipe breathes the true martial strain; And our hearts still the old Scottish valor retain."

Referenced in a lack of effeminacy and disdain for "luxurious tables," the virtues of Scots portrayed here, and still celebrated today, reflect a particular view of gender and national identity. The bagpipes are "truly martial" and "real Scots retain the old Scottish valor." As I became more familiar with popular ceilidh songs and campfire recitations of martial poetry, I was less surprised at the number of event participants with military backgrounds. Heritage events that celebrate the stereotyped Scot of the late eighteenth and early nineteenth centuries, by extension, celebrate the career path and something of the worldview of career military people.

Other nostalgic songs heard at heritage events focus on the Highland soldier's travels abroad and his longing for home. This is the central theme of an oft-heard tune called alternately "The Green Hills of Tyrol" or "The Scottish Soldier," which describes a "bold and victorious" man who has "soldiered far away" and is disheartened only at the thought of dying far from Scotland. The lyrics play on the exile's sense of place for "the Highland hills of home," which echoes heritage enthusiasts' own sense of displacement from "the homeland." As in musical celebration of the heritage, a focus on military history and lore predominates in Scottish Americans' travels to clan lands.

Touring "Scotland, Bloody Scotland"

Developing simultaneously with the growth of Highlandism, Scotland's tourism industry continues to promote militaristic themes and a sense of Scottish national identity rooted in defeat. Package tours and interpretation at historic sites and in museums confirm heritage celebrants' conceptions of "Scotland, Bloody Scotland." Community members making the pilgrimage to places "where clan history happened" focus on sites of military significance. This tendency is in accordance with heritage lore and with the romanticized interests in the tragic "death" of the Highland way of life. It was a fascination with the latter that, in the eighteenth century, began to attract Lowland Scots and non-Scots to clan territories as tourists and travel writers.[27]

Landscapes now valued for their particular "Scottishness" were reevaluated as such in conjunction with post-Culloden constructions of Scottish identity. Tourism based on landscape value and on the selling of a tumultous history is an established and significant element of the Scottish economy. When the landscapes are considered ancestral and specific historical events explain why heritage pilgrims do not dwell within them, visits to battlefields, locations of massacres, or Scottish military museums can poignantly affirm heritage versions of history.

Agents of tourism increasingly target Scottish Americans as a specific market for military-oriented heritage tours. Travel packages focus on the interests and experiences of particular generations and on the anniversaries of both general military events and those related to specific clan histories. During the 1990s, for example, touring companies and even airlines advertised carefully orchestrated fifty-year-tribute visits to World War II battlegrounds (complete with costume, period music, readings from Scottish soldiers' diaries, and samplings of soldiers' rationings) at American Highland Games and within Scottish-American literature. Companies within Scotland, often run by retired military personnel, offer specialized tours to clan-related battle sites. Many such tours incorporate the performance of a regimental band or the best-known touristic event in Scotland, the Edinburgh Tattoo, where contemporary demonstrations of Scottish military might seemingly authenticate perceptions of a Scottish warrior culture.

The centerpiece of the month-long Edinburgh Festival celebrating the arts, the Tattoo nonetheless features military demonstrations (of weaponry/machinery and physical agility) by Scottish regiments, interspersed with performances by military bands, Scottish dance troupes, solo bagpipers, and hymn-singing Gaelic choirs. The Edinburgh Tattoo has become a "must see" on the travel lists of heritage society members. Described by community members of all ages as a moving experience that made their heritage "come alive," the Edinburgh Tattoo has inspired emulators in the southern states.[28] Each year in May, the Montreat Scottish Society in western North Carolina has an annual Scottish festival that features the society's own pipe band and visiting bands in a massed-bands Tattoo. The "Super Military Tattoo," featuring American and international military bands, has become a hallmark of the annual Highland Games in Glasgow, Kentucky. Another military Tattoo takes place on the evening before Atlanta's Stone Mountain Games.

Begun in 1949, the Edinburgh Tattoo has been advertised as "the world's best known and best loved military spectacle." In the last days of the Empire, the Tattoo was a procession of Scottish soldiers dressed in their Highland best and accompanied by exotic animals, as well as "exotic peoples," from the lands they had been out conquering "for Crown and Country." Held nearly every evening through the month of August, the Tattoo is now a night of special-effects lighting at Edinburgh Castle as the castle esplanade becomes a parade ground. The most-visited site in Scotland, this Lowland castle is now home to the Army School of Piping, the Scottish United Services Museum, and the Scottish National War Memorial in addition to the headquarters for three Scottish regiments (the Royal Scots, the Royals Scots Dragoon Guards, and the Scots Guards). At the height of the tourist season, the Tattoo links the military with national and cultural identity, providing the tourist with more than just pictures to take home.

As a showcase for Scottish soldiery, Edinburgh Castle also houses the regimental museums of the Royal Scots and the Royal Scots Dragoon Guards. These and the nine other regimental museums in Scotland are a significant draw for Scottish Americans. Community members with military backgrounds schedule trips to Scotland around the locations and opening times of military museums and battlefields. Americans' interest in Scottish militaria is so well known that the Gordon Highlanders advertise in Scottish-American literature for donations to "display the social and military history of the North East of Scotland," asking, "Do help save part of Scotland's heritage now" (1994:27).

Members of SAMS express particular interest in visiting Blair Castle, home of the Atholl Highlanders (the Duke of Atholl's private army).

They explain that, as the last private army owing loyalty to an individual, the Atholl Highlanders are, in their view, the last remaining vestige of the clan system. True enthusiasts try to make the annual inspection and parade of the army (generally the last Saturday of May at the beginning of the tourist season). In nearby Blairgowrie are the headquarters of one of Scotland's best-known reenactment groups, "The White Cockade Society." Reenacting Jacobite period battles and giving tours "tracing Bonnie Prince Charlie's footsteps," the society's founder also heads "Alba's Adventure Tours," which provides illustrated lectures, treks through "remote Highland Glens," and guided walks describing the Jacobite invasion of Perth or fighting at the Pass of Killiecrankie. Tour company leaflets occasionally appear in displays at clan tents, especially when the clan has ties to the "remote Highland Glens" in question.

Clan Donald Society members have a particular interest in visiting Glencoe, where thirty-eight MacDonalds were massacred and at least three hundred driven from their homes by government troops under command of a Campbell, the MacDonalds' traditional rival. In 1992, American members of Clan Donald organized what has become an annual trip to attend a commemorative service on the event's 300th anniversary and view the clan-supported restoration of a memorial to the fallen MacDonalds in Glencoe village. The massacre occurred in the wake of the first Jacobite Rising, but scenes of later Jacobite events draw Scottish-American pilgrims of all clan affiliations.

Though the Scottish National Monuments Record notes over eighty clan battle sites, twenty-two Covenanting battle or skirmish sites, and thirteen sites of conflicts involving the ancient Picts, every Scottish battlefield with a visitor center, excepting Bannockburn, is of Jacobite origin (Ray 1991:48).[29] This almost exclusive emphasis on the Jacobite period, coupled with misperceptions of Jacobite conflicts as those between a unanimously Highland, anti-Hanoverian Scotland and England, both affirms a Scottish national identity constructed in the last century through Highlandism, and secures the importance of Jacobitism in lore for heritage tourists. Of all historic landscapes, battlefields perhaps most strongly evoke emotion according to how a visitor perceives the significance of the events they witnessed. As archaeologist William Lipe writes, battlefields "send broadly integrative messages, reminding the populace of . . . historical events that evoke common origins or experiences . . . [which] may serve as a kind of charter for a group or nation" (1984:5–6). Scottish Americans travel to Jacobite battlefields to experience why their ancestors "had to" come to America and to connect with their "heritage" and their "past" by visiting the scenes of their own clan history. The 250th anniversary of Culloden sparked not only a flurry of commemorative activities in America, but also numerous transatlantic visits by "returning exiles." The most-visited battlefield in Scotland and the fifth most-visited of all the National Trust for Scotland's over one hundred historic sites, Culloden's interpretation center received 25,000 visitors in the 1996 anniversary year, more than in any other year before or since (NTS 1997). The director of the battlefield's visitor center, Ross MacKenzie, spoke to North Carolina heritage groups in the pre-anniversary year, while reenactors and those traveling in clan groups held in-depth classes on the battle and the period in preparation for their pilgrimage. Visiting the battlefield allows heritage pilgrims to experience where specific persons fell or performed specific acts, and where the targes and claymores that now feature in replica at heritage events last served Prince Charlie. This "experience" is also important for clan members perhaps unfamiliar with who was positioned where, but who still revere the act of finding their clan stone among those monuments marking the dead on Drummossie Moor.

Monuments, and their visitation, maintain certain visions of a past "alive" and, as Alois Riegl has written, preserve a moment in the consciousness of succeeding generations (1982:38). Monuments define the field at Culloden; footpaths connect clan graves and memorials and mark the positioning of individual Hanoverian and Jacobite troops by name. For Scottish Americans, who preserve the memory of Culloden above most others as the moment that brought Highlanders to America, trips to Culloden can be quite emotional experiences. Many informants pack tissues for themselves and companions. Indeed, on my own trips there to interview Scottish-American visitors, many audience members sniffled through an emotive on-site audio-visual presentation. On clan or personal tours, days of immersion in clan history build up to the Culloden climax—the visit to the scene of "the death of the clan system." Often shopping days and lighter-themed excursions on organized tours are put off until travelers have undergone the Culloden experience.[30]

Sites of military importance rank high on Scottish Americans' travel plans because so much of the heritage, as told and retold at events and through song, involves these sites. For many Scottish Americans who view their Scottish heritage as that of a "warlike people," visiting these sites enhances their understanding and dedication to that heritage. The military emphasis in heritage lore is a Scottish inheritance, produced by and affirmed within touristic traditions that are also produced by Highlandism. Shaped by historical biases rather than cultural continuities, a perceived persistence of a Scottish warrior temperament shapes community membership and pervades both celebration and pilgrimage to the homelands of the clans. Focusing on a particular historic past also allows community members to maintain other identities (e.g., American, southerner) and a multifaceted patriotism that spans several time periods and territories. The following chapter addresses the combined celebration of southern and Scottish heritage.

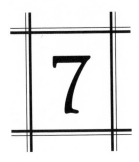

Scottish Heritage, Southern Style

Very late in the evening, but still early in the night, candles and flash-lights flicker across the Grandfather Mountain campgrounds as camp-ers visit and anticipate a night of fun and little sleep. Games events are done for the day, supper has been cleared away, the fiddles and pipes are brought out, and it is time for the fireside ceilidhs that animate the mountain into the wee hours. Campers freely wander between these parties, some annually hosted by particular clans, some growing spon-taneously around those with instruments or a good story to tell. At one tent someone recites Burns; at another a Cameron pipes his clan march, "The pibroch of Donald Dubh." I decide to stop where a lively discus-sion has ensued. Old friends and new acquaintances passionately debate Scottish immigrants' influence on America's regional cultures. The ex-change centers on where their influence was strongest. Someone spots me—the anthropologist—and laughingly asks me to decide between the cases presented.

With strength of conviction and the confidence of being among the majority that night, two southern men give a brief preamble and then launch into song:

> To the Lords of Convention 'twas Claverhouse spoke,
> Ere the King's crown go down there are crowns to be broke;
> So each Cavalier who loves honour and me,
> Let him follow the bonnets of Bonnie Dundee.

The song "Bonnets of Bonnie Dundee" was penned by Sir Walter Scott for the seventeenth-century Jacobite hero John Graham of Claver-house—Viscount Dundee, better known as "Bonnie Dundee." To the same tune, "The Band at a Distance," the men recommence:

'Tis old Stonewall, the Rebel, that leans on his sword,
And while we are mounting prays low to the Lord:
"Now each cavalier that loves Honor and Right,
Let him follow the feather of Stuart tonight."

Confederate cavalrymen created this second set of lyrics as a tribute to General "Jeb" Stuart. James Ewell Stuart was the rare model of the southern cavalier: pious, faithful to his wife, abstinent from alcohol, and something of a dandy wearing a plumed hat. Completing both songs in their entirety, the singers went on to contend that Stuart wore his feather in emulation of "Bonnie Prince" Charles Edward Stuart's white cockade and that Confederates reworked Sir Walter Scott's popular tune because they admired the Jacobite cause, lost as it was. As they triumphantly concluded, my neighbor turned to me on our shared log seat, contentedly stroked his beard, and asked what I made of *that* case for the South. His question, and the sparkle in his eye, prompts this chapter.

Scottish heritage celebrations have emerged across America, Canada, Australia, and other former British colonies, but in the southern United States, a unique and regional style flavors events and perceptions of Scottish origins. America's introduction to Scottish Highland Games and clan societies began predominantly in the North after the Civil War; however, these particular forms of ethnic awareness have grown most dramatically in the late-twentieth-century South. Currently, around 50 percent of all Scottish related societies in the country base their organizations in the South. Of over two hundred Highland Games and Scottish festivals scheduled across the country, more than one-third are in the southern United States.[1]

The popularity of the Scottish heritage movement in the South is partly due to its double celebration of a "reclaimed" Scottish ethnicity and its particular relationship to a southern regional identity. I have mentioned that Southern Scottish heritage societies emphasize kinship and bill clan society activities as family reunions. Scottish Highland Games in the South are more likely to have barbecue stands, fiddle competitions, and time designated for religious events. They are also more likely to take place at plantations.[2] At southern games, reenactors combine Confederate jackets and caps with the Scottish kilt, and bagpipe band renditions of "Dixie" leave crowds either cheering, in tears, or both.

Southerners take to Scottish heritage so well because its present shape draws on parallel mythologies, rather than actual cultural continuities, which underlie the construction of both Scottish and white southern identities. Both derive from historical injuries, strong attach-

Carl Ford combined Confederate and Scottish garb at the
1996 Scottish Games and Celtic Festival in Biloxi, Mississippi.

ments to place and kin, and links between militarism and religious faith.
Both also have internationally recognized, symbolic, material cultures.
The nineteenth-century Scottish identity inherited by Scottish Ameri-
cans blends harmoniously with folk memories of the South's Lost Cause.

Though history and community myths often diverge, I raise the
distinction between them, not to suggest the authenticity or inauthenticity of community lore, but to focus on the process of mythologizing
and, as Simon Schama writes, "to take myth seriously on its own terms,
and to respect its coherence and complexity" (1995:134). The integra-

tion of Scottish and southern lore provides a congruous and powerful sense of identity in relation to our particular time period.

Scottish heritage celebration in the South develops alternate interpretations of "southernness." Claiming Scottish ethnic origins, southern Scottish Americans also assert that their southern identity derives from more than the Civil War. In heritage lore, the southern experience and identity unfolds in continuous tradition from Scottish culture and history, rather than from a relationship to slavery or Jim Crow. In generational terms, the Scottish-American community in the South is largely composed of those who have experienced desegregation and the reinvention of "the new South." By attributing southern distinctiveness to Scottish roots, a celebration of southernness following the civil rights movement takes on an uncontroversial, multicultural dimension focused on ethnic rather than race relations. Mourning the Old South's defeat or displaying the Confederate battle flag acquires less problematic meanings in the Scottish heritage context. The "new southerner" involved in Scottish heritage is no longer just a white Anglo southerner, but an ethnically "Celtic" southerner with other reasons for being different and unassailable justification for celebrating that difference.

Elaborate articulations of historical and romantic premises have similarly constructed both the Scottish and southern identities now claimed as heritage. Parallels between them, and their easy merger in southern Scottish celebration, encourage many participants to perceive their ethnic and regional identities as part of a continuous, seamless heritage. Created by the battle-driven histories of Scotland and the South, both cultural stereotypes exhibit a certain inventiveness in explaining away defeat by emphasizing the virtues and chivalry of the losers and the romance of lost causes. In southern Scottish heritage celebration, "Scottish" heritage incorporates the main themes of the Old South Myth— themes originally borrowed from Scottish Highlandism.

The Integration of Parallel "Lost Causes"

In both the southern and Scottish cases, a region's military defeat becomes symbolic of the loss of distinctive agrarian ways of life. Folk models position the South's Civil War defeat as the end of an aristocratic, privileged, and carefree world for people who valued the extended family and maintained a love of the land and a sense of place. Likewise, Culloden marks the demise of Highland Gaelic society and a romanticized, though not prosperous, way of life for a people with clan ties to specific hills and glens. These defeats have become not merely significant in regional history, but the dates after which everything

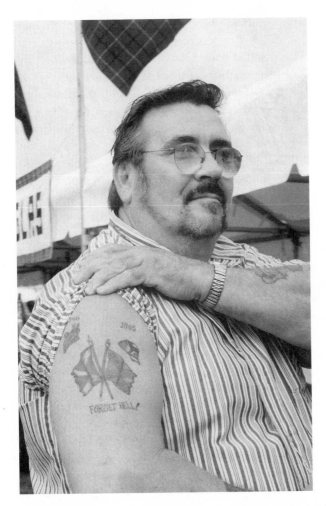

Tennessean Robert Wright and his tattoo commemorating the demise of two lost causes. With the dates of the Jacobite and southern defeats (1746 and 1865), the Confederate battle flag and cap cross the Scottish flag and glengarry. Underneath both is the familiar southern slogan, "Forget Hell!"

changed (for the worse). Southern antebellum houses, fashions, and manners always stand in opposition to the Reconstruction era. During the forty years following Culloden, legal proscriptions against tartan, the pipes, and communal clan land ownership accompanied the advent of exorbitant rents and large-scale emigration. Highlanders' sufferings during these years occupy a place in Scottish heritage literature and event oration comparable to that of Reconstruction in the lore of the South.

In both the plantation legend and Highlandism, the failures of the Confederacy and of Prince Charlie appear to cause major social and economic changes that nonetheless were well underway at the time of the events. Yet the myths portray both the Highland clan system and southern society as functioning smoothly until the dramatic demise of their respective causes at Culloden and Appomattox. The harmonious, pristine, and unchanging nature imputed to plantation and Highland ways of life in myth intensifies indignation at their loss. Southerners comforted themselves in defeat by imagining a noble past, a chivalric prewar Arcadia quite in contrast with northern industrial capitalism. The Highland way of life likewise acquired such romantic associations that even its privations polished nicely into stereotypical Highland sensibility, thriftiness, and efficiency.

In Scottish heritage lore, Culloden is the reason for broken clan ties and the forced exile of Americans' gallant Jacobite ancestors; in southern lore, the Civil War explains the fall of illustrious ancestors and their forced removal from the big house. Hence, within the southern Scottish-American community, "heritage" entails a double sense of loss. Much community literature and campfire discussion explores what might be now, had it just not been for event X in one's southern or Scottish past.

Beliefs that post-Culloden hardships resulted in ancestral immigration inculcates a certain sense of loss and injury—both for the transgenerational loss of a cultural heritage and homeland, and through a revived sense of indignity over ancestral sufferings. Already familiar with Lost Cause rhetoric and dispossession themes, southerners may easily incorporate the experiences of "wronged" Scottish ancestors. John Shelton Reed suggests that white southerners traditionally stand in a certain relationship to the Lost Cause and share what he calls a "grievance identity" because of that stance (Reed 1983:83). Such a grievance identity finds a corollary in these particular southerners' other heritage, of a Scottish identity constructed after Culloden and also grounded in defeat.

Taking on a Scottish identity, southerners of Highlander, Lowlander, or Scots-Irish backgrounds stand together on one side of another lost cause, "remember" the wrongs done to the Highlanders, and feel the pique—sometimes passionately—that the injury still smarts. Grievances of southern Scots include the saga of legal, economic, and cultural repression of Highlanders, the Hanoverian Duke of Cumberland's butchery, and subsequent eviction and forced emigration; southern stories relate parallel grievances of Sherman's March, Republican-implemented "reconstruction," and carpet-baggers. These motifs subtly

merge in commemorative rituals, storytelling, song, and general discourse about ancestral experience at the Highland Games.

A further lament, combining the above, is the tenet that the Civil War
also deprived the South of its Scottishness. In North Carolina, the use of
the Gaelic language for religious services does seem to have largely
ceased after the Civil War (MacDonald 1993:134). Following the war,
"Scotch fairs" (agricultural fairs) degenerated to occasions for gambling
and heavy drinking until their abolition about 1871. Community members suggest that Scottish consciousness succumbed to the overarching
implications of the war and the new identity forged by that experience.
According to heritage philosophy, coping with the war's devastation
meant sublimating Scottish ethnicity, not to an American identity, but to
a new southern unity. The significance of Culloden faded since almost
everyone had lost someone in the War of Northern Aggression.

These rationales pardon ancestors for "forgetting to remember."
Since heritage lore claims Scottish ancestors did not desert the ancient
clan homelands for adventure or profit, but under persecution, they may
not be accused of forsaking a heritage which their descendants now
value. Those ancestors preoccupied with the Civil War are no less
forgiven—their experience being an inheritance itself. Heritage celebration entails reverencing the ancestors; romanticized grievances maintain their venerability in public memory. That a heritage lost was forc-
ibly lost makes its reclaiming particularly potent.

As with Highlandism in Scotland, the plantation legend has become
"systemic" for southerners' sense of identity and in the world's conceptions of American southernness. To let go of grievances at this point, in
either the Scottish or southern case, would be to let go of the romance as
well. Attempts at "revising" regional identities, even grievance-based
identities, are not often popular, especially when such identities have
endeared their possessors to the outside world in legend, in public
culture, and through tourism.

The Southern Take on the Sir Walter Method

Highlandism developed between 1780 and 1860 with the major thrust
of Britain's empire-building. Drawing on antebellum origins, southern
postbellum lore developed mostly between 1880 and the first quarter of
the 1900s. While contemporary southerners recognize the familiar feel
and language of Scottish heritage, they credit this to cultural continuity
and, well, heritage. While not a continuous tradition, southern myths
are indeed built on a Scottish model.

Southern myths assumed a paradigm with which southerners were already well acquainted: that constructed by Highlandism and Sir Walter Scott. They named pets, plantations, and the occasional child after characters and places in Scott's novels. In Mississippi alone, the plantations and mansions of Waverley, Melrose, Montrose, Dunvegan, Monmouth, and Dunleith received their names from Sir Walter's appreciative readers.[3] Southerners generally identified with Scott's chivalrous castle- and glen-dwelling characters, who exhibited the best of courtly manners and hospitality, viewing them as models rather than as ancestors.[4] The motifs of Highlandism yielded many parallels for southerners based on assumed spiritual and intellectual kinship rather than heritage as is claimed today.

Making aristocrats of patriarchal chieftains, Scott medievalized and feudalized what had been an agro-pastoralist society in the Scottish Highlands. Southern mythologizing likewise revised a slave society into a courtly realm of knightly lords and beautiful belles.[5] The images and traditions made famous by Scott's Waverly novels provided a favorable analogy to fairly self-sufficient southern plantations in the Cameloting of the Old South. The chivalric moonlight-and-magnolias depiction of antebellum southern society evoked many of the same themes as Highlandism.

The lore of the Scottish heritage movement in the South has been over two centuries in the making. Romantic constructs developed in Highlandizing the Scottish identity proved popular with southerners, who drew from them in idealizing their own Lost Cause. This process produced many apparent similarities between the Scottish Highlands and the antebellum South that Scottish heritage celebration, and some scholarship, inflates to a belief in cultural continuity between the American South and Celtic lands.[6] Southerners, it is argued, are more Scottish than northern Scottish Americans because of these "authenticating" cultural ties that are claimed to extend hundreds, even thousands, of years. Certainly Scottish immigrants did contribute to southern culture, but as in the creation of the Old South model, the impact of Sir Walter Scott and Highlandism in current heritage lore cannot be overemphasized.

Scott's influence was much the same in Scotland and in the American South. In Scotland, it offered a Highland regional identity that appealed to the Scottish nation. In the South, it flavored a postbellum regionalism that appealed to northerner and southerner. Darden Pyron states that, across America, "the plantation legend functioned as a domestic version" of Scott's novels (1989:479). The romanticization of the Highlands and the South was a relief from the tragic consequences of both civil conflicts. It provided a means for reacceptance, as well as remasculinization, of the defeated as representatives of past but idyllic lifeways.

A Highlander and a Gentleman

In his classic *Romanticism and Nationalism in the Old South*, Rollin Oster-weis noted that even at the time of the Civil War, a Richmond newspaper editor commented on how southern chivalric ideals drew on a "military cult" and "polite notions of war" borrowed from Sir Walter Scott's novels (1949:90–91). The stereotypical image of a Scot as a bagpiping, kilted soldier certainly finds masculine parallels in the characters of southern myth. The Highland soldier is not unlike the military model of southern gallants: gentlemen and colonels.

Highlanders and southern men have somehow become both heroic in defeat and famed for loyal military service to their former enemies following those defeats. Both the South and the Scottish Highlands have disproportionately contributed to their national militaries since their respective disasters. While the Spanish-American War allowed south-erners to reaffirm their American patriotism, Scottish Highlanders, tak-ing "the King's shilling" rather than emigrating, transformed their reputation through their role in British empire-building. Valiance and military prowess are important components of male identities in both regions despite their ties to lost causes. Though succumbing at forma-tive historical moments, the stereotypical Highland soldier and south-ern gentleman remain ever-ready and clothed for battle. These male icons, prominent in both southern and Scottish defeat-generated my-thologies, are isomorphic in southern Scottish heritage celebration.

Military professionals within the Scottish-American community often credit their career paths and success to both their Scottish and southern ancestry, which in heritage lore entails genetic and cultural tendencies to a martial spirit. Heritage celebration compares and com-bines the legacies of these so-called "pugnacious" but "honorable and righteous" ancestors, and romanticization praises, yet tempers, south-ern and Highland bellicosity by directing it to the service of lost causes. Southern slave-owners have been transformed into gallant, chivalrous gentlemen, and Highlanders, once known to the outside world only as feuding bandits, are now "Prince Charlie's own loyal and gallant men," possessors of exemplary, noble virtues. The male ideal of southern Scot-tish heritage has developed as an alloy of the southern cavalier and the Highland warrior.

The southern cavalier is important in southern visions of Scottish heritage as a descendant, literally and spiritually, of the Highland clans-men. Scottish heritage enthusiasts celebrate this link as newly dis-covered, yet it appears in an earlier period of southern mythmaking. Heritage lore posits the eclipse of Scottish identity in the South by the

Lighting "the Fire on the Mountain" at Grandfather
Mountain. (Photograph by Hugh Morton)

Civil War, yet D. W. Griffith's 1915 film *Birth of a Nation* demonstrates
the survival of its less palatable associations. Eulogizing the Old South
and describing the origins of the Ku Klux Klan, Griffith originally titled
his film *The Clansman* after its inspiration, a 1905 novel by the Reverend
Thomas Dixon. The film links the KKK's use of a flaming cross to a similar device used by Highland chiefs for summoning clansmen to battle.

Griffith's derivation argument is not well known within the Scottish-
American community. Most whom I questioned had never heard of
Griffith or Dixon and were angered or dismissive about their sugges-
tions for a Scottish derivation of the KKK's flaming cross. Only older
community members indicated concern over the recent popularization
of the public ritual mentioned in Chapter 3 that incorporates fire and the
St. Andrew's cross at southern Highland Games. In the ritual gathering

of the clans on the evening before the Grandfather Mountain and Loch Norman Highland Games, representatives of each participating clan society symbolically answer the "summons" to their heritage. Positioned on the games field in the shape of a St. Andrew's Cross, each carries a flaming torch to be tossed onto a central bonfire as they announce their clan's presence. Participants seem unaware of the implications such an event might have had in Griffith's day. (In fact, heritage lore leaves a gap in southern-Scottish awareness between the Civil War and the revival of the late twentieth century.) Many were also surprised by interpretations that journalists try to force on the fire ritual today.

Recent British press accounts of the southern Scottish heritage movement have insinuated that the Southern League, a group advocating self-determination for the southern states, organizes Scottish heritage events as a part of a white supremacist movement in America (Roberts 1999). In nine years of fieldwork, a total of only seven informants (some of them photographed for this chapter) mentioned their support of the Southern League in our discussions, and they also stressed that they see their association as one dedicated to regional interests, not a racist agenda. Though they may be clansmen, as Peter Applebome notes, neo-Confederates are "not closet Klansmen (not most of them, anyway) and they've got some very valid gripes about their place in the American cultural landscape" (Applebome 1996:142). That white supremacists would be attracted to the heritage of people who happen to be white is obvious, but such people are not the organizers of Scottish heritage events and certainly do not represent the movement. Southern Scottish Americans are not celebrating whiteness. Had I encountered participants who advocated support for the KKK, my fieldwork would have yielded quite a different analysis. Scottish heritage participants explicitly distinguish clan from the Klan and link southerner and Highlander predominantly through ideal male virtues.

Exemplifying masculinity, both the gentleman planter and the chief became and remain central to the mythologies of the South and the Highlands. Much like the Highland chiefs, southern men, as Silber writes, "undoubtedly appeared as warriors who had failed, or perhaps refused, to adapt to a modern industrial society and thus would be forever linked to a soldierly, and masculine past. . . . In effect, the southern soldier became a more noble warrior precisely because his cause had been lost" (1993:173).

Both Foster and Silber stress how southern manliness became a major theme after Reconstruction. Southern participation in the Spanish-American War redeemed southerners as patriots, as international military service had done for Highlanders. A focus on manliness was also partly due to a general reemphasis of male superiority in the waning years of the Victorian age when women began to agitate for education, property rights, and the vote, and struggled to enlarge their realm beyond the domestic (Foster 1987; Silber 1993). The hoop-skirted belle featured in southern imagery knew her "place" and became exalted in her time as an example of humility, modesty, obedience, and patience. That Scottish celebrations also follow distinct gender lines at a time when gender roles are experiencing significant change in American society is suggestive.

Women may lead songs and dances or organize socials within the North Carolina community, but they do not often lead pipe bands, compete in Scottish athletics (other than marathons and dancing), emcee games, or participate in the discussions of military history that are common at any heritage event. Women's implicitly and explicitly limited roles in community spectacles reflect those of the generation that began the heritage movement in North Carolina and evidence that generation's upbringing on the roles of the southern belle and the southern gentleman, ideals modeled after Sir Walter's "Fair Maids" and "Waverlies." They also derive from the celebrated emphasis on male military traditions of the South and of Scotland and on heritage societies structured as hierarchical clans led by patriarchal heads with ultimate authority. Celebration of this heritage, when gender roles are undergoing dramatic change, portrays such masculine roles as both ancient and proper.

Within the Scottish heritage context, male identities are secure and their celebration is most expressive. It is the men who wear the elaborate tartan highland dress and who are "on the pedestal" and on display. Women, for whom true kilts are off-limits, lack a Scottish equivalent to the dress of a belle and have fewer options for exhibiting tartan in the Scottish style. However, southern women are blending traditions to develop new strategies for heritage dress. In Georgia, Alabama, and Mississippi, hostesses of antebellum home tours are increasingly incorporating their clan tartans in the costume of the hoop-skirted belle. Tartan is now a marker of "familial" affiliation, but, being worn in greatest abundance by males, it also signifies the traditional male role in perpetuating the family name and being the chief of his own family. Women's less prestigious roles in Scottish heritage societies and public ritual perhaps reflect southern conservativism to contemporary changes in this role.

The restoration of chiefships and the revived veneration for chiefs by clan societies has curiously accompanied these changes. However, like the southern plantation owner, the chiefs carried on a variety of un-

Beth Todd, tour director at Stately Oaks Mansion in Jonesboro,
Georgia, in a cotton version of the Gordon tartan, standing with
Virginia Military Institute cadet Daniel Hendrix in VMI's new tartan.

savory activities excluded from discussion at heritage events. Many
obtained pardons from the Crown for their part in the Jacobite Risings
by turning in their own clansmen or by paying taxes. The processes
they used to gather such revenue left thousands of their "kindred" with
no choice but to emigrate. Nevertheless, romanticization now exoner-
ates the clan chiefs as paternal and benevolent "grand old men" similar
to the "gallant gentlemen" of the Old South. For both, "chivalry" re-
volved around a belief in "honoring and protecting pure womanhood,"
yet in the Scotland of the chiefs, women could still be kidnapped and
married against their will in a practice called "marriage by capture," and

according to the actual behavior of "gentlemen" in the South, the designation of "pure womanhood" applied specifically to class and color. In current celebrations of Scottishness, however, southernness becomes an unproblematic outgrowth of ancestral proclivities. Without reference to the social realities from which they sprang, these romanticized identities interweave well. Any celebration of identity or "the past" necessarily produces a sparkling clean mirror in which to see ourselves flawlessly reflected. In Scottish heritage lore this is nowhere more evident than in the swirling of symbolic material cultures at heritage events.

Iconography: Tartan and the Confederate Flag

Material expressions of identity, lost causes, and the whole mythologies of Highlandism and the Old South meld in the combination of tartan and the Confederate flag. As markers of cultural identity, these icons visually reference the Highland and Old South legends, the concept of clan as family, and regional heritage. Both have become symbols of eras that met dramatic ends and "forgotten" parts of the American experience. Tartan and flag combine at Scottish heritage events in the reclaiming of identities once suppressed "for the greater good." As descendants of Scottish settlers replaced Scottish with southern identities, their descendants displaced both with a reaffirmed sense of American patriotism during the world wars. Those reclaiming a Scottish identity or displaying a Confederate flag do not consider themselves unpatriotic. Rather, the identities represented to them by the flag and the tartan embody those values that participants now feel make them "better" Americans.

Omnipresent in the heritage context, tartan symbolically evokes the whole history and mythology of the eighteenth-century Highlanders' experience, the "loss" of heritage, and its reclaiming. Clan tartans further represent "family" stories and connect participants as equal inheritors of the Highland heritage. The southern emphasis on "blood kinship" within the clan is a further elaboration of Highlandism: not only does each clan have a specific tartan, but all who wear the tartan are "kin." At large southern games such as those held at Stone Mountain, near Atlanta, or at Grandfather, well over one hundred clans represent themselves with tents on the games fields and banners in the tartan parades. In contrast, many northern games may field fewer than a dozen clan tents.

Associating clan with kin means that tartan operates as a type of heraldry. Pedigree-conscious southerners may obtain one through Scottish heritage. Simply by having a Scottish last name one acquires new "kin" through clan membership, an ancient and illustrious past, and a new sense of place in a "homeland" one may never visit—the historic landscapes of clan domains. As southern mythologizing supplies an elite planter background and plantation house for those whose ancestral greatness is no longer apparent "because of the war," Scottish heritage lore enhances the "backgrounds" of those planters with chieftains in the family tree and castles in the "family" lands.[7]

Yet Scottish Highlanders were far from aristocracy in the period since romanticized. Similarly, most southerners were pioneers with little of the extravagance now portrayed as antebellum standard. Those who provide the cavalier model were also overwhelmingly *English*. David Hackett Fischer notes that in Virginia many of the first settlers "were truly cavaliers . . . younger sons of proud armigerous families," but that the majority of Virginia's white population were indentured servants (1989:786–87). Most North Carolina farmers were yeomen; plantations were far less common in North Carolina than elsewhere in the South.

The large-scale Scottish heritage movement across the American South is such a relatively new thing that being the first of one's family to rediscover the "family Scottish heritage" elicits congratulations rather than condescension as might be expected. Newly reborn Scots tend to place a special emphasis on the long loss of "tradition" and ancestral grievances. Those claiming Scottish origins after discovering a Scottish surname in their genealogies also tend to display tartan with more enthusiasm than those with a transgenerational awareness of their Scottish ancestry. Southerners come to their Scottish roots in different ways, but what they share is a lifetime awareness of their southern identity—a kind of primary ethnic identity upon which the Scottish identity layers.

The familiar Confederate battle flag is also present at Highland Games and heritage events on T-shirts or lapel pins, on bumper stickers, and side-by-side with American and Scottish flags in clan society tents and in Highland Games campgrounds.[8] Believing their southern heritage to be "an extension of their Scottish heritage," members of the southern-oriented "Heritage Preservation Association" describe their flag-bearing association T-shirts as appropriate attire for Scottish events. They emphasize the flag's incorporation of the Scottish flag's St. Andrew's Cross.[9] For many, St. Andrew's Cross is a symbol of the Confederate states.

Both tartan and the Confederate flag encode beliefs about ancestry, but a difference in their symbolic power is obvious. Though proscribed for nearly forty years, tartan was resurrected through the British army's efforts to recruit Highlanders. In that context, tartan was transformed from the garb of rebels to that of valorous Highland soldiers loyal to the Crown. The meaning of the Confederate flag, in contrast, is still a source of contention. Those who fly the flag at Scottish events speak of the South in romanticized terms: of the cult of chivalry and southern belles, "aristocratic" southern manners, and Bonnie Robert E. Lee. For them, the Confederate flag symbolizes something quite different from what its detractors conceive. It symbolizes a shining simulacra of the Old South as the product of their idealized Scottish ancestors' accomplishments (rather than as a product of slave labor). Those displaying the flag also see it as representing the loss of both Scottish and southern traditions.

Likewise, tartan, gussied up in the nineteenth century, symbolizes the vision of Highland life from the Victorian period. Although those Highland Scots who came to the South adjusted their attire for the climate, the Scottish-American adoption of Highland dress and distinctive tartan setts provides an iconography to a generalized—and more easily assumable—heritage. Southern Scots were the first to don woven cotton tartans to fight the heat of summer games, and the first to initiate state tartans, the earliest being those of North Carolina, Georgia, and Texas. As mentioned in Chapter 1, Tennessee was the first state to set aside a tartan day in 1996. In 1997, a southern senator, Senator Trent Lott of Mississippi, proposed the adoption of Senate Resolution No. 155 designating April 6 as National Tartan Day. Also in 1997, the interweaving of Scottish and southern heritage found both literal and symbolic expression with the introduction of a Confederate Memorial Tartan. The tartan's originator, Georgian Mike Bowen of Clan Ewen and the Sons of Confederate Veterans, explained the symbolism of the sett as featuring a Confederate gray background with stripes of "Infantry blue," "Calvary yellow," and battle flag, or "Artillery" red.[10] In this way, through costume and imagery, the simplified, unproblematized visions of "Highlandness" and "southernness" are easily comparable and blended by those reared on the latter.

Scottish and southern identities do not mingle alone at southern Scottish heritage events. John Reed notes that southerners are more likely to claim Native American ancestry than are nonsoutherners (Reed 1997:111). Scottish heritage events in the South are more likely to reference Native American heritage and ancestry than similar events in the North. Southern Scottish Americans might send their children to both Highland dancing competitions at Scottish Games and Native American dancing competitions at southern powwows. Native American trading, social, and kin links with Scots find recognition in dress,

Mike Bowen displays the Confederate Memorial Tartan
at the Stone Mountain Highland Games in 1997.

reenactment, and story at southern Scottish gatherings. Scottish heritage is absorbed into the southern identity on the Old South model, but in the 1990s, even old mythologies can be further romanticized in a multicultural form.

Heritage and the "Faith of the Fathers"

Charles Reagan Wilson has called the ritual commemoration of "the Lost Cause" a civil religion (1980:170). Drawing on a system of beliefs that supports a sense of identity, southern Scottish heritage celebration might well be similarly labeled. Southern "Scots" have a cultural pre-

"Chief Chinnubbie," whose father was first president of the Clan
Macintosh Society and chief of the Creek, with Alex Beaton, one of
the most popular folk singers on the Highland Games circuit.

disposition for adopting and merging Scottish traditions and identity
with their own, as both operate on similar "root" paradigms. Beliefs
about the southern and Jacobite lost causes structure the southern and
Scottish identities. Public rituals (tartan parades, kirkins', and even the
games themselves) teach and affirm community "memories" of "ancestral experience," especially as connected to the Jacobite defeat. These
rituals are now practiced nationwide, but many developed in the post–
World War II South (specifically North Carolina), perhaps because the
South already had a Lost Cause ritual model.

Wilson notes that Civil War artifacts have a "sacred aura"; similarly

Ken Long of Charlotte dressed as a Shawnee. His third great-
grandmother, an Atkinson, was captured by the Shawnee; hence
the Gordon tartan (Atkinson is considered a sept of the Gordons).
Though initially scaring small children on the day I met him,
Mr. Long eventually assembled a group of fascinated children
as he explained his garb in detail. He regularly speaks on Native
American heritage in primary schools and attends powwows.

those of the Jacobite period (locks of Bonnie Prince Charlie's hair, sheets
on which he had slept, crystal glasses or jewelry with his image) are
venerated as "relics" today. Contemporary images of Charlie and Flora
MacDonald abound not only in Scottish representations of national
identity (from tourist advertising to shortbread packaging), but also in
heritage paraphernalia (in pictorial images "for the home," on desk sets

and stationary, on compact disc liner notes of "traditional" tunes, on tableware, and, of course, T-shirts). Like tartan and the Confederate flag, these images instantly invoke the whole of heritage lore.

The reverence and devotion accorded such symbols finds more explicit expression in actual worship services focused on the heritage of faith. Scottish heritage events in the South often have religious, especially Presbyterian, portions that affirm the importance of faith in a secular age and link faithfulness to ancestral virtues. Such events show the influence of southern Protestantism in the use of evangelical language and references to "finding" or "coming to" the heritage. Celebrants often speak of this discovery as a conversion experience. Community members claim converts and like to be acknowledged for shepherding new members into the Scottish fold. Many expressions used in the heritage movement are familiar to those enculturated in the southern evangelical tradition. Just as responding to God's will is answering, heeding, or hearing "the call," so too does one "hear the call" to one's own heritage.

Heritage language also mixes military with religious metaphors. The emphases on Presbyterianism and military prowess combine in the virtuous service of noble causes. The southern knight is a Christian soldier, and the Scottish Highlander of heritage lore becomes both the ideal warrior and Presbyterian. I have mentioned how today's Kirkin o' the Tartan honors the once-outlawed symbol of "rebel" Highland Jacobites with a service devised by once-outlawed Lowland Covenanters, though these two groups were historically opposed. A further convolution in the conventicle-style celebration of the tartan involves the stressed link between religious faith and faithful labors for lost causes. Fidelity to Prince Charlie made heroes of the Highlanders, but Prince Charlie was, at least until the "Forty-Five," loyal to Catholicism (an attachment that denied his father the crown).[11]

When history becomes heritage, Highland/Lowland and religious divides vanish in the face of the more emotive Culloden. Just as nineteenth-century southerners perceived themselves loyal to their faith despite the moral issues involved in their lost cause, their descendants likewise hold religion very dear and very flexible. Celebrations of the past often blend exactly what forebears found most divisive. In southern Scottish heritage celebration, participants fuse portions of the past into a unified heritage built on collective, rather than specific, grievances; on a particular faith, rather than historic diversity; and upon warrior ethics that also suit "gentlemen."

A heritage mythology, as Wilson notes, is not enough to start a civil religion; ritual is crucial (1989:169–70). Anthropologist Clifford Geertz has written that it is "out of the context of concrete acts of religious observance that religious conviction emerges on the human plane" (1966:28). In the South, Scottish celebratory rituals follow a root paradigm with which the South is already familiar—the celebration of that which was lost. Each clan and heritage society develops its own rituals with respect to its unique convictions about the meaning and form of its heritage. With the increasing numbers involved in the heritage movement and the expansion of the heritage to encompass their perspectives, the creation of new rituals is a continual process. (For example, blessings of tartans have grown to blessings of kilts, sgian dubhs, reenactors' claymores, dirks, new cairns, and so forth).[12] Acting out these new interpretations of the heritage through ritual authenticates their place in lore. Authenticating rituals work to spread new ideas and fortify communal beliefs about what was lost and what the past has to offer participants.

Community members speak reverently and often religiously about their perception of the past. As Scottish heritage frequently integrates sacred religious beliefs, many offer prayers at heritage events (both for protection at games competitions, and in thanksgiving for the model of the Scottish ancestors). Ministers in Kirkin' or games services make continual reference to family values, to people "knowing their places" and fulfilling their obligations, and to changing social norms, with instructive parallels always drawn from "the heritage." As Dr. A. Edwards reminded participants at the Longstreet Church homecoming in Fayetteville in a 1995 sermon, "Having the wind at your back never produced any heroes. . . . Scots were a people with the wind always in their face . . . and Christians are called to follow their example today, more than ever."

Wilson writes that "the constant application of biblical archetypes to the Confederacy and the interpretation of the Civil War experience in cosmic terms indicated the religious importance of the Lost Cause" (1989:172). Of the three major evangelical traditions in the South, the Presbyterian most emphasizes the Old Testament after the Scottish tradition, and it is the Presbyterian tradition that permeates the Scottish heritage movement. Given this southern and Presbyterian combination, I suggest that built into the heritage movement in the South is an even stronger emphasis on the traditions of the fathers and the importance of ancestors than elsewhere in the Scottish-American community.

Sermons, as well as speeches and conversation, call for "restorations," "renewals," and "rediscoveries" of ancestral values as a means of improving the present. Donald McCook's morning prayer at the 1995 Stone Mountain Games, for example, included the repetition of the following by the gathered crowd: "Too often the affairs of this world have prevailed in our lives . . . diverting us from the wholesome virtues which prompted our ancestors. . . . We long for the strength of human relationships experienced in the families and clans of old; we seek the fulfillment which came to those who experienced the joy of glen and mountain and sky. . . . As we discover our heritage, may our family relationships be renewed."

In the blessing of the tartan at the same games, participants read the following from a printed program: "We dedicate . . . these Tartans as symbols of the unswerving loyalty, steadfast faith, and great achievements of our Scottish forefathers. We take pride in their stamina as individuals in the face of adversity, in the tenacity of their loyalty to their families and clans." The minister said that tartan acknowledged not only the Scottish clan heritage, "but also a spiritual legacy," and that those who carried the tartans represented the "multitude of individuals who seek the restoration of a legacy of heritage." These quotes illustrate the moral guidance that community members draw from ancestral examples. The "great achievements of the Scottish forefathers" are attributed to their values that have, in turn, become a heritable "legacy"—equally instructive for today's community. Linking the sacred and secular heritages (the secular having become sacred for the community), the minister describes Scottish Americans as what Neville calls the Protestant pilgrim traveling "back into sets of ritual relationships" and seeking expiation and strength through "the way of the fathers" (1987:17).

Such ritualized repetitions of the "saving potential" of the heritage (in prayers, sermons, community literature, and songs) give southern Scottish heritage the quality of a civil religion. Contemporary individualism often entails a sense of alienation; heritage movements offer identity in the sea of mass culture and homogenizing media. In the Scottish case, heritage revival also calls for a return to community and individual responsibility. The mythology of the heritage movement is based on the Jacobite period, but accompanying the movement's numerical growth is the expansion of interest to other periods, both historic and prehistoric. At the heart of these new interests remains the basic tenet of heritage celebration and ritual: that the lifeways, values, and goals of the Scots and Celts are admirable and worthy of emulation.

Scholars too often study sense of place, ethnic identity, gender roles, literature, ritual, and religion as discreet entities. Their interconnectedness in southern Scottish heritage celebration allows us to explore the constant renegotiation of history, heritage, and interpretation that is involved in combining traditions and hyphenating one's identity. Southern aspects of Scottish heritage demonstrate how traditions are never really products of a singular "invention," but grow from the continual accretion of myth and the operation of root paradigms.

In the southern celebration of Scottish heritage we see the synthesis of two similar romantic traditions. Highlandism transformed the impoverished Scottish Highlands from a land of treacherous insurgents to one of the last bastions of true chivalry, gracious hospitality, and religious fortitude—something of the ideal that southerners claimed as their own after the Sir Walter model. The celebration of Scottish heritage in the South may overlook the Scottish Highland/Lowland cultural divide, but that between the American North and South still plays a powerful role in the claiming of identity.

Conclusion

Bagpipe music comes steadily from a variety of sources throughout any Highland Games, so that hours after leaving an event the pipes still echo in one's head. Halfway home you stop to gas up and over the click of the pump you are certain you hear pipes, and, because you have just been immersed in an environment where everything is Scottish, you actually look around for them. Then you realize you have the phenomenon known as "bagpipe head" and you have reentered the world where people will stare at your kilted passenger if you let him out of the car.

It is often the same when one tries to distill years of fieldwork and unique experiences into something representative of the whole of what one studies, yet accessible to the uninitiated. The late anthropologist Eric Wolf reminded us that "inquiries that disassemble [a] totality into bits and then fail to reassemble it falsify reality" (1982:3). Books are necessarily divided into easily digestible (and conceivable) chapters, but I have tried to emphasize what Wolf calls the bundles of relationships between the major themes and to stress that although Scottish heritage enthusiasts engage in activities for fun and sociability, they also take their rituals and interpretations of the past quite seriously.

An important part of ethnic identity formation and maintenance, selected traditions signify and reinforce the themes and symbols of a perceived common past that shapes group identity. As our identities are constantly renegotiated with regard to temporal and social context, traditions in support of those identities also evolve. As noted in the preface, this book is a product of a particular point in time. Writing in the summer of 1999, during which Scotland has its first parliament since 1707, I wonder how and if Scottish devolution will affect the celebration of Scottish roots abroad. Political redemption for Scotland today does not necessarily alter nostalgia about exiled ancestral immigrants, but might Scotland not develop a healthier self-image, breaking free of the "short-bread-tin" vision of itself imposed in Victoria's reign? New self-confidence for Scotland means a different emphasis in tourism and what pilgrims bring home as heritage. Perhaps only through independence, or at least devolution, will the lure of Jacobitism, and the defeatism its romance has instilled within the national identity, be itself defeated.

It seemed perhaps the major motifs of heritage celebration in America might be eclipsed in 1995 with the release of the film *Braveheart*. In the year that also saw the release of *Rob Roy* (set before the 1715 Jacobite Battle of Sheriffmuir), *Braveheart* (set in the late thirteenth century during the misnamed "Wars of Independence" and featuring the life of William Wallace) was the film preferred by almost all my informants. Discussion of the authenticity and inauthenticity of particular scenes in both films were prominent at 1995 heritage events, as were the tunes "We Shall Die or Be Free Cried the Bruce," and Robert Burns's "Scots Wha Hae." In *Braveheart*'s battle scenes, several actors wore blue paint on their faces, and many men began appearing at events in "blue face." In the ritual gathering of the clans at Highland Games, many clan representatives announcing their clan's presence also added "the right hand of William Wallace" or "from the land of Bravehearts." Movie posters and cardboard images of Mel Gibson as William Wallace appeared in many clan tent displays—not just Clan Wallace tents. Event conversation and community literature touted the larger-than-ever turnouts at games and credited attendance figures to the popularity of the 1995 films. Though 1995 and 1996 evidenced a feverish interest and pride in Scots who actually won wars, the heritage focus on the relatively more recent Jacobites has refused to succumb. Why anyone would prefer the ingrate Prince Charlie to William Wallace would mystify me if heritage lore and celebratory rituals were not so deeply invested in the Jacobite period and its connections with the immigrant experience.

The search for identity became an accepted part of life in the later twentieth century, not only "finding oneself," but also finding a group with which to identify, as people formed communities around specific interests often to replace community life in the geographic sense. Though celebration focuses on the past and revivifying traditions often long forgotten, a powerful sense of community emerges from public rituals affirming beliefs in shared kinship and common origins. As British anthropologist Anthony Cohen notes, "The reality of community lies in its members' perception of the vitality of its culture. People construct community symbolically, making it a resource and repository of meaning, and a referent of identity" (1985:118).

I do not interpret heritage celebration as necessarily entailing ethnocentrism. The celebration of any heritage or identity can lead, not just to cultural arrogance, but to hatred of any "other" and the cultural and social mediation of memory is inadequately understood for conflict res-

Keith Shelton, a member of Clan MacNeill, wears "blue
face" and demonstrates the detachable spike on his targe.

olution. I have presented those who compose the majority of the Scottish heritage movement as having an inclusive willingness to "adopt" non-Scots. Ironically, many multicultural movements of the 1990s, initiated to redress exclusivity, cannot make the same claim. Any movement to revive a "heritage lost" and maintain a grievance identity reveals a basic dissatisfaction with the order of things. The Scottish heritage movement, as expressed in the American South, corresponds with what anthropologists call a revitalization movement: an intentional and organized attempt to create a more satisfying state of existence.

In their conscious attempts to recreate community and retrieve a sense of identity that participants feel to be lost, heritage celebrations may be considered a response to our own time period. But here anthro-pologist Anthony Wallace's distinction between a revitalization move-ment and revivalism proves relevant. He defines the aim of the latter to be the "return to a former era of happiness, to restore a golden age, to revive a previous condition of social virtue" (1985:320). Celebrating the past and wanting to be in the past are vastly different phenomena. Scottish heritage celebration calls for a return only to ancestral values and the security that predecessors are presumed to have had in their identity—the type of security born in moments of societal drama. To-day's drama comes from within and plays out in culture change rather than lost causes. Southern Scottish heritage enthusiasts do not claim that the South or the Jacobites will rise again, but they do commemorate what they perceive to be southern and Scottish virtues as instructive for the present and as secure moorings at a point in history in which cul-tural change seems more rapid.

By definition, mythologizing processes construct contrasts to the present. As a revitalization movement, the celebration of Scottish heri-tage in the South reflects what participants feel is happening to their own society, especially with regard to kin ties, faith, and gender identi-ties. According to heritage tradition, Culloden dispersed the clans; de-localization of the American labor force, which southerners resisted for so long, distances families from each other and from southerner's pecu-liar attachment to place. Heritage pilgrims join clan ("family") societies and visit places made sacred by their historic ancestral associations—both in North Carolina and in the ultimate pilgrimage to the Scottish clan lands.

Stress of societal change impacts each generation differently, and this may explain the predominance of the retirement-age participants in a community celebrating ancestors and perceived pasts. Certainly the heritage movement evidences cosmological views of the first genera-tion, in the hierarchy within groups, in the emphasis on family, in the presumed leadership and authority of men, and in the emphasis on soldierly male ideals. Mainstream heritage celebrations construct an environment somewhat antithetical to contemporary emphases on the sensitive man, political correctness, women's leadership and achieve-ments, and changing familial structures. Yet this is more than simple re-actionism. Drawing upon the past, just as generations before us, the search for heritage is really a search for perspective, for models to recon-cile expectations of how "things should be" with our actual experience.

I view the heritage movement, not as homesickness for the past, but as an act of remembering for the improvement of the present. Far from being escapist, the romanticization of past failures and ancestral hardships that underpin heritage lore makes the present more acceptable. Heritage celebration involves a dialectical synthesis in the selection and merging of values and traditions from previous generations and those of the present. Viewing the dialectic in three steps—to cancel; preserve; transcend—I here infer that while celebrants may initially enter the community with overwhelming enthusiasm for discovering alternate identities and alternate pasts, they select from the various clan and other traditions available to them what they will incorporate into their worldview. A synthesis comes when they integrate several traditions, often assume a multifaceted patriotism, and transcend any either/or dichotomies to embrace a unified Scottish-American identity and heritage. In part, community rituals, revived or recreated (it matters not which), revere what is seen as a different and successful way of dealing with life problems. Operating in this stress-reduction role, celebration works as revitalization.

In practice, participation in community events such as the games not only revitalizes interest in ancestral values, but also community feeling by jolting members from their ordinary routines and prompting the creation of new traditions and new views of the heritage. Just as historian Gaines Foster viewed nineteenth-century Confederate celebrations as a kind of "Ghost Dance," the gathering of the clans at games in North Carolina may be thought of as a revitalization ritual, affirming beliefs in a heritable, shared past, kinship, and identity (1987:47). While competition regulations for standard events are set by an international body, the games demonstrate a variety of community innovations. As the Highland Games tradition continually grows, new games evidence the birth of new "old" events.

Sacred and secular revitalization movements involve the repetition of myth. Celebratory events and community literature focus on the recalling and retelling of that which makes Scottish Americans a distinctive people: their commitment to "noble causes," patriotism, a particular vision of the family, and, for many, their religious faith. The selection of certain traditions and memories transform history into heritage, and it becomes the heritage that is memorized and repeated. Tall tales about the living may raise eyebrows, but those about the dead may safely garner wistful and appreciative sighs. Models from the past, selected for their romantic appeal or instructive value, are encoded in heritage lore, thereby securing their perceived authenticity and continuity with each repetition. Material artifacts prominent in celebration become symbolic and indexical of these models.[1] Blessing the tartans at Grandfather in 1994, the games chaplain, Dougald Lachlan Maclean, prayed, "God bless the tartan, thank You for the tartan . . . as a symbol of Your love for us . . . as a symbol of the constancy of law and order . . . to remind us of our heritage and the rock from which we were hewn." A symbol of law and order was exactly what the now-fetishized tartan was not to Lowlanders and English of the eighteenth century; it was symbolic of quite the opposite. Yet in the claiming of a past, that past is refined, polished, and made exemplary.

Past-oriented referents are pan-human. If heritage celebration seems to be a postmodern, middle-class invention (Dorst 1989; Sanjek 1994; Schaefer 1996), this is only because the speed of technological change in the twentieth century and the culture lag it produced was without parallel; because we lack sufficient documentation, study, and appreciation of its role in other periods; and because the ease of communications and travel in the late twentieth century allowed its organization on a scale not before witnessed. Humans have always drawn precedents for living from social and cultural memories, the construction of which involves the articulation of pasts and presents, group and individual experiences, and ideals and realities in an ongoing process of synthesis.

Appendix

The Highland Dress Code

Correct attire for anyone in the Scottish-American community is Highland. Community publications ask, "Are you dressing properly?" and offer instruction booklets and even Scottish-dressed Barbie and Cabbage Patch–style dolls properly kitted. Many participants meticulously research period dress, but most learn the dress code through discussion at events and advice from community elders.

Event conversation frequently turns to who wears their kilts too short or too long, and which women have their tartan sashes on the wrong shoulder. Women nudge each other, whispering, "Right is right," when someone appears with a sash on her left shoulder. Wearing a tartan sash on the left shoulder means one is either a chief of a clan herself, the daughter or wife of a chief, or married to a man of a certain military rank. Rules become increasingly more intricate as interest in the Scottish-American community grows. According to informants Nita Sutherland and Abby Moffat, women who have married out of their clan but still wish to wear their "birth tartan" may do so if they tie the sash ends in a large bow at their left hip. Should someone appear with her sash improperly draped, she does not usually leave an event that way. Often the acknowledged local authority on such matters will approach the offender and correct her; some transgressors are even accompanied to the restroom for the sash to be properly pinned.

Women may wear floor or below-the-calf pleated tartan skirts, but they do not wear kilts (unless they are in a bagpipe band). Their dress is usually quite plain compared with the men's outfits, which have day and evening distinctions and are complete with the following:

kilt: The kilt should fall between the top and center of the knee. It may be worn in a variety of day and dress tartans.

kilt pin: The kilt pin secures the fabric so the kilt does not blow open and also serves an ornamental purpose. The day pin is plain; the evening pin may be jeweled.

belt: Belts have brass buckles for daywear; silver with the clan crest or other insignia for evenings.

shirt: Shirts vary in style from military to eighteenth-century white shirts with lace cravats.

jacket: Day jackets come in a variety of colors to match the day kilt (usually tweed). The jacket must not fall below the kilt seams.

plaid: A plaid refers to the length of one's tartan draped on top of the jacket and over one shoulder, secured with an ornamental brooch.

sporran: The sporran is a purse worn about the lower waist. Day sporrans are made of leather, while the more expensive evening sporrans are made from seal skin or horse hair and are trimmed in silver. Some men prefer a fur or "animal mask" sporran (the animal's head is the opening flap), as it can be worn day and night.

sgian dubh: Alternately spelled skean dhu, the sgian dubh (black knife) is a small knife tucked in a knee-high sock. Some men have both plain day versions and a more elaborate evening sgian dubh.

dirk: The dirk is a long knife, optionally worn on the side.

garter flashe: The flashe is usually a red or green string tied about the calf, three-quarters up each knee-high sock. Flashes may also be little flag-shaped attachments to the sock, the string more in keeping with an eighteenth-century style.

shoes: Men have the choice of brogues, wing-tips, or dancing shoes that lace several times about the ankle.

cap: Headwear may be worn in the Balmoral style of wool, possibly with feather or white cockade (bow) to show Jacobite sympathies, or in the Glengarry style worn with badges by military men and pipers.

additional accessories: Other accessories include military medals and/or cairngorm brooches of amethyst or amber-colored stones.

As important as what men wear is what they do not wear. Nothing is worn under the kilt. This is called "going regimental." One informant was photographed sitting, unknowingly, in such a way that his adherence to regimental standards was apparent to all. Male bystanders agreed that having underwear show instead would have been far more embarrassing.

For transporting the various outfits for day and night events, many men have individual cases for their accessories and allow a significant amount of time between events for the elaborate procedure of dressing. The Grandfather Mountain Highland Games Program describes the proper attire for the annual Games Tartan Ball (the most formal of Scottish events): "Formal dress is required. Men wear their best kilts with Prince Charles or Montrose jackets. Never is a Scottish gentleman more handsome than when appearing in his formal attire. The ladies come in their long evening dresses and sashes of their clan tartan. For the men who have not yet acquired their dress kilts, blacktie and tuxedo are acceptable" (Stewart 1992:43).

Though women's use of tartan is usually in a sash, for variety, some women wear the eighteenth-century style earasaid (or "arisaid"), which is basically a large tartan shawl. Women involved in reenacting or other specific interest groups are those who most commonly wear the earasiad. The earasaid is about three yards of sixty-inch tartan material gathered and belted at the width about the waist to look at first like a long skirt with a longer piece at the back. The two corners of that long piece are tied in a knot that can be worn over one shoulder so the cloth drapes like a man's plaid. Alternatively, the knot can be pulled over the head so that the cloth covers both shoulders like a wrap. Women may also wear "gaming" outfits of Victorian origin. These variations of tartan dress offer far fewer choices for women than the number available to men. The emphasis on male dress is perhaps largely associated with tartan's military use, and its revival in that context.

Glossary

Bonnie Prince Charlie: Charles Edward Stuart (1720–88), son of James Francis Edward Stuart and Clementina Sobieska and grandson of King James VII (King James II of England). Supported largely by Highland troops, Charles led the last Jacobite Rising. At first, it seemed that "the Forty-Five" might succeed in replacing a Stuart on the British throne, but such hopes died with Charles's defeat at Culloden in 1746.

Cead Mìle Fàilte (kee-ut meel-uh fal-chuh): 100,000 welcomes.

Celts: People sharing a language family, material culture, and to some degree cultural and religious practices whose origins are in Austria about 750–800 B.C. and who spread across the continent from Ireland to Spain to Poland and into Turkey. During the European Iron Age the continental Celts developed from a tribal society to a proto-state and built the first European towns (the oppida) north of the Alps before being conquered by the Romans in the first century B.C. In spite of the fact that the Celts originated in what is now Austria, and although we know the most about Celts in Gaul (France) because of the writings of Caesar and other classical authors, we tend to associate Ireland and Scotland with the Celts because the Romans never conquered Ireland or imposed their way of life in Scotland. Hence Celtic traditions survived there the longest on what was actually the fringe of the Celtic world.

ceilidh (kay-lee): An evening of song, dance, and music; a party; lit., "a visit."

claymore: The great sword, a Highland broadsword.

The Clearances: From the late 1700s through the 1800s, "the Clearances" removed tens of thousands of Highlanders from their homes so deer or sheep might graze in their place for the sporting and economic benefit of often absentee landlords. Forced evictions and resettlements led to poverty, mass emigration, and permanent change in land tenure and farming practices. Many Clearance victims went to Canada, and heritage celebration there reflects these reasons for immigration.

Covenanters: Having signed a "covenant with God" in 1638, the Covenanters were Lowland Scots who violently resisted attempts by Charles I and Charles II to impose Episcopal forms of worship in Scotland. Clan rivalry combined with religious fervor; while the Campbells of Argyllshire fought for the Covenanters, the majority of the Highland clans fought for the Crown.

creach (kree-ukh): A cattle raid; see under *tain.*

crofting: Subsistence strategy predominantly in the far western coastal Highlands and Islands of Scotland. After communal land holding among the clans became illegal (1747), and with the eviction of much of the Highland populace from the best arable lands, crofting developed as a farming strategy for small holdings (between two and four acres on average). Usually the land is poor for farming, often near the coast, and fishing and tourism must supplement income from sheep, cattle, or crops.

Culloden: The 1746 battle that lasted less than one hour on Drumossie Moor near Inverness between the troops of Bonnie Prince Charlie (Charles Edward Stuart) and William, Duke of Cumberland (second son of the Hanoverian King George II). The defeat of Charles Edward Stuart marked the last of the Jacobite Risings and the last great battle fought on Scottish soil.

Dal Riada: Earliest kingdom of the Scots in Scotland. Invading tribes from Antrim in Ulster began settling the southwest of the country (Argyll) in the late fourth century and from there further challenged the native Caledonians (Picts). The Dalriadic Scots brought Gaelic, and supposedly the kilt, bagpipes, and the Stone of Destiny (the Stone of Scone) with them from Ireland.

dinnsenchas (dind-hen-uh-kus): Folklore about topography.

The "Forty-Five" (1745–46): The last Jacobite Rising in support of "the Young Pretender," Bonnie Prince Charlie. The "Seven Men of Moidart" accompanied Charles from France to the Moidart Peninsula and raised the Jacobite Standard at Glenfinnan in August 1745, beginning the campaign that would end in April 1746 at Culloden Moor.

Glencoe: The 1692 slaughter of an aged chief, his family, and thirty-eight of their clansfolk who were suspected of Jacobite loyalties. That the victims belonged to a sept of the MacDonalds and the perpetrators were led by a Campbell has made this incident especially infamous in heritage lore.

Highlandism: A type of romanticism peculiar to late-eighteenth-century and nineteenth-century Scotland. Nineteenth-century Highlandism drew on the writings of Sir Walter Scott and transformed a regional Highland identity and material culture to that of the Scottish nation generally.

Jacobites: From the Latin *Jacobus*, meaning "James"; those who favored the return of the abdicated King James VII (James II of England) and later, his descendants, to the British throne. The first Jacobite Risings occurred in 1689–90 and were crushed by James's son-in-law William of Orange, who had claimed the throne with James's daughter Mary. A small campaign with French aid took place in 1708 after both James and William had died. Mar's Rebellion, known as "the Fifteen" (1715–16), failed to restore James's son to the throne after both his half-sisters Mary and Anne had reigned childless. Continued antagonism to the Hanoverian succession prompted a Spanish-assisted campaign in 1719, which was defeated at the Battle of Glenshiel. The last Rising, the "Forty-Five," drew support mainly from Scottish Highlanders and ended in defeat of the Jacobite Cause at Drumossie Moor, now called Culloden, in 1746.

kirk: A church; the Presbyterian Church of Scotland.

kirkin': A church service, most commonly Presbyterian in the United States; a kirkin' o' the tartan involves a parading and "blessing" of the tartan. Kirkin's often take place outdoors to emulate the open-air meetings of the Covenanters, though the ritual was actually created by U.S. Senate chaplain Peter Marshall. A native Scot, Marshall began the kirkin' as a service of prayer for all Britons during World War II. The ritual is now popular at Scottish heritage events throughout the southern states and has acquired much older origin stories.

pibroch (*piobaireachd*; pea-brock): "Pipe music." Refers to *ceòl mòr* (kyawl more)—

"big music," military marches, and elegiac compositions rather than dance tunes or "small music."

Picts: The aboriginal Caledonians. Known to the Romans as the Picti, "the painted ones," because they painted their bodies with woad. The Picts and invading Irish Celts (the Scots) only merged their kingdoms in 843 in the person of Kenneth MacAlpin, who inherited the Pictish crown through his mother and the Scottish crown through his father.

sett: The repeating pattern of a tartan in which the colors and width of the stripes are the same vertically (in the warp) and horizontally (in the weft). These patterns were once up to the individual weaver's fancy, skill, and the types of plant dyes available in the local area. They have now become standardized and associated with surnames, clans, districts, and even television stations and particular Highland Games or bagpipe bands. Over two thousand setts exist today.

sept: An associated clan or family of a larger clan.

sgian dubh (skian-doovh): "Black knife," a small knife worn in the top of a knee-high sock.

tacksmen: Military leaders of the clan chiefs who became their tenants after the 1747 Heritable Jurisdictions Act abolished communal clan lands. As tenants they were responsible for collecting rent from their subtenants and often organized and led them in emigrating.

tain (toy-n): A cattle raid; see *creach*.

targe: A circular shield of wood covered in cowhide, or occasionally pig or deer skin. Often ornamented with studs or tooled leather, the targe may be made an offensive weapon by the insertion of a spike.

tartan: What non–Scottish Americans call plaid. Tartan designations relate to purpose: clan, dress (usually with a white background), mourning (in black and white), hunting (for outdoor activities using less conspicuous colors), district (local designs from which clan tartans probably developed and now serve as an option for those without clan affiliation), military, and chiefs. Tartans also come in a variety of color schemes. "Modern" colors are usually darker and more vivid patterns than "muted" tartans. "Ancient" tartans are pale, resembling the faded samples from which older designs were documented. Color distinctions follow the name of the tartan as in "MacRae, muted" or "Dress, modern."

uisge-beatha (ishka-beyha): The "water of life," anglicized as *whisky*.

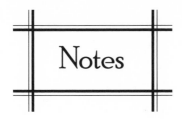

Notes

Introduction

1. According to Ned Landsman (1985), New Jersey was also a popular destination for Scots, but not predominantly Highland Scots. What Landsman's title (*Scotland and Its First American Colony*) downplays is that large numbers of Scots were transported to South Carolina earlier in the 1600s and failed to create a successful colony there. Additionally, communities of Scots-Irish settled on the coast of Maryland as early as 1649, and in Darien, Georgia, another less-known Highlander colony briefly flourished from 1735 to 1748. For information on the Darien settlement see Anthony Parker's *Scottish Highlanders in Colonial Georgia* (1997).

2. William Foote records an earlier 1729 settlement in his 1846 *Sketches of North Carolina*. Several subsequent works on the Highland Scots and the Scots-Irish repeat his claims. Meyer suggests that, having visited the Highlander settlements, Foote perhaps recorded surviving oral tradition about the early settlements (1961:177), or perhaps Foote had access to documents that are now lost to us.

3. In return for military and other services, chiefs granted the clan gentry pieces of land called tacks. These tacksmen, or *daoine uaisle*, led their underlings into battle, and occasionally into exile (Hunter 1994:13).

4. Anthropologist Victor Turner defines celebration as vivacity generated within crowds of people sharing common purposes and values (1982:16). I discuss Scottish heritage events, and the heritage movement itself, as celebration. However, I suggest that celebration commemorates and thus involves solemnity and reverence as well as—sometimes in conjunction with—vivacity.

5. For those in cultural studies, confident in their abilities to read cultural events as text, the role of feeling remains detached from thought (though we would hardly have ethnic conflicts if these were discrete in reality).

Chapter One

1. Despite Highlanders' fame for ardent Jacobitism, less than one-third of the estimated Highland fighting force actually fought for Prince Charlie (Cheape and Grant 1997:138).

2. Whether they had fought on the Hanoverian or Jacobite side, many Highlanders were ordered to swear an oath: "I do swear, and as I shall have to answer to God at the Great Day of Judgement, I have not nor shall have in my possession, any gun, sword, pistol, or arm whatsoever; and never use any tartan, plaid or any part of the Highland garb; and if I do so, may I be cursed in my undertakings, family, and property—may I never see my wife and children, father, mother and relations—may

I be killed in battle as a coward and lie without Christian burial, in a strange land, far from the graves of my forefathers and kindred" (Batty 1996:61).

3. The Stewart dynasty began with the son of Marjorie (daughter of King Robert the Bruce [d. 1329]) and Walter, the sixth High Steward of Scotland. At least two different views explain the change of spelling: either the name was anglicized to Stuart after 1603, or, more romantically, Mary Queen of Scots is thought to have dropped the "w" in recognition of her personal and the Stewart dynasty's close relationship with the French, whose language lacks a "w."

4. The House of Hanover acquired the British throne after William and Mary's successor, Mary's sister Anne, died without heirs in 1714. The German Elector of Hanover, a great-grandson of James VI & I, inherited the throne as George I.

5. In the 1970s many scholars began investigating the invention and reinvention of Jacobitism (Ash 1980; Cruickshanks 1979, 1982; Donaldson 1988). They have focused mostly on the Victorian period's creation of what is now labeled "Balmoralism" or "Highlandism." Excepting Nairn (1977), McCrone (1989), Jarvie (1991), and Harvie (1994), few writers investigate the meaning of those developments for contemporary Scottish identity, much less the transnational perpetuation of Highlandish views of Scotland through heritage movements in former British colonies.

6. The "Forty-Five" references the Jacobite Rising beginning in that year and culminating in 1746 at Culloden.

7. Brand notes that "Queen Victoria was not simply a formal member of the Church of Scotland, but took an active interest in it. She wrote to the Marchioness of Ely, 'I would never give way about the Scotch Church which is the real and true stronghold of Protestantism'" (Brand 1978:128).

8. Hugh Trevor-Roper suggests, somewhat simplistically, that an English Quaker, Thomas Rawlinson, "invented" the philibeg as a more industrial-friendly attire for workers in his iron-smelting operation near Inverness (1983:20–21). More likely, the kilt had a variety of manifestations before Rawlinson's revelation.

9. Since Caesar and other early ethnographers wrote most prolifically on Gaul (France of the Celtic period), the term "Gaulish" was often used interchangeably with Celtic by the eighteenth-century antiquarian writers and in popular culture of the time.

10. It is perhaps interesting to consider who wears tartan today (besides those in the tourist industry who sell Highlandism). Members of the Scottish Nationalist Party never appear in tartan; it is the late arch-conservative Member of Parliament Nicholas Fairburn who was known for his fabulous tartan creations.

11. This view still pervades much of the writing about Scotland and is a recurring motif in the heritage literature. A quintessential example: "The duel of Bonnie Prince Charlie and the Duke of Cumberland was to bring a climax to Scottish history. In its wake came massacre, torture, premeditated cruelty, persecution and ignominy to a degree sufficient to split two peoples for a thousand years. It was the love and understanding of Queen Victoria that was to wash away the blood-stain from the written tragedy of Drummossie Moor" (Duff 1968:20).

12. Scott actively disassembles the "Jacobite Highlander as traitor" and reconstructs him as the most loyal and honorable characters of his stories. He has villain figures such as the Duke of Albany (easily interpreted as the Duke of Cumberland) say of the Highlanders to his father the king, "These men are the pest of the Lowlands. . . . These are not loving subjects, but disobedient rebels" (1828:490). The

rest of the story disproves the validity of such opinions—to the king and to the reader.

13. However, even Queen Victoria notes how odd it is that she is enamored of the Highlands on her visit to the Glenfinnan monument (where Prince Charlie raised his standard) in 1873: "I thought I never saw a lovelier or more romantic spot, or one which told its history so well. What a scene it must have been in 1745: And here was I, the descendant of the Stewarts and of the very king whom Prince Charles sought to overthrow, sitting and walking about quite privately and peaceably" (Duff 1968:295).

14. Royalty loved Scott across Europe for his encouragement to loyalty and his strong monarchist leanings (at a time when Europe's thrones were being rattled in waves of anti-monarchic sentiment and nationalism). Nicholas I of Russia (ruled 1825–1855) personally censored Pushkin's works and encouraged him to write a good tale of Russia, after the style of Sir Walter Scott, to exemplify Russian life (Cowles 1971:162–4).

15. However, on April 6, 2000, the Scottish Tourist Board sponsored an "On-line Tartan Day Parade," featuring images of bagpipe bands in "the homeland" and virtual tours of Edinburgh for American celebrants.

16. Recent study of plaid fabrics found with the mummies of Urumchi suggests Celts, or proto-Celts, traveled east into Chinese Turkestan as well as west across Europe (Barber 1999).

17. The Romans delighted in critiquing Celtic fashions that employed colors prohibited for the average Roman citizen because of sumptuary laws. The Celts' use of checked and tartan trousers was a certain mark of barbarism to the Greco-Roman world.

18. Tartans are described according to purpose: "clan," "dress" (usually with a white background), "mourning" (in black and white), "hunting" (for sport and outdoor activities—the less conspicuous colors of the hunting setts act like camouflage), "district" (from which clan tartans probably developed and are now worn by those not entitled to wear a clan tartan), "military," and "chief's" (Bain 1961:28). Those of Scottish descent, but lacking a clan, family, or district tartan may wear one of the following: "Hunting Stewart" (originally a hunting tartan, named Stewart only ca. 1888); "Caledonia" (general "national" tartan); "Jacobite," for those with ancestors of that ilk; and "Black Watch" or "Government Tartan," which was initially a regimental tartan (Cory 1991:73–75).

19. Romanticization of the clan system projects a consciousness of the current meanings of tartan on to particular ancestors. In many retellings of the Battle of Culloden, one will hear about old Malcolm MacLachlan, who only missed killing his own kin by recognizing the "family" tartan. Actually at Culloden, Highlanders fought Highlanders—sometimes of the same clan—and one way they distinguished the enemy was by the color of the cockade, or bow, on their cap: white for the Jacobites, black for pro-Hanoverians.

20. Fires were built in the middle of the floor and the soot and smoke allowed to cover the walls and thatched roof; the latter being scattered around crops as fertilizer when roofs were rethatched.

21. "Modern" are usually the darker-colored tartans and "ancient" are those paler, often orangelike colors (actually those considered "ancient" had simply faded by the time they were recorded).

22. When referring to tartans with these new distinctions, colors should come after the name (MacRae, muted) and terms referring to the antiquity or use of the pattern should come before the name (e.g., Dress, modern).

23. At most games in recent years, the vendors' section may also host a booth where names may be entered into a "computer archive" and a printout purchased in certificate form of family name/history and the specifics of the tartan.

24. A complete outfit for a man (kilt, jacket, shoes, and accessories) is well over a thousand dollars. Usually the general clan or hunting tartan is obtained first for games and heritage events. The dress tartan (for tartan balls, weddings, and other formal functions) is more expensive and requires more costly accessories and a short doublet.

25. Replacing a small exhibition in Highlands, North Carolina, the museum's creation was promoted from both sides of the ocean by the late Dr. Gordon Teall of Teallach, former president of the Scottish Tartans Society in Scotland (which loaned the museum several artifacts) and by Franklin's Presbyterian minister Rev. Tyler Martin, whose church has its own "Tartan Hall." The museum's first curator, Charlie Rhodarmer, not only designed the layout of the museum, he also built much of the interior himself and annually brought Scottish speakers over for symposiums on the history and wearing of the tartan.

26. The crest is often taken from the chief's historically documented coat of arms. It generally relates to some event in clan history, a deed of an apical ancestor, or the clan's reputation for military strength.

27. Having signed a "covenant with God" in 1638, the Covenanters were Lowland Scots who violently resisted attempts by Charles I and Charles II to impose Episcopal forms of worship in Scotland. While the Campbells of Argyllshire fought for the Covenanters, the majority of the Highland clans fought for the Crown (Stevenson 1988:2).

28. The massacre included the slaughter of an aged chief, his family, and thirty-eight of their clansfolk who were suspected of Jacobite loyalties. That the victims belonged to a sept of the MacDonalds and the perpetrators were led by a Campbell has made this particular incident especially infamous in heritage lore on clan rivalries.

29. From the late 1700s through the 1800s, "The Clearances" removed tens of thousands of Highlanders from their homes so sheep might live in their place. Forced evictions and resettlements led to poverty, mass emigration, and permanent change in land tenure and farming practices. Many Clearance victims went to Canada, and heritage celebration there reflects these reasons for immigration.

Chapter Two

1. "Scots-Irish" has replaced the once commonly used term "Scotch-Irish"; "Scotch" denotes whisky, "Scots" refers to people.

2. While Scots-Irish immigrants wrote family back in Ulster of their homesickness, Trevor Parkhill characterizes their letters as emphasizing the freedom and independence to be found in America (Parkhill 1997:118–19).

3. While the Scottish Friendly Societies and St. Andrew's Societies followed Scots around the globe in the eighteenth century, the Ulster Protestant Orange Lodges reassembled in the urban American North with much later immigrants. The Orange Order was much more important in Canada in terms of settlement and politics (Houston and Smyth 1980).

4. The Cameronian Regiment of the British Army was originally formed by Covenanters for their own defense.

5. Presbyterianism (in which an elected presbytery ruled the church rather than monarch-appointed bishops) became the established Church of Scotland in 1690 and was secured as such in the 1707 Act of Union. In Martin Martin's second edition of *A Description of the Western Islands of Scotland* (1716), he mentions only the small islands of Benbecula, South Uist, Barra, Canna, and Eigg as still almost entirely Catholic. To these John Lorne Campbell adds Rum (Campbell 1994:90). The main areas from which the Cape Fear settlers came—Skye, Sutherland, and Argyll—were Protestant. Nova Scotia became the haven for persecuted Catholic Highlanders (Meyer 1961:67, 79).

6. For example, during "infant baptism" at the 1995 Stone Mountain Highland Games in Georgia, a child received coral beads to protect her from the evil eye (a custom of Roman Catholic origin in Scotland) and wore a packet hung around her neck containing bread and cheese (a version of what is called "crying kebback" in the North East of Scotland) (Bennett 1992:6). Explaining these traditions, the minister said, "We are collecting customs" to remind us of our Scottish ancestors.

7. "The Kirk" is the church in Scotland.

8. Though the Presbyterian clergy often did, surprisingly to our minds, support the "Catholic" Stuarts, that they blessed the tartan still seems doubtful. Historian Murray Pittock notes that in Aberdeen-shire and Banff-shire, a full third of the fifty-eight clergy who came out for the Jacobites in 1715 were Presbyterians (Pittock 1998:48).

9. Shortbread boxes/canisters are generally covered with tartan and images of Bonnie Prince Charlie/Flora MacDonald and other Highlandist themes.

10. "Some hae meat and canna eat / And some wad eat that want it / But we hae meat, and we can eat / And sae the Lord be thankit."

11. St. Andrew's Day, Burns's Night, and the consumption of haggis are events more celebratory in nature abroad than at home, as acknowledged in the "Address to a Twentieth Century haggis": "So, haggis, like the prophet's honour / In his own country, you're a gonner / Exported to expatriates / Or finely tickled hom palates. / Great chieftain O' the puddin' race, You've now acquired a different face" (Osoba 1994:7).

12. Some North Carolina heritage groups extend these evening festivities into a weekend of events; the New Bern-based Eastern North Carolina Scotish Society combines its St. Andrew's celebration with a parade "in kilts and other suitable Scottish regalia," followed by a Tartan Ball and a Sunday Kirkin' o' the Tartan. Reenactors and Scottish country dancing enthusiasts hold eighteenth-century-style dinners for both St. Andrew's and Burns's Nights.

13. The author even attended one banquet where the toast to the queen was given in three languages, English (so everyone could understand), Scots Gaelic, and in French in honor of the Scots' "Auld Alliance" against England.

14. Fearing her influence and Jacobite reputation in the coming war, the governor appointed her step-father, also in North Carolina, to raise a regiment of Highlanders for the Loyalist cause and appointed her husband a captain. Feeling bound by the oath of loyalty taken when entering the country, the MacDonalds took the Loyalist side and left America stripped of their possessions in 1779.

15. The unpublished and unfinished opera "Flora MacDonald," by Scottish composer Learmont Drysdale (1866–1909).

16. Attributed to Samuel Johnson (no fan of the Gael) after his introduction to Flora (Rogers 1993:137).

17. Many Highlanders who fought for the Crown left America for Barbados, Nova Scotia, and Britain. Near Skeabost on Skye is a place called "Carolina Hill," named by Captain Kenneth MacDonald who, having fought for the Loyalists at Moores Creek Bridge, was forced to return to his parents' native land (MacDonald 1980:58).

18. One state historical marker on Highway 73 between Ellerbe and Mt. Gilead was moved a few miles north in 1959 to a site on Cheek's Creek. Another state sign was erected in 1972 on NC 24/27 near Cameron Hill in Harnett County, which notes that Flora spent the winter of 1774—75 there. At least four other private markers have been erected at various sites by individuals.

19. The invited speaker was Dr. James A. MacDonald, president of the Scottish Society of America.

20. One informant recalled sitting on the campus grave of Flora's "son." According to the state's Office of Archaeology, officials of the college had the remains of two children, purported to be MacDonald's, reinterred on college grounds in 1937. Red Springs locals told me that Flora herself was buried there—a slab said to be her original gravestone from Skye is in the college garden. Memories of Flora may be confused, but not forgotten.

21. In the 1960s, a family of MacRaes on the Isle of Lewis were still called "the Carolinas," because their ancestors had briefly settled there in the Napier project (J. MacDonald 1993:240).

22. Written in the 1960s by Roy Williamson of the Scottish folk band, The Corries, "Flower of Scotland" is actually about a Scottish victory—that of Robert the Bruce over English King Edward's troops at Bannockburn. It asks when "the likes" of those Scots will be seen again to lead Scotland to independence.

23. Transcribed as sung by Donald MacDonald.

Chapter Three

1. The past four years have witnessed an explosion of Scottish clan pages and journals on the World Wide Web that will continue to grow and perpetuate, or perhaps challenge, certain definitions of heritage.

2. Odom Library in Moultrie, Georgia, serves as the national repository for over 110 clan societies' publications.

3. The Campbells' ancient rivals the MacDonalds suggest that "cam beul" referred less to the physical appearance of a mouth than to the falsity of words that issued from it!

4. "Broken" is also a term used to describe "Scots" whose families emigrated from Scotland.

5. Though Major C. J. Shaw of Tordarroch was the first chief of Clan Shaw in four hundred years, he was the twenty-first chief of the clan.

6. Outside the South, California has one of the most rapidly developing Scottish heritage movements. In recent years, California has also become the home to more British expatriates than any other state.

7. Older members of Clan Mackintosh related how two disputatious Clan Mackintosh societies united through the 1973 American visit of "Mackintosh of Mackintosh."

8. Clan commanders may be elected from among armigerous families in line for the chiefship.

9. Clan MacGregor may be one of the only clans whose members actually are biologically related. James VI abolished the name of MacGregor in 1603 and executed the clan chief. The MacGregor's persecution lasted until laws against them were finally repealed in 1774, at which time only 826 MacGregors were recorded under their own name. Part of the MacGregors' return to vogue was the work of Sir Walter Scott, who gave MacGregor history a spotlight in *The Lady of the Lake* and in his tale of Rob Roy MacGregor. Today, Scotland boasts a Rob Roy Visitor Center.

10. Clan Donald grants membership to anyone with a surname found in the region under MacDonald control at its height in the 1400s, which opens membership to a multitude of septs, including those who allied with other clans once the MacDonalds were no longer the "Lords of the Isles." However, clan literature and events also suggest that all MacDonalds share a lineage and may wear the tartan by natural right.

11. "Native men" actually refers to all inhabitants of the clan's territorial base (Way 1994:28).

12. I have never met an active heritage or clan society member who could not claim a Scottish relative, a Scottish surname, or a spouse with one.

13. Of course Lowlanders stole cows and committed worse crimes as "reivers."

14. In a Clan Donald newsletter article emphasizing the beauty of the ritual "smooring chant" (said by Highland women as a blessing each night while smothering their fires), Mary Gillies disdainfully adds, "Such were the people represented as savage barbarians who knew nothing better than killing each other and stealing cattle" (Gillies 1993:26).

15. The MacFarlanes have a "plundering pibroch" (pipe tune) called "Thogail Nam Bo Theid Sinn" (To Lift the Cattle We Go) and ask unsuspecting anthropologists riddles about "MacFarlane's Lantern" (the full moon, so called because their creachs often took place in its light).

16. Featuring Robert the Bruce's image with the caption "The Ancestor We Honor," Clan Bruce's literature would seem that of a Robert the Bruce historical society rather than a clan society. This was the impression of some Grandfather Games visitors; when I asked which clan tents they had seen, they included "the Robert the Bruce tent."

17. St. Andrew's Societies organized to help poor newcomers from Scotland, but as immigration slowed, they became social clubs for second- and third-generation Scots—and now those with vaguely Scottish ancestry or a Scottish surname. Male-only organizations in many states, including North Carolina, maintain a "charitable purpose" by granting scholarships, and cultivate a Scottish theme by inviting speakers on Scottish traditions and Scottish performers to events. One must be invited to join, and because in North Carolina the four hundred memberships are for life, this usually means waiting until someone either moves away or dies. A member of Clan MacLachlan invited to a St. Andrew's affair in Raleigh was amazed that "few of the men, and none of the women guests, wore tartan and they don't know their clans." Members of North Carolina's society are generally elite professionals and two ex-governors, eight judges, and a number of bank presidents. With few individuals as exceptions (such as John Kerr, former president of the society, who helped design North Carolina's tartan), the St. Andrew's society has little involvement with the clan and heritage societies on whose events I have focused.

Chapter Four

1. Jeffry Gantz suggests that the Cycles of Early Irish literature may preserve visions of the earlier Iron Age period in Ireland (1981).

2. Taking advantage of the power vacuum left by Roman withdrawal from Britain, the Irish Scotti began raiding the western British coasts and eventually established permanent settlements in the southwest of Scotland. Their kingdom (ca. A.D. 400–800) is called Dalriada after a Northern Irish tribe. (Until approximately the tenth century, "Scotia" referred to Ireland.) The native inhabitants, the Picts, did not politically merge with the Scots until Kenneth MacAlpin, king of the Scots, inherited the Pictish throne through his mother in 843.

3. In one of the few social studies of Highland Games, Jarvie draws on Gramsci in a class analysis of the events as they developed in Victorian times, rather than on what the games mean to people today. He examines the impact of emigration on their development in the homeland, but does not follow the growth of the games tradition across the water among emigrants' descendants.

4. The Flora MacDonald Games are the only games in the state in a Highlander-settled area; it is in conjunction with these games that the North Carolina Scottish Heritage Society holds its annual meeting and "genealogy day."

5. The Grandfather Games give a nod to growing Celtic interests with a Friday, pre-games "Celtic Music Jam." As this event occurs on the same evening as the Scottish Country Dance Gala, the Games Ceilidh, the annual Bagpipe concert, and the Sponsors' Reception, the musicians also play during the games in one of the three shaded "Celtic Groves" off from the field. Following Grandfather's lead, Loch Norman has also instituted a "Celtic Entertainment" stage away from its games field.

6. "Gathering" may also refer to the smaller size of an event and the amateur rather than professional status of athletic competitions.

7. In North Carolina, many feel that professional competition at the large games trivializes the nonprofessional locals' performances. Referring to the original competitions' relevance for the chief's "army," one Campbell informant even compared the professionals to mercenaries (their travel expenses often being paid by games organizers).

8. Each year the Flora MacDonald Games' promotional leaflets describe Highland Games as based on the ordinary expected skills of any Highlander. The leaflets also note, "The never-ending housework of women gave rise to competition for them in areas such as baking and sewing," though no related competitions occur at the games (1995:2).

9. This is a growing trend with the further development of heritage tourism and as overseas Scots plan more clan gatherings in the homeland. In 1998, Clan Rattray held its gathering in conjunction with the Blairgowrie and Rattray Highland Games. Clan Grant's Society Gathering coincided with the games at Abernethy; the Menzies Clan Society Gathering visited the Aberfeldy Breadalbane Highland Games; and the Lochcarron Highland Games in Ross-shire hosted the Gathering of Clan Matheson. Four weekends of games at Loch Ness and three in Edinburgh are now largely exhibition events at the height of the tourist season.

10. Braemar would be excluded as typical of Scottish Gatherings because it is so large and such a tourist spectacle.

11. Most medium to large Highland Games hold bagpipe-band competitions and organizers choose, or form, a local band to host the events.

12. Marking personal stages of life among assembled "Scots" is an increasing trend. In 1998 alone, three weddings took place at the weekend Loch Norman Highland Games.

13. Unexpectedly, in a country where tartan and tourism are major industries, even the gathering most attended by tourists in Scotland, that at Braemar, has only an "overseas" tent where visitors may examine maps for regional clan associations.

14. Anthropologists would find this a classic rite of intensification.

15. Goffman calls those areas that are neither front nor back "the outside region" (1959:135). All games participants have different front, back, and outside regions of activity on the games field. For clan society members solely involved with clan activities, the rest of the games site beyond the clan tent is their "outside" where their performance changes from representative in the front area or insider in the back area to spectator and even visitor to the front areas of other tents. For dancers and musicians without involvement or parental involvement in a clan society, all areas beyond their competition platforms and viewing areas are "outside."

16. Though Loch Norman has a small area for camping, the grounds have not yet acquired the popularity or lore that those at Grandfather have. Though reenactors may camp at one-day events such as Waxhaw or the Flora MacDonald Games, the practice is not communitywide.

17. Other community members promote museums and interpretation at historic sites connected to the ancestral experience, or encourage developments in cultural policy and education that reflect the heritage of an area. The full impact of heritage revival beyond community celebrations remains to be seen.

18. The Welsh Eisteddfod is a competition in music, drama, and poetry. The revived Eisteddfod is claimed by some to be a tradition from Roman times. Dr. William Price standardized and romanticized the format in the late nineteenth century and introduced the wearing of "druidic robes."

19. How the image is created is a topic of light-hearted debate among those who have witnessed the display.

20. This legend has evolved during my 1990s fieldwork, from first a lone bag-piper (thought to be an unknown soldier) to "the spirit of the ancestors," and finally in 1997 to Alexander MacRae.

Chapter Five

1. Victor Turner has described pilgrimage as a replacement for initiation into a belief system (1974:65). I discuss heritage tourism in Scotland and heritage enthusiasts' travel to local, national, or international community events (such as Highland Games) as pilgrimage and as initiation into heritage beliefs and practices. Both draw community members away from their ordinary existence to identify with and learn about sets of beliefs, experiences, and places that compose their Scottish heritage. Scottish-American pilgrimages bring participants into an active form of liminality, or separateness, in which to explore beliefs through celebratory ritual, as well as their own identities as Scots, a sense of kinship, and a sense of *communitas*.

2. Sir Walter Scott's use of landscape and the picturesque in his novels had a great influence on contemporary thinking about nature. James Reed notes that Dorothy Wordsworth's 1803 *Recollections of a Tour Made in Scotland* is "probably the last literary record of Scotland before the irreversible changes which came about as a result of the direct influence of Scott's writing on the Scottish tourist trade"

(1980:18). James Holloway writes that "the mountains of Scotland were never painted before the middle of the eighteenth century," before they were considered "of the wildest and most hideous aspect" (1978:3). Yet with Robert Nories, John Sanger, and Alexander Nasmyth, those wild features of the Highland landscape, now considered typically Scottish—dramatic mountains, streams, and waterfalls—became the dominant subjects in Scottish landscape painting after 1750. Painters took up themes from James Hogg's late-eighteenth-century "Jacobite" ballads. Nostalgic tourists and artists searching for safe subjects considered the areas of Scotland connected with Jacobite treachery in the 1740s (and even Jacobitism itself) as peculiarly representative of a pacified Scotland by the 1770s.

3. With the purchase of Balmoral Castle, Victoria began the tradition of an annual Royal visit to Scotland. Her court, and any who considered themselves fashionable, followed her and built country estates throughout the eastern Highlands. (This area was considered the "tamest" and least Gaelic in the mid-nineteenth century; later Victorians and Edwardians came to the more "exotic" heart of the Gaelic West.) The laying of rail in Scotland corresponded to the needs of these Victorian sporting landlords, who influenced the direction of the lines through the most scenic areas to their estates. They also had the funds to clear "unsightly" tenant settlements from the path and surroundings of the tracks, so that the romantic views of this "untamed" land would be unbroken. With the arrival of the sporting landlords also came Cheviot sheep (for their profit) and deer (for their sport), replacing the Highland people through what are now called "the Clearances." Landscape paintings and tourism literature, though artistic in construction, are invaluable records of changes in the post-Culloden landscape. In the later eighteenth century, kilted figures or flocks of sheep appear in landscapes, and in the nineteenth century such artists as Edwin Landseer replaced human figures of stereotypical Highlanders altogether with the "Monarch of the Glen" (the stag), a romanticized portrayal of very real changes in the Highlands.

4. Where chunks of arable land were available (glacial till fragments farming space in the Highlands), infields and outfields composed a "runrig" system so that all residents of the clachans (clustered dwellings in the Highland form of dispersed settlement as opposed to village settlement) had equal access to good land.

5. As Kirshenblatt-Gimblett notes, this has been a primary concern in the works of Edward Said, Michel Foucault, and James Clifford, among others (1992:304).

6. The largest number of visitors to Scotland by country of origin is from the United States. In the mid-1990s approximatley 420,000 Americans annually visited Scotland. Other countries to which Scots immigrated during "the Clearances," Canada and Australia, contributed 130,000 and 120,000 tourists, respectively, during the same period (Turnbull 1998:5).

7. In his much-quoted work, *The Tourist: A New Theory of the Leisure Class,* folklorist Dean MacCannell has suggested that staged performances are often interpreted as spontaneous authentic acts by the tourist (1976).

8. See Erik Cohen's work on emergent authenticity (1988).

9. Americans' Saint Patrick's Day Parades are a centuries-old tradition, yet they only began to become popular in Ireland three decades ago. Likewise, the American innovation of clan tents at Highland Games is an idea Scottish Games (in Scotland) may eventually consider adopting.

10. Distinguishing between types of tourism, I agree with sociologist Erik Cohen that tourism we can label pilgrimage is a movement toward a "sacred Center"—or

what defines oneself—while tourism we would simply call travel is "a movement in the opposite direction toward the Other"—what one sees as exotic and apart from oneself (Cohen 1992:50).

11. Clan Henderson even lists in its stated objectives "encouraging travel to Scotland."

12. The Clan Douglas Society notes twenty-seven historical sites connected with clan history for members to find when in Scotland. In preparation for the first annual Gathering of MacGillivrays in 1992, the clan newsletter provided a map and description of points of interest in "the heart of the ancestral homelands . . . to put the local geography and history of the clan in useful perspective" (1992:1–7). The Shaw Society informs clan visitors that "every house and hillock hereabouts has played some part in the story" of the Shaws (MacDonald [1994]:2).

13. Individuals may also buy symbolic pieces of the homeland. American owners of Scottish land have begun marketing square-foot parcels in community literature. "MacKenzie & MacKenzie" out of New York advertise such parcels at Ullapool: "Attention all Scottish ex-patriots and descendants! Own a piece of your heritage . . . overlooks the departure point of the 'Hector' [a famed immigrant boat leaving Scotland in 1773]" (*The Family Tree*, January 1997:6A).

14. Some clan society foundations are designed to purchase properties as close to the original site of a clan stronghold as possible. The Clan MacGillivray newsletter advertised an offer to the clan of a Victorian stone cottage near "the presumed location . . . occupied and used by the chiefs of the Clan for perhaps 400 years" as "a possible opportunity for the Clan MacGillivray to return, in a sense, to the ancestral home of its chiefs in Scotland" (1994:6).

15. Local museums also play a role in documenting clan heritage; in 1993, the town of Castle Douglas opened the Douglas Heritage Museum, and the Moffat Museum in the borders tells the story of "clan warfare" and provides "family trees" for the Clans Johnstone and Moffat.

16. Clan Leslie planned its first all-Leslie gathering in clan territories in 1995 to "celebrate 925 years of Leslies on the site."

17. In 1992, the Burnett "family" gathered at the "clan-home," Crathes Castle, to celebrate the four hundredth year of Burnetts on the site. They organized lectures on the history of the castle and clan, attended the Aboyne Highland Games, and visited Culloden Moor. In 1994, though lacking a clan castle, the Urquharts held the first annual gathering of the clan "called by a clan chief in modern times" at a castle nonetheless (Craigston Castle near Turriff, owned by a clan member).

18. Many fringers go seeking experience of the "traditional" Celtic folk music scene and also bring home new tunes to perform at games.

19. Gwen Kennedy Neville has excluded clan gatherings in the United States and in Scotland from her analysis of Protestant pilgrimage, as she considers clan societies "secular voluntary associations," but the point I wish to make is that participants do not always see their involvement as voluntary or secular (Neville 1987). They describe themselves as "answering the call" to their heritage, which is often inseparable from their religious traditions.

20. Cameron Hill is well known among community members as the location of the 1791 burial of a young Highlander named Cameron. Having settled in the flat lands and not wanting to bury his son "where there were no mountains," his father carried him west to the first hill he encountered.

21. The name derives from its location on the same "prong" of Raft Swamp as

McPhaul's Mill. As one of the few remaining houses known to have been built by an immigrant Highland Scot, the house is on the National Register and receives restoration funds from descendants of Mill Prong's owners, allied families, and other community members.

22. At the 1980 dedication of the Grandfather Mountain Memorial Cairn, the late Nestor MacDonald read from Sir Walter Scott's "The Lay of the Last Minstrel" (1805)—an appropriate choice in view of how Scott impacted perceptions of Scottish landscapes, Scottish national identity, and today's heritage movement.

23. A cairn is literally a heap of stones used by Highlanders, generally as a grave marker to which each visitor would add a stone, hence the Gaelic saying "Cuiridh mi clach 'nad Charn" (I'll add a stone to your cairn). Heritage lore has created many other romantic interpretations including, the idea that soldiers deposited a stone to a cairn as they answered their chief's call to battle, or that deparing emigrants raised a cairn to leave a mark in a landscape to which they never expected to return.

Chapter Six

1. Though a small engagement, Moores Creek Bridge significantly squelched Loyalist support in Carolina and played an important role in ending British hopes for success in the South. Highlanders immigrating from North Carolina after Moores Creek included the heroine Flora MacDonald.

2. For example, Clan MacRae's war cry is also the title of the North American society's newsletter: *Sgurr Uaran* (a war cry which invokes a sense of place for a mountain in the MacRae homeland in Kintail). The Lochbuie Maclaines call their newsletter *The Battle-ax*.

3. Informants and the literature also note the fame of the "Galloglas" (Scottish mercenaries employed across Europe from the late Middle Ages to the time of Napoleon) and the Scottish reputation for valor within the British army. Certainly, it is their battlefield exploits that are mentioned, not the off-field activities for which mercenaries are more infamous.

4. Though subject to debate at their publication, their enduring popularity as authoritative references illustrates the way in which cultural heritage is always a heritage of ideas.

5. Logan romantically suggests that Highlanders lost Culloden not because of ineptness, exhaustion, or any practicality, but on a point of honor in Highland military tradition:

> The Highlanders have always been most jealous of their accustomed right to certain positions in the line of battle, and rather than submit to the indignity of being placed in any other situation . . . they would allow their army to be disgraced in defeat. . . . On the field of Culloden, the MacDonalds were unfortunately placed on the left instead of the right wing, to which they asserted an ancient right, and not a man . . . would draw a sword that day. (1851:153)

Though later writers, such as John Lorne Campbell, repudiate this story, it has surfaced in the many discussions of the Battle of Culloden to which I have been privy during fieldwork (attributed to various sources and with varying characters) (Campbell 1994:99).

6. McWhinney's followers and their works include James Michael Hill's 1986 *Celtic Warfare* and Perry Jamieson's 1982 *Attack and Die: Civil War Military Tactics*

and the Southern Heritage. For further hyperbolic arguments that the Scots-Irish identity and "mentality" derive from events even further removed than the Celtic invasion of Britain, see Rodger Cunningham's 1987 *Apples on the Flood.*

7. Logan does not explain how or why an aliterate society would keep muster rolls.

8. Of enduring interest since Plato's era, the nature-versus-nurture debate attempts to explain individual and group behaviors by pitting instinct and biological proclivities against socialization and cultural environment as if either alone could adequately explain human action.

9. The beginning of the Celtic period is dated to the mid-700s B.C. with the most famous Celtic archaeological site at Hallstatt, Austria. This is one of the earliest datable find sites, but the Celts may have prospered in Europe long before. Hallstatt designates the early Iron Age, and La Tene, named after an archaeological find at Lake Neuchatel, Switzerland (450 B.C.), designates the different artistic styles and technological advancements characteristic of the later European Iron Age. Though never establishing an empire in the classical sense, the Celts evolved from chiefdoms to proto-states, establishing the oppida—the earliest large European towns beyond Greece and Italy.

10. It might seem difficult to get an American soldier into anything like a skirt, but kiltmaker Bob Martin has no problem once they learn of Highland soldiers' reputation as "the ladies from Hell."

11. The words are attributed to Major Patrick Ferguson, a Scot from Aberdeenshire on the Lowland side of the Highland/Lowland divide. Leading the largest contingent of Patriots at King's Mountain was another Scot, Colonel William Campbell.

12. At least one American military division, the 245th Artillery of the Army, has also adopted the Scottish belt and buckle crest with the motto, "Pro Patria Armamus."

13. Clan Gunn not only professes its American patriotism, but calls itself "Discoverers of America," claiming to have reached America before Columbus. The claim stems from a rock carving of a "crusader knight" near Westford, Massachusetts. The knights' shield is thought to bear the fourteenth-century arms of a cadet branch of the clan.

14. As I write this, a new, official, national anthem is being planned for Scotland.

15. The many Highland regiments and clans who fought for the Hanoverians during the Jacobite Risings are, however, rarely mentioned.

16. Layers of oak or pine covered with cowhide or, less often, pig or deer skin, formed the original Highland targe. The leather would be studded and tooled in simple or quite ornate designs (Grant and Cheape 1997; Moran 1996:55-59).

17. The longbow more likely came with the Normans (Borg 1986).

18. Many other military living history groups that are named after their clan, such as Clan Chattan (actually a federation of clans), or that have adopted such titles as "the Wild Highlanders," or "the Colonial Light Brigade," have become a regular presence as specific games or events. All focus on the late medieval period to either 1746 or approximately 1780.

19. I use this quote as sufficient argument against applying Richard Handler and William Saxton's deconstruction of reenactments and living history to Scottish heritage events (1988:243). Though Handler and Saxton write that reenactors and living historians seek an alternate reality to their "unauthentic existence," many of

the reenactors I met in the context of Scottish events were celebrating a belief in the continuity of their heritage from ancestral Scottish settlers of North Carolina. As David Lowenthal notes, "Celebrating continuity, as distinct from antiquity, is profoundly anti-escapist. The accretive past is appreciated less for its own sake than because it has led to the present" (1985:61).

20. The combination of the kirkin', as an American innovation, and American Presbyterianism, being an inheritance from the Covenanters, causes reflection on the military origins of the Covenanters. Their 1639 Articles of Militarie Discipline note that each regiment should have a minister and that "for doing of service and worship to God Almightie, the Lord of hosts, for whose Covenant this war is undertaken, from whom we look for assistance and on whom the success of war depends; it is thought necessary that there be publick prayers every day, morning and evening" (1969:7). Scottish Presbyterianism was born through the armed struggle of the Lowlander, nontartan wearing Covenanters, but the association of tartan, clan identification, religion, and a military presence is an interesting evolution of meanings.

21. Unlike the Irish dancing style, Highland dancers perform in soft shoes and make no sound with their feet and travel very little on stage.

22. Those accepting a much earlier Celtic origin for the dances told me that the hand and finger positioning used in Highland dancing actually suggests deer antlers and, therefore, deference to some long-forgotten hunting god akin to the English Herne or the Gauls' Cernunnos. Highland society was primarily cattle-based; deer imagery, however was predominant in the Victorian fascination with the "Monarch of the Glen." Such an association between finger positioning and the reverence of deer may or may not be connected to Highlandism, but I mention it here as an example of the many and varied attempts to link current practice with an ever-more ancient past.

23. The standardization of country dancing began with efforts to preserve it as a living tradition. Jane Milligan founded the Royal Scottish Country Dance Society in 1923 and it has since documented thousands of dances and has become the foremost authority on their "proper" performance.

24. Many American military units have pipe and drum bands that also wear specially designed tartans like those that now exist for the Navy and Marines. A general U.S. Armed Forces tartan now exists in addition to several for military academies such as the Virginia Military Institute. Scottish regimental bands exist in many commonwealth and former commonwealth countries such as Australia and New Zealand. In the last decade, Canada still had sixteen Scottish regiments with pipe bands and each adopting a particular tartan.

25. Individuals also compete in solo piping competitions playing military marches, dances, and the classical and oldest music of the Highland Bagpipes, the emotive Piobaireachd (pronounced pea-brock). The Piobaireachd is often described in exclusively male terms as being played to "welcome the chief's new [male] heir into the world or to mourn the passing of a great warrior" (Jones 1994:60).

26. Known as "the government soldiers" during the last Jacobite rising, the pro-Hanoverian Black Watch developed in the southern Highlands of Campbell territory. The six independent companies raised in 1725 to quell the continuing unrest following the 1715 Jacobite rising were incorporated into the Black Watch in 1740.

27. Martin Martin was one of the first "travel writers" on the Scottish Highlands, publishing explanations of topography and culture from 1697 to 1716. The major-

ity of exploratory texts appeared well after Culloden, however, when Highland society was experiencing rapid change and emigration. Their travels were made possibly by General Wade's military roads (the Highland's first planned network of roads, built to aid Hanoverian troop movements during the Jacobite period). English and Scottish intellectuals undertook several "tours" in the later half of the eighteenth century (see Pennant 1771; Johnson 1775; Knox (1787) cited in Grant 1961; Hogg 1803), but the themes of Scottish tourism became set with the works of Sir Walter Scott and the travels of his readers (especially Queen Victoria) to the physical scenes of the histories he embellished.

28. Tattoos occur elsewhere in the United States, such as the memorial tattoo at New York's Fort Ticonderoga, where French troops decimated the Scottish Black Watch in 1758.

29. It is too early to predict if the 1995 release of the Mel Gibson film *Braveheart*, set in the misnamed "Wars of Independence" during the thirteenth century, will permanently influence the Scottish-American heritage movement and widen interests beyond the Jacobite period. Michael King has designed a Braveheart or "Warrior" tartan. Immediately after the film's release, the Wallace Clan Trust planned to develop a Braveheart monument and information center explaining the life and times of Sir William Wallace. The newsletter of SAMS's Post #7 is called *The Braveheart Beat*. Songs about the period, including "We Shall Die or Be Free Cried the Bruce" and Burns's "Scots Wha Hae," have become more prominent at ceilidhs and games performances. In the battle scenes of the film, actors portraying William Wallace and his supporters wore blue paint on their faces, and many men appeared for the Gathering of the Clans at Grandfather in "blue face." (Never mind that the use of blue woad in battle was a Pictish practice, and unless Wallace had studied classical texts referencing Pictish encounters with the Romans, he was unlikely to know this and therefore unlikely to have created a symbolic reference to independence by invoking Pictish traditions.) The historical accuracy of the face-painting went curiously undiscussed at events. The 1995 releases of both *Braveheart* and *Rob Roy* (set just before the 1715 Jacobite Battle of Sheriffmuir) are credited with increasing attendance at all of the major Highland Games in the United States and significantly impacting tourist numbers traveling to Scotland.

30. The attraction of the tragic site for Scottish descendants has led at least one enterprising neighbor to attempt to rent pieces of his adjoining property to American clan societies.

Chapter Seven

1. The figure of 50 percent is taken from *The Highlander 1999 Directory* 37, no. 2a (April 1999), edited by Sharon Kennedy Ray. Figures on games and festivals are based on games listings annually compiled by Jim Finegan of the Clan MacLachlan Association of North America. I include the following twelve states under the rubric of "southern": Alabama, Arkansas, Florida, Georgia, Kentucky, Louisiana, Mississippi, North Carolina, South Carolina, Tennessee, Texas, and Virginia.

2. Visitors to either a Highland Games or a southern plantation visit our polished visions of particular pasts—some may even get to do both simultaneously. The Loch Norman Highland Games near Charlotte take place at Rural Hill Plantation. Boone Hall Plantation in South Carolina hosts the Charleston Scottish Games and Highland Gathering. The Monticello Highland Games in the panhandle of northern

Florida occur at Trelawn Plantation. Following the Flora MacDonald Highland Games, community members supporting the restoration of Mill Prong House (home of a Scottish immigrant) host a "plantation party." The Stone Mountain Games in Atlanta take place near the mountainside carvings of Robert E. Lee, Stonewall Jackson, and Jefferson Davis. The southern settings of these games consciously affirm links between southern and Scottish heritage.

3. Scott was not alone in publishing popular works on the Highlands that influenced Americans. Jane Porter's 1810 *The Scottish Chiefs*, a historical romance about William Wallace, had great popularity in Britain and America and surely influenced John Pendleton Kennedy's 1832 southern romance *Swallow Barn*. Tindall notes that the plantation myth "pattern appeared full-blown" in Kennedy's influential work (1989:4).

4. Though Sir Walter Scott and other Scots referred to the English people negatively as "Southrons," American southerners (familiar with the term from Scott's works) applied it positively to themselves during the Confederacy.

5. Inspired by Scott's stories, southerners held jousting tournaments, in which local young men in medieval attire challenged each other as "knights." Guion Griffis Johnson notes that such tournaments became popular in North Carolina in the late 1850s (1937:184). Today, some of the same plantations that hosted the tournaments host another sport spectacle inspired by Scott's writings—the Highland Games. The site of the Loch Norman Highland Games, Rural Hill Plantation, was once the site of such jousting tournaments.

6. As mentioned in Chapter 6, a small school of thought has developed around this hyperbole. See McWhinney 1988; McWhinney and Jamieson 1982; Hill 1986. (Michael Hill is the founder of the Southern League that advocates peaceful self-determination for the southern states.) Many critiquing the work of McWhinney et al. aim not for their untenable claim that any culture could maintain such continuity over millennia, but instead assume the Celtic character thesis is really a thinly veiled argument for some sort of racial purity. While I have found the wacky claims of the McWhinney school to be popular with some Scottish Americans, it did not follow that they had racist reasons for accepting his theory. Rather, for them, it explained why they had such strong interest and emotional attachments to things Scottish.

7. A popular T-shirt for several clan societies features the "clan castle" with the words, "My other home."

8. In 1997, southern participants in the first annual "North vs. South" Scottish athletic competition tucked battle flag bandanas in the backs of their kilts and displayed a larger flag beside their games tent in Kalamazoo, Michigan.

9. The Cross of Saint Andrew was adopted in the second National Flag of the Confederate States of America on May 1, 1863. It remained on the third and last national flag and on the battle flag symbolic of the Lost Cause today.

10. The tartan's creators, Mike Bowen and Phillip Smith, note that the size of each color stripe within the sett is proportional to the size of the historical units that they represent.

11. By many accounts, Charles had declared himself a Protestant by 1750 while living secretly in London. Property manager for the National Trust for Scotland's visitor center at Culloden, Ross MacKenzie notes that it would be reductionistic to see the "Forty-Five" as a "Catholic v. Protestant contest . . . the large Episcopalian element in Charlie's army had more in common with the Anglicans of Cumberland's

army than they did with the Presbyterian Campbells, also in the government army, but that did not save them in the atrocities after the battle" (MacKenzie 1996:11).

12. The Loch Norman Games organized its first annual Kilt Christening ceremony in 1997. Each novice who had obtained a first kilt in the year since the last games was called before the review stand. A "kinsman" of each novice served as "Tartan Banner Bearer" and, from "a wee sma' christening glass," administered a sprinkling of either Scottish spring water or uisge beatha (whisky) to the new kilt. Christening performed, all novices and standard bearers paraded once around the games field.

Conclusion

1. A symbol depends on a conventional relationship between the sign and its signified, whereas an index is a sign that points to further meanings (Atkinson 1990:84). Tartan, for example, is now symbolic of clan heritage; it is also an index to conceptions of Scottish heritage in general.

Bibliography

Adam, Frank. [1908] 1970. *The Clans, Septs, and Regiments of the Scottish Highlands*. Edinburgh: Johnston and Bacon.

Agnew, John A., and James S. Duncan. 1989. *The Power of Place*. Boston: Unwin Hyman.

Alba, Richard D., ed. 1989. *Ethnicity and Race in the U.S.A.: Toward the 21st Century*. London: Routledge.

Allen, Barbara. 1990. "The Genealogical Landscape and the Southern Sense of Place." In *Sense of Place: American Regional Cultures*, edited by Barbara Allen and Thomas J. Schlereth, 152–63. Lexington: University Press of Kentucky.

Anderson, Benedict. 1983. *Imagined Communities*. New York: Verso.

Anstruther, Ian. 1986. *The Knight and the Umbrella: An Account of the Eglinton Tournament 1839*. Gloucester: Alan Sutton.

Applebome, Peter. 1996. *Dixie Rising*. New York: Times Books.

Ardener, Edwin. 1989. "The Construction of History." In *History and Ethnicity*, edited by Elizabeth Tonkin et al., 22–33. London: Routledge.

Arensberg, Conrad. 1961. "The Community as Object and as Sample." *American Anthropologist* 63:241–64.

———. 1965. *Culture and Community*. New York: Harcourt, Brace and World.

Arensberg, Conrad, and Solon Kimball. 1968. *Family and Community in Ireland*. Cambridge, Mass.: Harvard University Press.

Armstrong, Dewitt. 1994. "Flowers of the Forest." *Armstrong Chronicles* 13 (2): 7.

———. 1994. "Generals Armstrong." *Armstrong Chronicles* 13 (2): 8–10.

Ash, M. 1980. *The Strange Death of Scottish History*. Edinburgh: Ramsay Head Press.

Atkinson, Paul. 1990. *The Ethnographic Imagination: Textual Constructions of Reality*. London: Routledge.

Babcock, Barbara, ed. 1978. *The Reversible World*. Ithaca, N.Y.: Cornell University Press.

Bain, Robert. [1938] 1961. *The Clans and Tartans of Scotland*. Edited by Margaret MacDougall. London: Collins.

Banel, Ronald. 1995. "Home Win." *The Scotsman*, December 30, Weekend sec., p. 17.

Banta, Dana. 1994. Waxhaw Gathering of the Clans Program. Monroe, N.C.

Barber, Elizabeth. 1999. *The Mummies of Urumchi*. New York: W. W. Norton.

Barth, Fredrik. 1994. "A Personal View of Present Tasks and Priorities in Cultural and Social Anthropology." In *Assessing Cultural Anthropology*, edited by Robert Borofsky, 349–61. New York: McGraw-Hill.

Batty, John. 1996. "Some Notes on Firearms and Their Collectors." In *The Swords and the Sorrows*, 60–64. Edinburgh: National Trust for Scotland.

Bauman, Richard, ed. 1992. *Folklore, Cultural Performances, and Popular Entertainments*. New York: Oxford University Press.

Baynes, John. 1988. *Soldiers of Scotland*. London: Brassey's Ltd.

Becker, Jane S. 1988. "Revealing Traditions: The Politics of Culture and Community in America, 1888–1988." In *Folk Roots, New Roots: Folklore in American Life*, edited by Jane S. Becker and Barbara Franco, 19–60. Lexington, Mass.: Museum of Our National Heritage.

Beeman, William O. 1993. "The Anthropology of Theater and Spectacle." *Annual Review of Anthropology* 22:369–93.

Bendix, Regina. 1989. "Tourism and Cultural Displays: Inventing Traditions for Whom?" *Journal of American Folklore* 102:131–46.

Bennett, Margaret. 1992. *Scottish Customs from the Cradle to the Grave*. Edinburgh: Polygon.

Berthoff, Rowland. 1982. "Under the Kilt: Variations on the Scottish-American Ground." *Journal of American Ethnic History* 1 (2): 5–29.

Billings' Sutlers (advertisement). 1993. *Highlander* 31:57.

Bintliff, John. 1991. *Annal School and Archaeology*. New York: New York University Press.

Blethen, Tyler, and Curtis Wood. 1983. *From Ulster to Carolina: The Migration of the Scots-Irish to Southwestern North Carolina*. Cullowhee, N.C.: Western Carolina Mountain Heritage Center.

Bloch, Marc. 1953. *The Historian's Craft*. New York: Vintage Books.

Bohannan, Paul, and Dirk van der Elst. 1998. *Asking and Listening: Ethnography as Personal Adaptation*. Prospect Heights, Ill.: Waveland Press.

Boon, James. 1982. *Other Tribes, Other Scribes*. Cambridge: Cambridge University Press.

Borg, Alan. 1986. *Arms and Armour in Britain*. London: Her Majesty's Stationery Office.

Bourdieu, Pierre. 1977. *Outline of a Theory of Practice*. Cambridge: Cambridge University Press.

Bradburd, Daniel. 1998. *Being There: The Necessity of Fieldwork*. Washington, D.C.: Smithsonian Institution Press.

Brand, Jack. 1978. *The National Movement in Scotland*. London: Routledge and Kegan Paul.

Brander, Michael. 1992. *The Essential Guide to Highland Games*. Edinburgh: Cannongate.

Braudel, Fernand. 1992 [1949]. *The Mediterranean*. London: HarperCollins.

Brettel, Caroline, ed. 1993. *When They Read What We Write: The Politics of Ethnography*. Westport, Conn.: Bergin and Garvey.

Buchan, David. 1972. *The Ballad and the Folk*. London: Routledge and Kegan Paul.

Buckley, Anthony. 1989. "We're Trying to Find Our Identity: The Uses of History among Ulster Protestants." In *History and Ethnicity*, edited by Elizabeth Tonkin et al., 183–97. London: Routledge.

Burke, Peter. 1990. *The French Historical Revolution: The Annales School, 1929–89*. Stanford, Calif.: Stanford University Press.

Calder, Jenni. 1987. *The Story of the Scottish Soldier 1600–1914*. Edinburgh: Her Majesty's Stationery Office.

Calhoun, Craig. 1991. "Indirect Relationships and Imagined Communities: Large-Scale Social Integration and the Transformation of Everyday Life." In *Social*

Theory for a Changing Society, edited by Pierre Bourdieu and James Coleman, 95–
120. San Francisco: Westview Press.

Cameron, Ed. 1992. "History of Cameron Hill." Unpublished Cameron Hill
Presbyterian Church bulletin insert.

Campbell, Alastair. 1993. "Names and Clans—a Closer Look, Part IV." *Highlander*
31:54–57.

———. 1994a. "Names and Clans—a Closer Look, Part VI." *Highlander* 32:54–58.

———. 1994b. "Tartan and Highland Dress." In *Scottish Clan and Family
Encyclopedia*, edited by George Way of Plean, 31–42. Glasgow: HarperCollins.

Campbell, John Lorne. 1994. *Canna: The Story of a Hebridean Island*. Edinburgh:
Cannongate.

Carmack, Robert. 1972. "Ethnohistory: A Review of Its Development, Definitions,
Methods, and Aims." *Annual Review of Anthropology* 1:227–43.

Carr, Edward Hallett. 1961. *What Is History?* New York: Vintage Books.

Cash, Wilbur J. 1968. *The Mind of the South*. New York: Alfred A. Knopf.

Charlton, Thomas H. 1981. "Archaeology, Ethnohistory, and Ethnology:
Interpretive Interfaces." In *Advances in Archaeological Method and Theory*, edited
by Michael B. Schiffer, 4:129–76. New York: Academic Press.

Cheape, Hugh. 1995. *Tartan the Highland Habit*. Edinburgh: National Museums of
Scotland.

Cheney, Charles, ed. 1994. "Tartan Ball Tops Expectation." *Loch Norman Piper* 2
(6): 1.

Clan Burnett. 1993. *Breagh Burnett Gazette* 9:1.

Clan Currie. 1994. Clan Currie Society Historical Overview leaflet, 4.

Clan Davidson Society. 1993. Information leaflet.

Clan Ferguson. 1993. "What Is a Clan Society?" Information leaflet, 4.

Clan Forrester. 1993. Information leaflet, 1.

———. 1994. "Clan Forrester Will Be at Grandfather Mountain Games." *Corstorphine
Journal* 8 (4): 1.

Clan Fraser. 1994. Information leaflet.

Clan Gunn Society. 1994. Information leaflet, 1.

Clan Henderson Society. 1990. "Ceilidh Song Book." *An Canach*, January, 4–11.

Clan Henderson Society. 1994. Information leaflet.

Clan Leslie. 1995. Information leaflet.

Clan Leslie. 1993. "Leslie Gathering." *GripFast: The Newsletter of the American Clan
Leslie Society* 4 (3): 3.

Clan Lindsay. 1994. Information leaflet, 1.

Clan MacFarlane Society. 1995. Information leaflet, 2.

Clan MacGillivray. 1992. "Clan Country Beckons." *Clan MacGillivray U.S.
Commissioner's Newsletter* 1 (2): 1–7.

———. 1994. "Dunmaglass Farmhouse Offered to Clan." *Clan MacGillivray U.S.
Commissioner's Newsletter* (Fall / Winter): 6.

Clan MacGregor. 1994. Information leaflet, 2.

Clan Mackintosh Society. 1993. Information leaflet, edited by Carolyn Clark.
Madison, Ind.

Clan Maclaine of Lochbuie. 1992. "Who Are We?" Information leaflet, 2.

Clan Moffat Society. 1995. Information leaflet, 3.

Clan Montgomery. 1993. *Be Part of a Thousand-Year Tradition*. Information
booklet.

Clan Napier Society. 1995. "Who We Are." Clan Napier Society information leaflet, 2.

Clan Urquhart Association. 1994. *North American Branch Newsletter* 5 (1): 1.

Clark, Victor, ed. 1982–90. *Argyll Colony Plus* (serial). N.p.

Clark, Victor, and Louise Curry, eds. 1989. *Colorful Heritage Documented.* N.p.

Clifford, J., and G. E. Marcus, eds. 1988. *Writing Culture: The Poetics and Politics of Ethnography.* Berkeley: University of California Press.

Cohen, Anthony P. 1985. *The Symbolic Construction of Community.* London: Tavistock Publications.

Cohen, Erik. 1988. "Authenticity and Commoditization in Tourism." *Annals of Tourism Research* 15:377–86.

———. 1992. "Pilgrimage and Tourism: Convergence and Divergence." In *Sacred Journeys: The Anthropology of Pilgrimage,* edited by Alan Morinis, 47–61. Westport, Conn.: Greenwood Press.

Collinson, Francis. 1966. *The Traditional and National Music of Scotland.* Nashville, Tenn.: Vanderbilt University Press.

———. 1975. *The Bagpipe: The History of a Musical Instrument.* London: Routledge and Kegan Paul.

Comaroff, Jean. 1985. *Body of Power, Spirit of Resistance.* Chicago: University of Chicago Press.

Comaroff, John, and Jean Comaroff. 1992. *Ethnography and the Historical Imagination.* Boulder, Colo.: Westview Press.

Condry, Edward. 1983. *Scottish Ethnography.* Edinburgh: Association for Scottish Ethnography.

Cory, Kathleen. 1991. *Tracing Your Scottish Ancestry.* Edinburgh: Polygon.

Council of Scottish Clans and Associations, Inc. 1994. Annual Contribution Form.

[Covenanters]. 1639 [1969]. *Articles of Militarie Discipline.* Amsterdam: Theatrum Orbis Terrarum Ltd.

Cowles, Virginia. 1971. *The Romanovs.* New York: Harper and Row.

Craig, Maggie. 1997. *Damn Rebel Bitches: The Women of the '45.* Edinburgh: Mainstream.

Cruickshanks, Eveline, ed. 1979. *Political Untouchables: The Tories and the '45.* Edinburgh: John Donald Publishers.

———. 1982. *Ideology and Conspiracy: Aspects of Jacobitism, 1689–1759.* Edinburgh: John Donald Publishers.

Crumley, Carole L. 1987. "A Dialectical Critique of Hierarchy." In *Power Relations and State Formation,* edited by Thomas C. Patterson and Christine Ward Gaile, 155–68. Washington, D.C.: American Anthropological Association.

———, ed. 1994. *Historical Ecology.* Sante Fe, N.M.: School of American Research.

Crumley, Carole, and William H. Marquardt, eds. 1987. *Regional Dynamics.* San Diego, Calif.: Academic Press.

Dobson, David. 1984. *Directory of Scottish Settlers in North America.* Baltimore, Md.: Genealogical Publishing.

———. 1989. *The Original Scots Colonists of Early America, 1612–1783.* Baltimore, Md.: Genealogical Publishing.

Dodgshon, Robert. 1995. "Modelling Chiefdoms in the Scottish Highlands and Islands Prior to the '45." In *Celtic Chiefdom, Celtic State,* edited by Bettina Arnold and Blair Gibson, 99–109. Cambridge: Cambridge University Press.

Donaldson, Emily Ann. 1986. *The Scottish Highland Games in America*. Gretna, La.: Pelican.

Donaldson, William. 1976. "Bonny Highland Laddie: The Making of a Myth." *Scottish Literary Journal* 3:30–50.

———. 1988. *The Jacobite Song: Political Myth and National Identity*. Aberdeen, Scotland: Aberdeen University Press.

Dorst, John. 1989. *The Written Suburb: An American Site, an Ethnographic Dilemma*. Philadelphia: University of Pennsylvania Press.

Duff, David. 1968. *Victoria in the Highlands*. New York: Taplinger Publishing.

Dunbar, John Telfer. 1981. *The Costume of Scotland*. London: B. T. Batsford Ltd.

Duncan, A. A. M. 1975. *The Edinburgh History of Scotland*. Vol. 1, *The Making of the Kingdom*. Edinburgh: Oliver and Boyd.

Eliade, Mircea. 1961. *Images and Symbols*. Kansas City, Kans.: Sheed Andrews and McMeet.

Ellis, Peter Berresford. 1985. *The Celtic Revolution: A Study in Anti-Imperialism*. Cerredigion, Wales: Y Lolfa.

Epstein, A. L. 1978. *Ethos and Identity*. Chicago: Aldine Publishing Company.

Fenton, Alexander, and Bruce Walker. 1981. *The Rural Architecture of Scotland*. Edinburgh: John Donald Publishers.

Finegan, Jim, and Michaele Finegan. 1996. Promotional material and correspondance for the "United Regiment of MacLachlans and MacLeans, circa 1745."

Fischer, David Hackett. 1989. *Albion's Seed: Four British Folkways in America*. New York: Oxford University Press.

Fitzpatrick, Rory. 1989. *God's Frontiersmen: The Scots-Irish Epic*. London: Weidenfeld and Nicolson.

Flora MacDonald Highland Games promotional leaflet. 1995. Red Springs, N.C.: Flora MacDonald Highland Games, Ltd.

Foote, William H. 1845. *Sketches of North Carolina*. New York: Robert Carver.

Foster, Andrew. 1995. "Stone Mountain Highland Games and Scottish Festival Program." Atlanta, Ga.: Scott Lithographing Co.

Foster, Gaines. 1987. *Ghosts of the Confederacy: Defeat, the Lost Cause, and the Emergence of the New South, 1865–1913*. New York: Oxford University Press.

———. 1989. "Lost Cause Myth." In *Encyclopedia of Southern Culture*, edited by Charles Reagan Wilson and William Ferris, 3:509–10. New York: Doubleday.

Fowler, Malcolm. 1976 [1955]. *They Passed This Way: A Personal Narrative of Harnett County History*. N.p.

———. 1986. *Valley of the Scots: A History of the First Scottish Settlers in North Carolina*. Raleigh, N.C.: W. Fowler.

Gallamore, Alexander. 1998. Interview, January 25, Charlotte, N.C.

Gaston, Paul M. 1970. *The New South Creed: A Study in Southern Mythmaking*. Baton Rouge: Louisiana State University Press.

Gantz, Jeffrey. 1981. *Early Irish Myths and Sagas*. Middlesex, Eng.: Penguin Books.

Gatherer, Nigel. 1986. *Songs and Ballads of Dundee*. Edinburgh: John Donald Publishers.

Geertz, Clifford. 1966. "Religion as a Cultural System." In *Anthropological Approaches to the Study of Religion*, edited by Michael Banton, 1–46. New York: Basic Books.

———. 1973. *The Interpretation of Cultures*. New York: Basic Books.

Gellner, Ernest. 1987 [1973]. *The Concept of Kinship: And Other Essays on Anthropological Method and Explanation*. Oxford: Basil Blackwell.

Gerster, Patrick, ed. 1989. *Myth and Southern History*. Urbana: University of Illinois Press.

Gibson, Grace Evelyn, ed. 1990. *The Pocket John Charles McNeill*. Laurinburg, S.C.: St. Andrew's University Press.

Gillies, Mary. 1993. "Smooring Chant." *By Land and By Sea* 17 (2): 26.

Goffman, Erving. 1959. *The Presentation of Self in Everyday Life*. New York: Anchor Press.

Goldman, Robert. 1992. *Reading Ads Socially*. London: Routledge.

Gordon Regiment. 1994. Advertisement. *Highlander* 32:27.

Graham, Ian. 1956. *Colonists from Scotland: Emigration to North America, 1707–1783*. Ithaca, N.Y.: Cornell University Press.

Gramsci, Antonio. 1971. *Selections from the Prison Notebooks*. Edited by Quitin Hoare and Geoffrey Nowell Smith. New York: International Publishers.

Grant, I. F. 1961. *Highland Folkways*. London: Routledge and Kegan Paul.

Grant, I. F., and Hugh Cheape. 1997. *Periods in Highland History*. London: Shepheard-Walwyn Publishers.

Greenwood, D. J. 1977. "Culture by the Pound." In *Hosts and Guests*, edited by Valene L. Smith. Philadelphia: University of Pennsylvania Press.

Grimble, Ian. 1973. *Scottish Clans and Tartans*. New York: Harmony Books.

Grimes, John. 1993. "AYO Gurkhali!" In *The Book of the Braemar Gathering*, edited by George S. Shepherd, 57–61. Arbroath: Herald Press.

Haley, Alex. 1977. *Roots*. London: Hutchinson.

Handler, Richard, and William Saxton. 1988. "Dyssimulation: Reflexivity, Narrative, and the Quest for Authenticity in 'Living History.'" *Current Anthropology* 3:242–60.

Hanna, Charles. 1902. *The Scotch-Irish*. New York: G. P. Putnam's Sons.

Harvey, David. 1989. "Time-Space Compression and the Postmodern Condition." In *The Condition of Postmodernity*, 284–307. Oxford: Basil Blackwell.

Harvie, Christopher. 1994. *Scotland and Nationalism: Scottish Society and Politics, 1707 to the Present*. 2d ed. New York: Routledge.

Healey, Joseph. 1997. *Race, Ethnicity, and Gender in the United States*. Thousand Oaks, Calif.: Pine Forge Press.

Henley, Nettie McCormick. 1989. *The Home Place*. Laurinburg, S.C.: St. Andrew's University Press.

Hesketh, Christian. 1961. *Tartans*. New York: G. P. Putnam's Sons.

Hewison, Robert. 1983. *The Heritage Industry: Britain in a Climate of Decline*. London: Methuen.

———. 1989. "Heritage: An Interpretation." In *Heritage Interpretation*. Vol. 1, *The Natural and Built Environment*, edited by David Uzzell. London: Belhaven Press.

Hill, James Michael. 1986. *Celtic Warfare*. Edinburgh: John Donald Publishers.

Hobsbawm, Eric, and Terence Ranger, eds. 1983. *The Invention of Tradition*. Cambridge: Cambridge University Press.

Hogg, James. [1986]. *A Tour in the Highlands in 1803*. Edinburgh: Mercat Press.

Holloway, James. 1978. *The Discovery of Scotland*. Edinburgh: National Gallery of Scotland (Her Majesty's Stationery Office).

Houston, Cecil, and William Smyth. 1980. *The Sash Canada Wore: A Historical Geography of the Orange Order in Canada*. Toronto: University of Toronto Press.

Hubert, Jane. 1994. "Sacred Beliefs and Beliefs of Sacredness." In *Sacred Sites, Sacred Places*, edited by David L. Carmichael et al. New York: Routledge.

Huddleston, Joe. 1998. "The Highlander: Definition and Description." *Highlander* 36 (1): 56–61.

Hunter, James. 1976. *The Making of a Crofting Community*. Edinburgh: John Donald Publishers.

———. 1994. *A Dance Called America: The Scottish Highlands in the United States and Canada*. Edinburgh: Mainstream.

Hunter, John Michael. 1985. *Land into Landscape*. London: George Godwin.

Innes, Sir Thomas. [1938] 1971. *Tartans of the Clans and Families of Scotland*. Edinburgh: Johnston and Bacon.

Jackson, Anthony. 1987. *Anthropology at Home*. London: Tavistock Publications.

Jarvie, Grant. 1989. "Culture, Social Development and the Scottish Highland Gatherings." In *The Making of Scotland*, edited by David McCrone, Stephen Kendrick and Pat Straw. Edinburgh: Edinburgh University Press.

———. 1991. *Highland Games: The Making of the Myth*. Edinburgh: Edinburgh University Press.

Johnson, Guion Griffis. 1937. *Ante-Bellum North Carolina: A Social History*. Chapel Hill: University of North Carolina Press.

Johnson, Samuel. 1985 [1775]. *A Journey to the Western Islands of Scotland*. Edited by J. D. Fleeman. Oxford: Clarendon Press.

Jones, Alwyn. 1982. *Scottish Roots: A Step-by-Step Guide for Ancestor Hunters*. Gretna, La.: Pelican.

Jones, Henry. 1993. *Psychic Roots: Serendipity and Intuition in Genealogy*. Baltimore, Md.: Genealogical Publishing.

Jones, Sandy. 1994. "Piping at Grandfather Mountain Highland Games." Grandfather Mountain Highland Games Program 60.

Kincardine and Deeside Tourist Board. 1993. *Victorian Heritage in Kincardine and Deeside*. N.p.

Kirshenblatt-Gimblett, Barbara. 1988. "Authenticity and Authority in the Representation of Culture: The Poetics of Tourist Production." In *Kuturcontakt / Kulturkonflikt*, edited by Ina-Maria Greverus, Konrad Kostlin, and Heinz Schilling. *Notizen* 28 (1): 59–69.

Knapp, Bernard. 1992. *Archaeology, Annales, and Ethnohistory*. Cambridge: Cambridge University Press.

Krech, Shepard. 1991. "The State of Ethnohistory." In *Ethnohistory* 20:345–75.

Landsman, Ned. 1985. *Scotland and Its First American Colony, 1683–1765*. Princeton, N.J.: Princeton University Press.

Layton, Robert. 1989. *Who Needs the Past?: Indigenous Values and Archaeology*. London: Unwin Hyman.

Lefler, Hugh Talmage, and Albert Ray Newsome. 1954. *North Carolina: The History of a Southern State*. Chapel Hill: University of North Carolina Press.

Leslie, Bob. 1995. "Why Should I Become a Member?" American Clan Leslie Society, information leaflet, 1.

Lesser, Alexander. 1978. *The Pawnee Ghost Dance Hand Game*. Madison: University of Wisconsin Press.

Lévi-Strauss, Claude. 1966. *The Savage Mind*. Chicago: University of Chicago Press.

Leyburn, James G. 1962. *The Scotch-Irish: A Social History*. Chapel Hill: University of North Carolina Press.

Lieberson, Stanley 1989. "Unhypenated Whites in the United States." In *Ethnicity and Race in the U.S.A.: Toward the 21st Century*, edited by Richard D. Alba, 159–80. New York: Routledge.

Lindsay, J. M. 1980. "The Commercial Use of Woodland and Coppice Management." In *The Making of the Scottish Countryside*, edited by M. L. Parry and T. R. Slater, 271–90. London: Croom Helm.

Lipe, William. 1984. "Value and Meaning in Cultural Resources." In *Approaches to the Archaeological Heritage*, edited by Henry Cleere, 1–12. Cambridge: Cambridge University Press.

Loch Lomond, Stirling and Trossachs Tourist Board. 1991. *Follow the Highland Gateway Trail*. Promotional leaflet. Stirling: Tourist Board.

Loch Norman Highland Games Program. 1994.

Logan, James. 1848. *The Scottish Gael; or Celtic Manners as Preserved among the Highlanders*. Hartford, Conn.: S. Andrus and Son.

Lowenthal, David. 1982. "Revisiting Valued Landscapes." In *Valued Environments*, edited by John Gold and Jacquelin Burgess. London: George Allen and Unwin.

———. 1985. *The Past Is a Foreign Country*. Cambridge: Cambridge University Press.

Ludwig, Mary A. 1992. "The Invention of Tradition among Irish-Americans." In *Celtic Languages and Celtic Peoples: Proceedings of the Second International Congress of Celtic Studies*, edited by Cyril Byrne et al. Halifax, N.S.: St. Mary's University Press.

Lumley, Robert, ed. 1988. *The Museum Time-Machine*. London: Routledge.

MacAloon, John, ed. 1984. *Rite, Drama, Festival, Spectacle: Rehearsals toward a Theory of Cultural Performance*. Philadelphia: University of Pennsylvania Press.

McBain, S. W. 1988. "The Royal Scots (The Royal Scots Regiment)." In *Soldiers of Scotland*, edited by John Baynes, 139–45. New York: Barnes and Noble Books.

MacCannell, Dean. 1976. *The Tourist: A New Theory of the Leisure Class*. New York: Schocken Books.

McCrone, David, ed. 1989. *The Making of Scotland: Nation, Culture, and Social Change*. Edinburgh: Edinburgh University Press.

McDavis, Jeff. 1998. Scottish District Families Association, information leaflet, 2.

MacDonald, D. 1992. "These Are Your People: The Shaws." Clan Shaw Society handout, 2.

MacDonald, Donald. 1980. "Changing the Map of Scotland." In Grandfather Mountain Highland Games Program, 57–59.

———. 1982. Grandfather Mountain Highland Games Program, 44.

———. 1993. Interview, August 27, Inverurie, Scotland.

———. 1994. Interview, April 17, Charlotte, N.C.

———. 1995. Interview, June 28, Charlotte, N.C.

———. 1995. Interview, July 10, Linville, N.C.

———. 1998. Interview, February 24, Charlotte, N.C.

McDonald, Forrest, and Ellen Shapiro MacDonald. 1980. "The Ethnic Origins of the American People, 1790." *William and Mary Quarterly* 37 (2): 179–99.

MacDonald, James. 1993. "Cultural Retention and Adaptation among the Highland Scots." Ph.D. diss., University of Edinburgh.

——. 1993. Interview, Inverurie, Scotland.

MacDonald, Micheil. 1993. "The Routes to Your Roots." *Scottish Quest* (Fall): 44–48.

McIan, R. R., and James Logan. 1845 [1980]. *The Clans of the Scottish Highlands: Costumes of the Clans.* New York: Alfred A. Knopf.

MacInnes, Allan. 1992. "Scottish Gaeldom: The First Phase of Clearance." In *People and Society in Scotland, Vol. 1: 1760–1830,* edited by T. M. Devine and Rosalind Mitchison, 70–90. Edinburgh: John Donald Publishers.

McKee, Christian. 1989. *Scottish Character and Lifestyle.* Landisville, Pa.: N.p.

Mackenzie, James. 1969. *A Colorful Heritage: An Informal History of Barbecue and Bluff Presbyterian Churches.* Edited by Victor Clark and Louise Curry. Dallas, N.C.: Argyll Printing Center.

MacKenzie, John. 1990. "David Livingstone: The Construction of the Myth." In *Sermons and Battle Hymns: Protestant Popular Culture in Modern Scotland,* edited by Graham Walker and Tom Gallagher, 30–37. Edinburgh: Edinburgh University Press.

MacKenzie, Ross. 1996. "Foreword: The Origins of Jacobitism and the Course of the '45." In *The Swords and the Sorrows,* 4–11. Edinburgh: National Trust for Scotland.

McKinney, Margaret. 1997. Interview, October 11, Monticello Celtic Festival and Highland Games.

MacKinnon, Charles. 1984. *The Scottish Highlanders.* New York: Barnes and Noble Books.

MacLean, John P. [1919]. "An Historical Account of the Settlements of Scotch Highlanders in America prior to the Peace of 1783." Unpublished manuscript.

McLellan, Julia. 1994. "Clans Tour." *Highlander* 32 (2): 7.

MacNaughton, John. 1994 [1978]. "The Clan Macnachtan." Clan MacNachtan information leaflet, 1.

MacRae, David. 1868. *The Americans at Home: Pen and Ink Sketches of American Men, Manners, and Institutions.* New York: E. P. Dutton.

McWhinney, Grady. 1988. *Cracker Culture: Celtic Ways in the Old South.* Tuscaloosa: University of Alabama Press.

McWhinney, Grady, and Perry D. Jamieson. 1982. *Attack and Die: Civil War Military Tactics and the Southern Heritage.* Tuscaloosa: University of Alabama Press.

Manning, Frank E. 1992. "Spectacle." In *Folklore, Cultural Performances, and Popular Entertainments,* edited by Richard Bauman, 291–99. Oxford: Oxford University Press.

Marcus, George. 1998. *Ethnography through Thick and Thin.* Princeton, N.J.: Princeton University Press.

Marks, Stuart A. 1991. *Southern Hunting in Black and White: Nature, History, and Ritual in a Carolina Community.* Princeton, N.J.: Princeton University Press.

Martin, Bob. 1994. *All about Your Kilt.* Bruceton Mills, W.Va.: Unicorn Ltd.

Martin, Martin. 1970 [1716]. *A Description of the Western Islands of Scotland.* Edinburgh: Mercat Press.

Martine, Roddy. 1988. "Clan Gathering." In *The Scottish Field,* 36–37.

Maxwell, Murvan. 1980. "The Parade of Tartans." Grandfather Mountain Highland Games Program, 55.

——. 1989. "History of Parade of Tartans." Grandfather Mountain Highland Games Program, 31.

Meyer, Duane. 1961. *The Highland Scots of North Carolina, 1732–1776*. Chapel Hill: University of North Carolina Press.

Mitchell, Andy. 1992. "The Father of America's Braemar." In *Scotland Now*, 3. Edinburgh: East Lothian Tourist Board.

Moore, Sally Falk. 1994. "The Ethnography of the Present and the Analysis of Process." In *Assessing Cultural Anthropology*, edited by Robert Borofsky, 362–75. New York: McGraw-Hill.

Moran, Jackie. 1996. "Highland Targes." In *The Swords and the Sorrows*, 55–59. Edinburgh: National Trust for Scotland.

Morinis, Alan, ed. 1992. *Sacred Journeys*. Westport, Conn.: Greenwood Press.

Morrison, Iain. 1991. "Guest of Honor." Orlando Highland Games Program.

Morrison, Gary. 1999. "Celtic Groves." Grandfather Mountain Highland Games Program, 43.

Nadel-Klein, Jane. 1997. "Crossing a Representational Divide: From West to East in Scottish Ethnography." In *After Writing Culture: Epistemology and Praxis in Contemporary Anthropology*, edited by Allison James, Jenny Hockey, and Andrew Dawson, 86–102. London: Routledge.

Nairn, Tom. 1977. *The Break-up of Britain: Crisis and Neo-Nationalism*. London: NLB.

Nantista, Frances. 1995. Interview, March 18, Culloden, Ga.

National Trust for Scotland. 1993. *62d Annual Report*. Edinburgh: National Trust.

———. 1997. *66th Annual Report*. Edinburgh: National Trust.

Neville, Gwen Kennedy. 1971. "Annual Assemblages as Related to the Persistance of Cultural Patterns: An Anthropological Study of a Summer Community." Ph.D. diss., University of Florida.

———. 1979. "Community Form and Ceremonial Life in Three Regions in Scotland." *American Ethnologist* 6 (1).

———. 1987. *Kinship and Pilgrimage: Rituals of Reunion in American Protestant Culture*. Oxford: Oxford University Press.

———. 1994. *The Mother Town: Civic Ritual, Symbol, and Experience in the Borders of Scotland*. New York: Oxford University Press.

Neville, Gwen Kennedy, and John H. Westerhoff. 1978. *Learning through Liturgy*. New York: Seabury Press.

Newsome, A. R., ed. [1934] 1989. *Records of Emigrants from England and Scotland to North Carolina 1774–1775*. Raleigh, N.C.: Division of Archives and History.

Nichols, Larry, ed. 1994. *Patriot* 12 (2).

Nicolaisen, W. F. H. 1976. *Scottish Place-Names*. London: B. T. Batsford.

O'Brien, Michael. 1989. "Southern Regionalism." In *Encyclopedia of Southern Culture*, edited by Charles Reagan Wilson and William Ferris, 3:486–88. New York: Doubleday.

Osoba, Margaret. 1994. "Address to a 20th Century Haggis." *Gunn Salute* 24 (1): 7.

Osterweis, Rollin G. 1949. *Romanticism and Nationalism in the Old South*. New Haven, Conn.: Yale University Press.

Parker, Anthony. 1997. *Scottish Highlanders in Colonial Georgia: The Recuitment, Emigration, and Settlement at Darien, 1735–1748*. Athens: University of Georgia Press.

Parkhill, Trevor. 1997. "Philadelphia Here I Come: A Study of the Letters of Ulster Immigrants in Pennsylvania, 1750–1875." In *Ulster and North America:*

Transatlantic Perspectives on the Scotch-Irish, edited by Tyler Blethen and Curtis Wood, 118–33. Tuscaloosa: University of Alabama Press.

Parman, Susan. 1990. *Scottish Crofters: A Historical Ethnography of a Celtic Village*. London: Holt, Rinehart and Winston.

Peacock, James. 1986. *The Anthropological Lens: Harsh Light, Soft Focus*. Cambridge: Cambridge University Press.

Pennant, Thomas. 1979 [1771]. "A Tour of Scotland in 1769." Perth, Scotland: Melven Press.

Pittock, Murray. 1998. *Jacobitism*. New York: St. Martin's Press.

Pope, Arnold. 1995. Interview, May 2, Fayetteville, N.C.

Porter, Jane. 1810. *Scottish Chiefs*. London: Collins.

Pound, Ezra. 1986. *The Cantos*. New York: New Directions.

Powell, T. G. E. 1986. *The Celts*. London: Thames and Hudson.

Prebble, John. 1961. *Culloden*. Middlesex, Eng.: Penguin Books.

———. 1984. *The Highland Clearances*. Middlesex, Eng.: Penguin Books.

Pyron, Darden A. 1989. "Plantation Myth." In *Encyclopedia of Southern Culture*, edited by Charles Reagan Wilson and William Ferris, 3:477–80. New York: Doubleday.

Ramsey, Robert. 1964. *Carolina Cradle: Settlement of the Northwest Carolina Frontier, 1747–1762*. Chapel Hill: University of North Carolina Press.

Rankin, David. 1987. *The Celts and the Clasical World*. Routledge: London.

Rappaport, Roy A. 1992. "Ritual." In *Folklore, Cultural Performances, and Popular Entertainments*, edited by Richard Bauman, 249–60. Oxford: Oxford University Press.

Ray, Angus John, ed. 1994. *The Highlander Directory Issue 32* (2a). Chicago: Angus J. Ray Associates.

———. 1995. *The Highlander Directory Issue 32* (2a). Chicago: Angus J. Ray Associates.

Ray, Celeste. 1991. "Scottish Battlefields: Images of National Identity in the Presentation of Historic Landscapes." Master's thesis, University of Edinburgh.

Reed, James. 1980. *Sir Walter Scott: Landscape and Locality*. London: Athlone Press.

Reed, John Shelton. 1983. *The Social Psychology of Sectionalism*. Chapel Hill: University of North Carolina Press.

———. 1986. *The Enduring South: Subcultural Persistence in Mass Society*. Chapel Hill: University of North Carolina Press.

———. 1997. "The Cherokee Princes in the Family Tree." *Southern Cultures* 3 (Spring): 111–13.

Relph, Edward. 1976. *Place and Placelessness*. London: Pion Limited.

Riegl, Alois. 1982 [1928]. "The Modern Cult of Monuments: Its Character and Its Origin." *Oppositions* 25:20–51.

Roberts, Diane. 1999. "Your Clan or Ours?" *Oxford American* 29:24–30.

Robson, Ralph. 1989. *The English Highland Clans*. Edinburgh: John Donald Publishers.

Rogers, Pat, ed. 1993. *Johnson and Boswell in Scotland: A Journey to the Hebrides*. New Haven, Conn.: Yale University Press.

Rosie, George. 1988. "The Great Tartan Monster." In *Scotland*, edited by Brian Bell, pp. 76–81. Singapore: APA Publications.

———. 1991. "What I Hate about . . . Clans, Kilts, and Celtic Kitsch." *Scotsman Weekend*, April 6, p. 2.

Sanjek, Roger. 1994. "The Enduring Inequalities of Race." In *Race*, edited by Steven Gregory and Roger Sanjek, 1–17. New Brunswick, N.J.: Rutgers University Press.

Scarlett, James. 1981. *Scotland's Clans and Tartans*. London: Lutterworth Press.

Schaefer, Richard. 1996. *Racial and Ethnic Groups*. 6th ed. New York: HarperCollins.

Schama, Simon. 1995. *Landscape and Memory*. New York: Alfred A. Knopf.

Schmidt, Leigh Eric. 1989. *Holy Fairs: Scottish Communions and American Revivals in the Early Modern Period*. Princeton, N.J.: Princeton University Press.

Scott, James C. 1985. *Weapons of the Weak: Everyday Forms of Peasant Resistance*. New Haven, Conn.: Yale University Press.

Scott, Walter. [1828]. *The Waverley Novels*. Vol. 12, *The Fair Maid of Perth*. Philadelphia, Pa.: John D. Morris.

———. 1990 [1814]. *Waverley*. Oxford: Oxford University Press.

———. 1993 [1826]. *Manners, Customs, and History of the Highlanders of Scotland and Historical Account of the Clan MacGregor*. New York: Barnes and Noble Books.

Seigler, Morris G. 1993 [1966]. Church leaflet excerpt from "A History of St. Andrew's-Covenant Presbyterian Church, November 11, 1858, to December 31, 1966."

Shaw, Tom. 1994. Interview, October 29, Waxhaw, N.C.

Sheperd, George, ed. 1993. *The Book of the Braemar Gathering*. Arbroath, Scotland: Herald Press.

———. 1994. *The Book of the Braemar Gathering*. Arbroath, Scotland: Herald Press.

Sher, Richard, and Jeffery Smitten, eds. 1990. *Scotland and America in the Age of Enlightenment*. Princeton, N.J.: Princeton University Press.

Shils, Edward. 1981. *Tradition*. London: Faber and Faber.

Silber, Irwin. 1960. *Songs of the Civil War*. New York: Columbia University Press.

Silber, Nina. 1993. *The Romance of Reunion: Northerners and the South, 1865–1900*. Chapel Hill: University of North Carolina Press.

Simpson, Grant G., ed. 1992. *The Scottish Soldier Abroad: 1247–1967*. Edinburgh: John Donald Publishers.

Sinclair, Cecil. 1990. *Tracing Your Scottish Ancestors*. Edinburgh: Her Majesty's Stationery Office.

Slater, T. R. 1980. "The Mansion and Policy." In *The Making of the Scottish Countryside*, edited by M. L. Parry and T. R. Slater, 223–48. London: Croom Helm.

Sloan, Douglas. 1971. *The Scottish Enlightenment and the American College Ideal*. New York: Teachers College Press.

Smith, Anthony. 1991. *National Identity*. London: Penguin Books.

Smith, Stephen. 1984. "Food for Thought: Comestible Communication and Contemporary Southern Culture." In *American Material Culture: The Shape of Things Around Us*, edited by Edith Mayo, 208–17. Bowling Green, Ohio: Bowling Green State University Popular Press.

Smout, T. C. 1969. *A History of the Scottish People, 1560–1830*. London: Collins/Fontana.

Snadon, Patrick A. 1989. "Gothic Revival Architecture." In *Encyclopedia of Southern Culture*, edited by Charles Reagan Wilson and William Ferris, 1:120–25. New York: Doubleday.

Steinberg, Steven. 1981. *The Ethnic Myth: Race, Ethnicity, and Class in America*. New York: Atheneum.

Stevenson, David. 1988. *The Covenanters*. Edinburgh: Saltire Society.

Stewart, A. I. B. 1985. "The North Carolina Settlement of 1739." *Scottish Genealogist 32*.

———. 1992. "Who Are the Scots?" *Argyll Colony Plus 6* (2): 88–97.

Stewart, Jacqueline P., ed. 1992. Grandfather Mountain Highland Games Program.

———. 1994. Grandfather Mountain Highland Games Program.

———. 1995. Grandfather Mountain Highland Games Program.

Stoeltje, Beverly J. "Festival." In *Folklore, Cultural Performances, and Popular Entertainments*, edited by Richard Bauman, 261–71. Oxford: Oxford University Press.

Stone, Linda Ann, and Cheryl Wilson, eds. 1993. Flora MacDonald Highland Games Program. Red Springs, N.C.

———. 1995. Flora MacDonald Highland Games Program. Red Springs, N.C.

Strathern, Marilyn. 1981. *Kinship at the Core*. Cambridge: Cambridge University Press.

Swangren, Jean. 1994. "Happy That She Found Us." In *MacLaren Standard* (Winter): 9.

Swann, Chuck, ed. 1994. "An Introduction to the Clan Gunn Society." Unpublished manuscript.

Taylor, Richard. 1994. Editorial. *Loch Norman Piper 2* (6): 3.

———. 1995. "Torchlight Ceremony Narration for the Grandfather Mountain Highland Games." July 6, Linville, N.C.

Taylor, Keets, ed. 1995. Loch Norman Highland Games Program.

Taylor, Robert M., and Ralph J. Crandall, eds. 1986. *Generations and Change: Genealogical Perspectives in Social History*. Macon, Ga.: Mercer University Press.

Taylor, William R. 1961 [1957]. *Cavalier and Yankee: The Old South and American National Character*. New York: George Braziller.

———. 1989. "Cavalier and Yankee: Synthetic Sterotypes." In *Myth and Southern History*, edited by Patrick Gerster and Nicholas Cords, 133–45. Urbana: University of Illinois Press.

Teall, Gordon, and Philip Smith. 1992. *District Tartans*. London: Shepeheard Walyn.

Thomas, Keith. 1983. "Chapter VI: The Human Dilemma." In *Man and the Natural World: A History of Modern Sensibility*, 242–303. New York: Pantheon.

Tindall, George B. 1989. "Mythology: A New Frontier in Southern History." In *Myth and Southern History*, edited by Patrick Gerster and Nicholas Cords, 2:1–16. Urbana: University of Illinois Press.

Tonkin, Elizabeth, et al., eds. 1989. *History and Ethnicity*. London: Routledge.

Trevor-Roper, Hugh. 1983. "The Invention of Tradition: The Highland Tradition of Scotland." In *The Invention of Tradition*, edited by Eric Hobsbawm and Terence Ranger, 15–41. Cambridge: Cambridge University Press.

Troxler, Carole. 1976. *The Loyalist Experience in North Carolina*. Raleigh, N.C.: Division of Archives and History.

Tuan, Yi-Fu. 1974. *Topophilia: A Study of Environmental Perception, Attitudes, and Values*. Englewood Cliffs, N.J.: Prentice-Hall.

Turnbull, Michael. 1998. *Scotland: The Facts.* Glasgow: Neil Wilson Publishing Ltd.

Turner, Newell. 1989. "Kappa Alpha Order." In *Encyclopedia of Southern Culture,* edited by Charles Reagan Wilson and William Ferris, 1:495. New York: Doubleday.

Turner, Victor. 1969. *The Ritual Process.* Chicago: Aldine.

———. 1974. *Dramas, Fields, and Metaphors: Symbolic Action in Human Society.* Ithaca, N.Y.: Cornell University Press.

———. 1978. *Image and Pilgrimage in Christian Culture.* New York: Columbia University Press.

———. 1982. Introduction to *Celebration: Studies in Festivity and Ritual.* Washington, D.C.: Smithsonian Institution Press.

———. 1985. "Symbols in African Ritual." In *Magic, Witchcraft, and Religion,* edited by Arthur Clehmann and James E. Myers, 55–63. London: Mayfield.

Vandagriff, G. C. 1993. *Voices in Your Blood: Discovering Identity through Family History.* Kansas City, Kans.: Andrews and McNeel.

Van Gennep, Arnold. 1909. *Les Rites de Passage.* Paris: Émile Nourry.

Wallace, Anthony. 1985. "Nativism and Revivalism." In *Magic, Witchcraft and Religion,* edited by Arthur Clehmann and James E. Myers, 319–24. London: Mayfield.

Wallace, Michael. 1986. "Visiting the Past: History Museums in the United States." In *Presenting the Past: Essays on History and the Public,* edited by Susan Porter Benson, Stephen Brier, and Roy Rosenzweig, 137–61. Philadelphia, Pa.: Temple University Press.

Waters, Mary. 1990. *Ethnic Options: Choosing Identities in America.* Berkeley: University of California Press.

Watson, Alan. 1996. *Society in Colonial North Carolina.* Raleigh, N.C.: Division of Archives and History.

Way, George. 1994. *Scottish Clan and Family Encyclopedia.* Glasgow: HarperCollins.

Whyte, Ian, and Kathleen Whyte. 1986. *Exploring Scotland's Historic Landscapes.* Edinburgh: John Donald Publishers.

Wicker, Rassie Everton. 1952. *Highland Settlements in Anson County.* Pinehurst, N.C.: N.p.

Wiedman, Dennis, ed. 1986. *Ethnohistory: A Researcher's Guide.* Williamsburg, Va.: Studies in Third World Societies.

Williams, Ronald. 1997. *The Lords of the Isles: The Clan Donald and the Early Kingdom of the Scots.* Isle of Colonsay, Argyll, Scotland: House of Lochar Press.

Wilson, Buddy, and Cheryl Wilson, eds. 1992. Flora MacDonald Highland Games Program. Red Springs, N.C.

Wilson, Charles Reagan. 1980. *Baptized in Blood: The Religion of the Lost Cause: 1865–1920.* Athens: University of Georgia Press.

———. 1989. "The Religion of the Lost Cause." In *Myth and Southern History.* Vol. 1, *The Old South,* edited by. Patick Gerster and Nicholas Cords. Urbana: University of Illinois Press.

Wolcott, Harry. 1995. *The Art of Fieldwork.* London: Altamira.

———. 1995. "Making a Study 'More Ethnographic.'" In *Representation in Ethnography,* edited by John Van Maanen, 79–111. Thousand Oaks, Calif.: Sage.

Wolf, Eric. 1982. *Europe and the People Without History.* Berkeley: University of California Press.

Wolf, Mary MacDougall. 1994. "MacDougalls Enjoy Recent Trip to Scotland."
 Tartan 11 (28): 2.
Woodward, C. Vann. 1960. *The Burden of Southern History*. Baton Rouge: Louisiana
 State University Press.
Wright, Patrick. 1985. *On Living in an Old Country*. London: Verso.

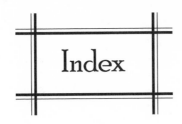

Index